The Competition Between Overt Suffixation and Zero-Affixation in Present-Day English Nominalisation

Language and Text Studies

Edited by
Alexander Brock & Daniela Pietrini

Volume 25

Cristina Lara-Clares

The Competition Between Overt Suffixation and Zero-Affixation in Present-Day English Nominalisation

PETER LANG
Berlin · Bruxelles · Chennai · Lausanne · New York · Oxford

Library of Congress Cataloging-in-Publication Data
A CIP catalog record for this book has been applied for
at the Library of Congress: LCCN : 2025003365

Bibliographic Information published by the Deutsche Nationalbibliothek
The Deutsche Nationalbibliothek lists this publication in the Deutsche Nationalbibliografie; detailed bibliographic data is available in the internet at http://dnb.d-nb.de.

This publication is supported by the project PID2020-119851GB-I00, funded by the Spanish Ministry of Science, Innovation and Universities and the State Research Agency, MICIU/AEI /10.13039/501100011033.

MINISTERIO
DE CIENCIA
E INNOVACIÓN

AGENCIA
ESTATAL DE
INVESTIGACIÓN

ISSN 0941-4134
ISBN 978-3-631-93063-2 (Print)
ISBN 978-3-631-93064-9 (E-PDF)
ISBN 978-3-631-93065-6 (E-PUB)
DOI 10.3726/b22566

Published by Peter Lang GmbH, Berlin (Germany)

info@peterlang.com

This publication has been peer reviewed.

www.peterlang.com

Contents

Typographical conventions 11

List of Figures 13

List of Tables 17

Acknowledgements 19

List of Abbreviations 21

Abstract 23

Resumen 25

1. Introduction 27

1.1. Introduction 27

1.2. Justification 28

1.3. Aims and research questions 29

1.4. Methodological background 30

1.5. Structure and contents 31

2. Research on competition in morphology 33

2.1. Introduction 33

2.2. Competition in inflection (overabundance) 35

2.3. Competition in word formation 37

2.3.1. The emergence of competition in derivation 39
2.3.2. Definition 41
2.3.3. The resolution of competition 43
2.3.3.1. Phonological factors 44
2.3.3.2. The profile of the base 46
2.3.3.2.1. The origin of the base 46
2.3.3.2.2. The word class of the base 47
2.3.3.2.3. The morphological structure of the base 48
2.3.3.2.4. The semantics of the base 48
2.3.3.3. Frequency and productivity 49
2.3.3.3.1. Availability 50
2.3.3.3.2. Profitability 51
2.3.3.4. Register distribution 52
2.3.3.5. Non-structural factors 54
2.3.3.6. Blocking: type and token 55
2.3.3.7. Analogy 56
2.3.4. Research on competition in English affixation 58
2.3.4.1. Competing patterns in nominalisation 60
2.3.4.1.1. Class-changing: *-ity*/*-ness* 61
2.3.4.1.2. Class-maintaining: *-ship*/*-dom*/*-hood* 63
2.4. Summary 64

3. Method 67
3.1. Introduction 67
3.2. Data source selection: corpus and dictionary data 67
3.2.1. Corpus selection 67
3.2.2. Dictionary selection 69
3.3. Samples 70
3.3.1. Sample1: the frequency list 70
3.3.1.1. Sample extraction 70
3.3.1.2. The analysis of Sample1 72

3.3.1.3. Methodological decisions 76
3.3.1.4. An illustration of data analysis of Sample1 77
3.3.1.5. The selection of competing patterns 78
3.3.2. Sample2 79
3.3.2.1. Sample extraction 79
3.3.2.2. The analysis of Sample2 81
3.3.2.2.1. Semantic concordance analysis 81
3.3.2.2.1.1. Manual semantic annotation: ACTION 83
3.3.2.2.1.2. Manual semantic annotation: AGENTIVE 83
3.3.2.2.1.3. Manual semantic annotation: INSTRUMENT 84
3.3.2.2.1.4. Manual semantic annotation: STATE 85
3.3.2.2.1.5. Automatic semantic annotation: a test 85
3.3.2.2.2. Profile of the affixes: constraints and Naturalness 86
3.3.2.2.2.1. *-ation* 87
3.3.2.2.2.2. *-er* 87
3.3.2.2.2.3. *-ness* 87
3.3.2.2.2.4. Zero-affixation 88
3.3.2.2.3. Productivity: the Referenced Index of Competition 88
3.3.2.2.4. Register distribution 89
3.3.2.2.5. Cooccurrences 94
3.4. Summary 97

4. The competition between overt affixation and zero-affixation 99

4.1. Introduction 99
4.2. Overview: competing patterns in PDE 99

4.3. Historical tendencies ... 102
4.3.1. Introduction ... 102
4.3.2. *-ation* vs. zero-affixation: ACTION ... 102
4.3.3. *-er* vs. zero-affixation: AGENTIVE ... 104
4.3.4. *-er* vs. zero-affixation: INSTRUMENT ... 105
4.3.5. *-ness* vs. zero-affixation: STATE ... 106
4.3.6. Discussion ... 107
4.4. Resolution of competition in PDE ... 109
4.4.1. Introduction ... 109
4.4.2. *-ation* vs. zero-affixation: ACTION ... 109
4.4.3. *-er* vs. zero-affixation AGENTIVE ... 114
4.4.4. *-er* vs. zero-affixation: INSTRUMENT ... 118
4.4.5. *-ness* vs. zero-affixation: STATE ... 123
4.4.6. Discussion ... 127
4.5. Competition by competitor ... 132
4.5.1. Introduction ... 132
4.5.2. *-ation* vs. zero-affixation: ACTION ... 132
4.5.3. *-er* vs. zero-affixation: AGENTIVE ... 136
4.5.4. *-er* vs. zero-affixation: INSTRUMENT ... 142
4.5.5. *-ness* vs. zero-affixation: STATE ... 148
4.5.6. Discussion ... 154
4.6. The clash between two models ... 159
4.7. Methodological aspects ... 160
4.7.1. Versions of the OED ... 161
4.7.2. Discrepancies between dictionary and corpus data ... 161
4.7.3. Corpus frequencies ... 163
4.7.4. Restriction to doublets ... 165
4.8. Summary ... 166

5. Conclusions ... 169
5.1. Introduction ... 169

5.2. Conclusions 169
5.2.1. Methodological 170
5.2.2. Descriptive 171
5.3. Limitations and future research 172

Appendices 175

References 193

Subject index 213

Typographical conventions

The typographical conventions used in this book are:

i) Small capitals for semantic categories (e.g. INSTRUMENT).
ii) Italics for:
   a. names of dictionaries and corpora when first mentioned (e.g. *Oxford English Dictionary*),
   b. emphasis (e.g. *roughly* the same semantic content),
   c. examples (e.g. *sweep*), and
   d. terminology when first presented and defined in the text (e.g. *cluster* in footnote 2).
iii) Double quotation marks (“ ”) for:
   a. quotations (e.g. the definition of blocking as “the non-occurrence of one form due to the simple existence of another” in Aronoff 1976: 43), and
   b. complete or partial lexicographic definitions of word senses (e.g. *dark* as “absence of light”).
iv) Single quotation marks (‘ ’) for glosses (e.g. *singer* ‘a person who Vs’).
v) The source of the examples extracted from dictionaries and corpora is specified between brackets at the end of each example (see example (16), §4.7.2: *Dvorak pursued the hyperrealities of tribal cultures, the structured ceremonies at the tenable borders of civilization in a small town, imagined tribal music as an instance of nationalism, and worried about his daughter too close to* ***savagism*** (COCA)).
vi) Numbers of tables and figures are preceded by their chapter number (e.g. the second table in Chapter 3 is Table 3.2).
vii) Citation of bibliographical references, both in-text and on the list of references, is in accordance with The Generic Style Rules for Linguistics (Haspelmath 2014), available at https://www.eva.mpg.de/lingua/pdf/GenericStyleRules.pdf.

List of Figures

Figure 3.1:	The association plot of the relation between the competing pattern (*-ation*/zero-affixation with the sense ACTION) and mode (spoken/written). Black represents higher frequencies than expected, and grey lower than expected.	94
Figure 3.2:	Graph of the cooccurrences of *importation* and *import* for the sense ACTION.	97
Figure 4.1:	Timeline of potentially competing clusters by suffix obtained from the sample for the expression of ACTION in the period 500–2020, where zero-affixation is represented by a continuous dark blue line and diamond ends, and *-er* is represented by a light blue discontinuous line and arrow ends.	103
Figure 4.2:	Timeline of potentially competing clusters by suffix obtained from the sample for the expression of AGENTIVE in the period 500–2020, where zero-affixation is represented by a continuous dark blue line and diamond ends, and *-er* is represented by a light blue discontinuous line and arrow ends.	104
Figure 4.3:	Timeline of potentially competing clusters by suffix obtained from the sample for the expression of INSTRUMENT in the period 500–2020, where zero-affixation is represented by a continuous dark blue line and diamond ends, and *-er* is represented by a light blue discontinuous line and arrow ends.	105
Figure 4.4:	Timeline of potentially competing clusters by suffix obtained from the sample for the expression of STATE in the period 500–2020, where zero-affixation is represented by a continuous dark blue line and diamond ends, and *-ness* is represented by a light blue discontinuous line and arrow ends.	107
Figure 4.5:	Distribution in terms of mode of *-ation* (blue) and zero-affixation (patterned blue) for the sense ACTION. The size of each mode in the BNC is presented in dotted yellow for easier comparison.	111

Figure 4.6: Register distribution of *-ation* (blue) and zero-affixation (patterned blue) for the sense ACTION. The size of each register in the BNC is presented in dotted yellow for easier comparison. 112
Figure 4.7: Association plot of the relation between the competing pattern (*-ation*/zero-affixation) and register, where black represents higher frequencies than expected, and grey represents lower frequencies than expected. 113
Figure 4.8: Distribution in terms of mode of *-er* (blue) and zero-affixation (patterned blue) for the sense AGENTIVE. The size of each mode in the BNC is presented in dotted yellow for easier comparison. 116
Figure 4.9: Register distribution of *-er* (blue) and zero-affixation (patterned blue) for the sense AGENTIVE. The size of each register in the BNC is presented in dotted yelow for easier comparison. 117
Figure 4.10: Distribution in terms of mode of *-er* (blue) and zero-affixation (patterned blue) for the sense INSTRUMENT. The size of each mode in the BNC is presented in dotted yellow for easier comparison. 121
Figure 4.11: Register distribution of *-er* (blue) and zero-affixation (patterned blue) for the sense INSTRUMENT. The size of each register in the BNC is presented in dotted yelow for easier comparison. 122
Figure 4.12: Distribution in terms of mode of *-ness* (blue) and zero-affixation (patterned blue) for the sense STATE. The size of each mode in the BNC is presented in dotted yellow for easier comparison. 125
Figure 4.13: Register distribution of *-ness* (blue) and zero-affixation (patterned blue) for the sense STATE. The size of each register in the BNC is presented in dotted yellow for easier comparison. 126
Figure 4.14: Register distribution of *importation* (blue) and *import*^{N} (patterned blue) for the sense ACTION. The size of each register in the BNC is presented in dotted yellow for easier comparison. 133
Figure 4.15: Graph of cooccurrences of *importation* and *import*^{N} for the sense ACTION. Cooccurrences of *import*^{N} are in light blue and those of *importation* in dark blue. 135

Figure 4.16: Register distribution of *cheater* (blue) and *cheat*^{N} (patterned blue) for the sense AGENTIVE. The size of each register in the BNC is presented in dotted yellow for easier comparison. 138

Figure 4.17: Register distribution of *sweeper* (blue) and *sweep*^{N} (patterned blue) for the sense AGENTIVE. The size of each register in the BNC is presented in dotted yellow for easier comparison. 138

Figure 4.18: Graph of the cooccurrences of *cheater* and *cheat*^{N} for the sense AGENTIVE. 142

Figure 4.19: Graph of the cooccurrences of *sweeper* and *sweep*^{N} for the sense AGENTIVE. 142

Figure 4.20: Register distribution of *clipper* (blue) and *clip*^{N} (patterned blue) for the sense INSTRUMENT. The size of each register in the BNC is presented in dotted yellow for easier comparison. 143

Figure 4.21: Register distribution of *wrapper* (blue) and *wrap*^{N} (patterned blue) for the sense INSTRUMENT. The size of each register in the BNC is presented in dotted yellow for easier comparison. 144

Figure 4.22: Graph of the cooccurrences of *clipper* and *clip*^{N} for the sense INSTRUMENT. 147

Figure 4.23: Graph of the cooccurrences of *wrapper* and *wrap*^{N} for the sense INSTRUMENT. 148

Figure 4.24: Register distribution of *alertness* (blue) and *alert*^{N} (patterned blue) for the sense STATE. The size of each register in the BNC is presented in dotted yellow for easier comparison. 150

Figure 4.25: Register distribution of *darkness* (blue) and *dark*^{N} (patterned blue) for the sense STATE. The size of each register in the BNC is presented in dotted yellow for easier comparison. 150

Figure 4.26: Graph of the cooccurrences of *alertness* and *alert*^{N} for the sense STATE. 153

Figure 4.27: Graph of the cooccurrences of *darkness* and *dark*^{N} for the sense STATE. 154

List of Tables

Table 3.1:	Simplified version of a competing cluster in the template with the base *bother*^{V}	75
Table 3.2:	A list of 20 rows of Sample1 of the BNC, showing the row number of the complete frequency list, the entry and the absolute frequency	77
Table 3.3:	Filters in the OED advanced search	80
Table 3.4:	Number of concordances analysed by competing pattern	82
Table 3.5:	Computation of the C value of the cluster *coolness/cool/coolth* with the sense STATE	89
Table 3.6:	Absolute frequencies of *-ation*/zero-affixation competitors with the sense ACTION by register	90
Table 3.7:	Standardised residuals of the chi-square test for *-ation* and zero-affixation for the sense ACTION in the spoken and written modes (BNC)	93
Table 4.1:	Competing patterns identified from Sample1 by semantic category (PDE)	101
Table 4.2:	Diachronic profiles of resolution of the competing patterns according to OED data	108
Table 4.3:	C* values of the competitors from the sample for the sense ACTION	110
Table 4.4:	C* values of the competitors from the sample for the sense AGENTIVE	114
Table 4.5:	C* values of the competitors from the sample for the sense INSTRUMENT	119
Table 4.6:	Standardised residuals of the chi-square test for *-er* and zero-affixation for the sense INSTRUMENT across registers in the BNC	123
Table 4.7:	C* values of the competitors from the sample for the sense STATE	124
Table 4.8:	Standardised residuals of the chi-square test for *-ness* and zero-affixation for the sense STATE across registers in the BNC	127
Table 4.9:	Forms in PDE competition classified as pertaining to a specific register or domain in the OED	129
Table 4.10:	Results from the statistical analysis of the competing patterns as regards register	130

Table 4.11: Standardised residuals of the chi-square test for *importation* and *import*^{N} for the sense ACTION across registers in the BNC 133
Table 4.12: The sense ACTION in the gloss of *importation* and *import*^{N} in dictionaries 134
Table 4.13: Cooccurrences of *importation* and *import*^{N} for the sense ACTION (BNC) 136
Table 4.14: Standardised residuals of the chi-square test for *cheater* and *cheat*^{N} for the sense AGENTIVE across registers in the BNC 139
Table 4.15: Standardised residuals of the chi-square test for *sweeper* and *sweep*^{N} for the sense AGENTIVE across registers in the BNC 139
Table 4.16: The sense AGENTIVE in the gloss of *cheater* and *cheat*^{N} in dictionaries 140
Table 4.17: The sense AGENTIVE in the gloss of *sweeper* and *sweep*^{N} in dictionaries 140
Table 4.18: Standardised residuals of the chi-square test for *clipper* and *clip*^{N} for the sense INSTRUMENT across registers in the BNC 144
Table 4.19: Standardised residuals of the chi-square test for *wrapper* and *wrap*^{N} for the sense INSTRUMENT across registers in the BNC 145
Table 4.20: The sense INSTRUMENT in the gloss of *clipper* and *clip*^{N} in dictionaries 145
Table 4.21: The sense INSTRUMENT in the gloss of *wrapper* and *wrap*^{N} in dictionaries 146
Table 4.22: Standardised residuals of the chi-square test for *alertness* and *alert*^{N} for the sense STATE across registers in the BNC 151
Table 4.23: Standardised residuals of the chi-square test for *darkness* and *dark*^{N} for the sense STATE across registers in the BNC 151
Table 4.24: The sense STATE in the gloss of *alertness* and *alert*^{N} in dictionaries 152
Table 4.25: The sense STATE in the gloss of *darkness* and *dark*^{N} in dictionaries 152
Table 4.26: Results obtained from computation of the C value by competing pattern 155
Table 4.27: Results from the statistical analysis of the competing patternsas regards mode 160
Table 4.28: Absolute frequencies of the competing cluster *savage*^{N}/*savageness*/*savagery*/*savagism* in PDE corpora without sense separation 162
Table 4.29: Number of clusters where both members, no member or only one member attest(s) the competing sense in the BNC 164

Acknowledgements

This publication has been supported by the project PID2020-119851GB-I00, funded by MICIU/AEI/10.13039/501100011033.

I would like to thank the supervisors of my thesis, Dr. Paul Thompson, and Dr. Salvador Valera, as well as the evaluating committee of my thesis, for their comments and suggestions in earlier versions of this book. I would also like to extend my gratitude to Cristina Fernández-Alcaina, Alicia Lara-Clares and Alba E. Ruz for their continuous support.

List of Abbreviations

Adj	adjective
Adv	adverb
BNC	*British National Corpus*
COCA	*Corpus of Contemporary American English*
N	Noun
NM	Natural Morphology
OE	Old English
OED	*Oxford English Dictionary*
PDE	present-day English
RQ	research question
V	verb

Abstract

In the field of linguistic morphology, competition is expected to be resolved, as it is not economical for a system to keep two or more processes for the same purpose (Hock & Joseph 2009: 213). Research on competition in word formation has focused on the variables that may promote or constrain the resolution of competition (Aronoff 1976; Plag 1999; Bauer et al. 2010; Bauer et al. 2013).

This book takes on a restrictive view of competition, whereby competitors derive from the same base and express the same meaning. It researches overt suffixation and zero-affixation for the nominalisastion of the semantic categories ACTION, AGENTIVE, INSTRUMENT and STATE aiming at hints of resolution, diachronically and in present-day English (henceforth, PDE). The analysis is based on senses instead of by lemmas.

The diachronic analysis explores the earliest and latest attestation dates of the competing sense of each form in the *Oxford English Dictionary*. The findings indicate that in nearly 50% of cases both forms in the set of competitors (here named *cluster*) fall out of use, and one of the forms falls out of use only in c. 15% of clusters.

The analysis in PDE examines resolution in terms of specialisation regarding mode, register, and meaning. For this, the frequency of use of the competing sense in the *British National Corpus* is computed for every competitor. Statistical analysis reveals a significant association between mode and word-formation process and also between register and word-formation process. The exploration of semantic specialisation in individual clusters reveals uneven results for each pattern: some clusters show semantic specialisation, others still overlap clearly in meaning.

The results obtained further support the idea that competition may take place at varying degrees (Huyghe & Wauquier 2021; Huyghe & Varvara 2023a) and prove that it needs to be researched at a sense level.

Keywords: affixation, morphological competition, nouns, resolution

Resumen

En morfología lingüística, se espera que la competición se resuelva, dado que no es económico para un sistema mantener dos o más procesos para un mismo propósito (Hock & Joseph 2009: 213). Los estudios sobre la competición en la formación de palabras se han centrado en las variables que pueden promover o restringir su resolución (Aronoff 1976; Plag 1999; Bauer et al. 2010; Bauer et al. 2013).

Este libro mantiene una visión restrictiva de la competición, en la que los competidores derivan de la misma base y expresan el mismo significado. Se estudia la sufijación explícita y la afijación cero para la nominalización de las categorías semánticas ACCIÓN, AGENTIVO, INSTRUMENTO y ESTADO en busca de indicios de resolución, diacrónica y en inglés contemporáneo. El análisis se basa en sentidos, no en lexemas.

El análisis diacrónico explora las fechas de primer y último registro del sentido que compite de cada forma en el *Oxford English Dictionary*. Los resultados muestran que las dos formas del grupo de competidores dejan de usarse en casi el 50% de los casos, y que una de las formas cae en desuso en alrededor del 15% de los grupos de competidores.

El análisis del inglés contemporáneo explora la resolución en términos de especialización con respecto al modo, registro y significado. Para cada competidor, se calcula la frecuencia de uso del sentido que compite en el *British National Corpus*. El análisis estadístico revela una asociación significativa entre modo y proceso de formación de palabras, y entre registro y proceso. El análisis de pares de competidores señala que algunos pares muestran especialización semántica, mientras que otros mantienen un claro solapamiento semántico.

Los resultados ahondan en la idea de que la competición puede darse en distintos grados (Huyghe & Wauquier 2021; Huyghe & Varvara 2023a) y demuestran que es necesario investigarla por sentidos.

Palabras clave: afijación, competición morfológica, sustantivos, resolución

1. Introduction

1.1. Introduction

Competition has been the subject of research in one way or another since Sanskrit grammars (Gardani et al. 2019: 5–6), even if it did not become a more central topic until the 1970s, both in inflectional and in derivational morphology.

In word formation research, it has become more prominent over the past few years, both for its relevance within studies on the productivity of processes and within research of paradigms. Thus, four volumes have been published on competition in derivational morphology in the last decade (MacWhinney et al. 2014; Santana-Lario & Valera 2017; Rainer et al. 2019; Bagasheva, Nagano & Renner 2024), as well as a themed issue in *Word Structure* (Huyghe & Varvara 2023b), and it has also been the topic of the 17th *International Morphology Meeting* in Vienna (2016) and of a workshop at the International Conference *Word-Formation Theories VI/Typology and Universals in Word-Formation V* in Košice (2022).

These and other references lead to two general conclusions. The first is that there is a remarkable degree of variability on how the concept of competition is defined, as there are differing opinions on whether two processes are in competition if they have a similar meaning, even if they do not derive from the same bases, or if they produce synonymous outputs (at least in one sense), derive from the same base, and are used in the same domains. The second, more restrictive view, is the one taken in this book.

The second conclusion is that there is considerable agreement that, whenever competition takes place, it is expected to be resolved, because it is not economical for a system to have two (or more) processes for the same purpose (Bauer et al. 2010: 15; cf. also Plag 2000). Resolution may take place variously under the influence of a number of factors that are still not fully understood (Bauer 2009: 188):

i) one (or all) of the processes may fall out of use,
ii) one (or all) of the processes may become specialised, or
iii) both processes may remain in use for a sustained period of time.

As is the case with morphological competition in general, the competition between overt affixation and zero-affixation,[1] the topic of this book, ultimately appeals to the choice between a more transparent process, to prime easier perception and pronounceability, or a more economical process, to prime shorter forms. Previous research on competition has thus focused on exploring:

i) the ways in which competition is resolved, both diachronically and synchronically, and
ii) the factors that may determine the resolution of competition between specific word-formation processes.

As an introduction to the research on the above, which is the subject of this book, this chapter is structured as follows: §1.2 summarises previous research on competition, §1.3 presents the aims of this book, §1.4 outlines the method followed for data extraction and analysis and §1.5 outlines the structure of this book.

1.2. Justification

Previous research on competition deals with the competition between affixal processes for the formation of nouns (Romaine 1985; Aronoff & Cho 2001; Arndt-Lappe 2014; Fradin 2019), verbs (Plag 1999; Gottfurcht 2008; Lindsay 2012) and adjectives (Kaunisto 2007, 2009; Smith 2020; Nagano 2022), but few references explore the competition between overt affixation and zero-affixation (e.g. Cetnarowska 1993; Iordăchioaia 2022; Lieber & Plag 2022 on the formation of nouns; Bauer et al. 2010; Fernández-Alcaina 2017 on the formation of verbs), partly for the methodological difficulties that research on zero-affixation poses. Research on competition between these two processes for the formation of nouns is thus very limited.

Besides, competition is usually investigated without restriction:

i) to forms derived from the same base (e.g. Plag 1999; Arndt-Lappe 2014; Díaz-Negrillo 2017; Bonami & Thuilier 2019; Rodríguez-Puente et al. 2020), and
ii) regarding their semantics, that is, comparing the productivity of the processes without sense separation (e.g. Kwon 1997; Baayen & Lieber 1991; Gaeta & Ricca 2003a, 2003b; Lindsay 2012).

---

1 In this book, the term used for this word-formation process (referred to variously as conversion, zero-derivation, functional shift, etc.) is *zero-affixation*. No theoretical stance is taken in this regard. Whenever a reference is cited, the terminology used by the author(s) in this regard is maintained.

To the best of my knowledge, only a few studies have dealt with competition at a sense level (e.g. Kaunisto 2007; Díaz-Negrillo 2017; Fernández-Alcaina & Čermák 2018; Fernández-Alcaina 2021a, 2021b), and only three references compute the frequencies of use of a particular sense for the analysis of the competition between word-formation processes in English (Lara-Clares 2017; Lara-Clares & Fernández-Alcaina 2024; Lara-Clares & Thompson 2019).

1.3. Aims and research questions

This book aims to explore whether and how the competition between overt affixation and zero-affixation in present-day English for the formation of nouns (henceforth, PDE) is resolved. To this end, this book identifies clusters[2] of competition, grouped according to competing pattern,[3] and it focuses on four patterns in particular:

i) *-ation*/zero-affixation for the expression of ACTION,
ii) *-er*/zero-affixation for the expression of AGENTIVE,
iii) *-er*/zero affixation for the expression of INSTRUMENT, and
iv) *-ness*/zero-affixation for the expression of STATE.

This book sets out to answer the following research questions:

i) RQ1: Is there any historical tendency in the resolution of the competition for the patterns under study? If so, does it agree with PDE corpus data?
ii) RQ2: Does synchronic data point to any of the possibilities of resolution of competition for the patterns under study? Specifically, is any pattern expected to fall out of use or to become specialised?
iii) RQ3: If a resolution tendency is identified for any given pattern, does each competition cluster follow that tendency?

---

2 A *cluster* is defined in this book as a set of *forms* with the same base but derived with a different affix (or word-formation process) for the expression of the same semantic category, for example, *clipper* and *clip*^{N} for the expression of INSTRUMENT (see Fernández-Alcaina 2017: 168).

3 A competing *pattern* is defined in this book on a morphosemantic basis, that is, it refers to a pair (or group) of *affixes* (or word-formation processes) that compete for the expression of a specific semantic category, for example, *-er* suffixation and zero-affixation for the expression of INSTRUMENT. This definition is slightly different to Fernández-Alcaina's (2017: 168) and Fernández-Alcaina's (2021a: 22), in that these references view individual word-formation processes for the expression of a semantic category as a pattern (e.g. *-er* suffixation for the expression of INSTRUMENT).

iv) RQ4: Does the data analysed reflect a preference for transparency or for economy in cases of competition? If so, is it dependent on the context of use?

1.4. Methodological background

The data used in this book is extracted from two main sources:

i) a general corpus (the *British National Corpus*, henceforth BNC), used:
   a. for extraction of a preliminary sample intended as the experimental basis for an overview on competition between nouns; a sample which is used to select the competing patterns to be analysed in this book, and
   b. for frequency and distribution analyses of competing patterns and competitors, and
ii) a historical dictionary (the *Oxford English Dictionary*, henceforth OED), used:
   a. for extraction of a second sample intended to identify potential competitors for the four patterns under analysis, and
   b. to obtain information as regards etymology, a description of senses over time, and the lifespan of forms and senses.

Once the four patterns of competition have been selected among the most prevalent in the preliminary sample, pairs of competitors[4] (doublets) where both forms are attested in the BNC are selected for further analysis.

The first step in the analysis is to carry out a semantic analysis of the concordances of the doublets. This is because the analysis of competition is at a sense level, and it is necessary to ensure that the frequencies recorded are of the competing sense (i.e. ACTION, AGENTIVE, INSTRUMENT or STATIVE, according to the pattern under analysis), so other senses or tagging errors are not included in the count. This is done manually for most of the sample, although a test is also performed on a pair of competitors for automatic semantic analysis using a large language model, which yielded promising results.

After obtaining the frequencies of attestation of each sense for every competitor, the aim is to identify hints on resolution by means of extinction or by means of specialisation, either as regards

4 This book explores the competition between pairs of word-formation processes via the analysis of clusters of competitors. This is because the competition between individual words would resolve the competition between word-formation patterns: "[…] if sufficient doublets are formed and word-formation x wins out the majority of cases, then word-formation process x will become the dominant process" (Bauer 2009: 181).

i) context of use, or
ii) semantics.

The former, context of use, is analysed through the register distribution of the competitors, also using statistical measures, namely Pearson's chi-square test, standardised residuals and effect size measures (Cramer's *V*). Competitors are also grouped according to competing process, so the two processes analysed within each competing pattern can be compared. The latter, semantic specialisation, is examined by means of the information contained in PDE reference dictionaries, and also by the cooccurrences of the competitors in the BNC, considering only the concordances classified as showing the competing sense.

1.5. Structure and contents

This book is divided into five chapters, each containing several sections, and Chapters 2 to 5 include an introduction and a summary each. Specifically, the thesis is structured as follows:

i) The present introduction is Chapter 1.
ii) Chapter 2 reviews the literature on the interplay between economy and transparency, and also previous research on morphological competition, with a focus on competition in word formation.
iii) Chapter 3 describes the method used for data collection and analysis.
iv) Chapter 4 presents the results obtained, discusses the methodological limitations and addresses the research questions.
v) Chapter 5 draws conclusions from the results.

2. Research on competition in morphology

2.1. Introduction

The existence of *competition* (or rivalry) is as an "inherent universal feature of natural languages" (Štekauer 2017: 15). According to Gardani et al. (2019: 14), it takes place at all language levels (e.g. phonological, morphological) and also across levels (e.g. the suffix *-er* competes with the syntactic comparative construction with *more*).

The first reference to competition probably is found in Pāṇini's view of Sanskrit grammar as a rule-governed system where exceptions are not violations but the consequence of the overlap of competing rules (Gardani et al. 2019; see Fernández-Alcaina 2021a: 14 and Fernández-Alcaina 2021b: 20–22 for a review of the concept). Since then, many studies have dealt with the topic indirectly, by comparing the productivity of word-formation processes (e.g. Plag 1999; Bauer 2001; §2.3.3.3) or their semantics (e.g. Lieber 2004), but it was not until Aronoff's (1976)[5] description of word formation that competition became a research topic by itself. The concept has since been applied both to research on inflection (§2.2) and on word formation (§2.3), but it operates differently in each field, because inflection is determined by morphosyntax (Aronoff 2019) and derivation is mainly driven by semantic needs (Fernández-Alcaina 2021a: 13).

In word formation, competition has of late received increasing attention. Several volumes and a themed issue in *Word Structure* have been published on the topic since 2014 (i.e. MacWhinney et al. 2014; Santana-Lario & Valera 2017; Rainer et al. 2019; Huyghe & Varvara 2023b; Bagasheva, Nagano & Renner 2024), and it was also the leitmotif of the 17th *International Morphology Meeting* (Vienna 2016) and the topic of a workshop at the International Conference *Word-Formation Theories VI/Typology and Universals in Word-Formation V* (Košice 2022).

Despite the number of recent publications on morphological competition, no unequivocal definition has been given of the concept. This is both the cause and the consequence of the problems arising from its study. Hoekstra & Versloot (2016) claim that "[c]ompetition is always between two different forms competing

5 Aronoff (1976) has been described in the literature as following a generative approach. However, the author has recently acknowledged that, despite his generative background and against what he believed at the time, his analysis was not generative, but it crosses the synchronic-diachronic boundary that has been central in structural linguistics after de Saussure (Aronoff 2018: 11).

for roughly the same semantic content". Although this definition captures the essence of what is usually understood as *competition*, it is unclear in that it does not specify what "two different forms" are and to what extent the semantic content should be "the same" (Lara-Clares 2017: 207; see §2.3.2). Still, it seems that a certain degree of semantic overlap is what defines competition, even if the limitations inherent to semantic analyses do not allow for a clear-cut categorisation of what degree counts as competition and what degree does not. Besides, the very existence of semantic overlap goes against the *Principle of Synonymy Avoidance*, which governs the resolution of competition: "[o]ne would expect [...] that complete synonymy – where two phonetically distinct words would express exactly the same range of meanings – is highly disfavored" (Hock & Joseph 2009: 225; see also Bréal 1897; Benveniste 1948; Marchand 1969; Kiparsky 1982; 1983; Haiman 1983: 800; Lindsay & Aronoff 2013; Štekauer 2017; see also §2.3.3.6 on blocking).

Also, it is widely accepted that this principle applies to individual words, but the question remains whether it also applies to morphological patterns: while synonymous patterns might be attested, these affixes tend to be in complementary distribution (Rainer et al. 2014: 22 for examples in Spanish that can be extended as a general principle; cf. Aronoff & Lindsay 2014: 72 for a discussion against synonymy avoidance as a driving force in competition). The *Principle of Synonymy Avoidance* is related to a universal tendency that has been described in the literature towards the preservation of the principle of one meaning/one form, as in Vennemann's account of Humboldt's universal (Anttila 1972: 92, 98, 100–101; see also, among others, Kiparsky 1971; Aronoff 1976: 8–14; Mayerthaler 1988: 97; Pounder 2000: 134; Carstairs-McCarthy 2010: 211ff.). In derivational morphology, this principle implies that the phonological form of a derivative should match a semantic component (e.g. *-er* in *singer* to mean 'a person who Vs').[6] However, form-meaning mismatches are widespread (see, e.g., Lloyd 2011; Hathout & Namer 2012; Rainer et al. 2014: 18ff.), even if there is a tendency in languages to screen them, because they require additional effort in morphological processing (Bolinger 1977: 9; Crocco Galèas 2001: 3). This strategy is behind the resolution of competition in word formation: in principle, it is not economical for the system to keep more than one form to express exactly the same range of meanings (Hock & Joseph 2009: 213; Bauer et al. 2010). In the choice of one process over another, there are two antagonistic (or competing) forces at play on the part of the speaker and the listener, which von der Gabelentz (1901: 181–185, cited in Körtvélyessy et al. 2021: 1022) originally named *Bequemlichkeit* 'comfort,

6 This principle has also been applied to inflection (e.g. in Cameron-Faulkner & Carstairs-McCarthy 2000).

laziness' and *Deutlichkeit* 'clarity'. The former, that is, to say more with fewer elements (economy of expression), would be preferred by the speaker, whereas the latter, that is, to receive a clear message to process (transparency of expression), would be the listener's preference (Štekauer 2017: 17–19).

The competition could, however, "[...] also be located within the speaker, whose endeavor to minimize effort may at times conflict with the desire to be witty or otherwise rhetorically effective" (Gardani et al. 2019: 4). In word formation, this choice would be governed by an inherent conflict between the tendency towards morphotactic transparency and the (opposite) tendency towards phonological productivity (Dressler 1985a: 250). The competition between overt affixation and zero-affixation, which is the focus of this book, evidences the conflict between the transparent model (overt affixation) and the economical model (zero-affixation).[7] Why these two models of word formation have coexisted for so long despite their redundancy and their apparent violation of the one-to-one preference of the two dimensions of the linguistic sign is partly explained by the evolution of English over time (§2.3.1), but many other factors may have also had an influence (§2.3.3).

This chapter examines the emergence of competition and the co-existence between economy and transparency in morphology (§2.3.1), with a focus on over affixation and zero-affixation. Then, it discusses the concept of competition in §2.3.2, and focuses on the literature on competition in inflection (§2.2) and competition in word formation (§2.3), with a focus on the competition between overt affixation and zero affixation. Section §2.4 is a summary of the chapter.

2.2. Competition in inflection (overabundance)

The term *overabundance* was first described in Thornton (2011: 360) as "[...] a non-canonical[8] situation in which certain lexemes exhibit cell-mates, that is, more than one inflected form to fill one and the same cell of their paradigm (realize the same set of morpho-syntactic features)", as in Spanish *cantara/cantase* (both being past subjunctive third person singular forms of *cantar* 'sing') (see Thornton 2019

---

7 This clash could also be viewed as one between the Germanic model, where words tend to be shorter, and the Romance model, where words tend to be longer (Zipf 1949: 112).

8 *Canonicity* is described here in terms of Corbett's canonical morphology, where it is expected that, for any given lexeme, the stem and the inflection will be predictable (Corbett 2005: 33).

for a typology of overabundance). The so-called cell-mates may have (Thornton 2012: 254):

i) different composition/structure (i.e. means of exponence), such as Dutch *drukste/meest drukke* (superlative of 'busy'),
ii) different lexical material (i.e. shape of the stem), for example, English plural forms *cacti/cactuses*, or
iii) different inflectional material (i.e. shape of inflection), such as Latin *fēcĕrunt/fēcērunt/fēcēre* (third person plural perfect of indicative of the verb 'do').

If the canonical approach is applied to overabundance, then cell-mates must comply with at least two criteria to be considered canonical (Santilli 2014: 10):

i) they must be used interchangeably, and
ii) they must have a frequency ratio of 1:1.

Italian verbal paradigms have been shown to be fairly canonically overabundant (e.g. Thornton 2012), but an analysis of comparison in Italian (e.g. *più buono/migliore* 'better') showed that doublets could hardly be used interchangeably, and the overall ratio for both comparatives of majority and relative superlatives was far from the ratio 1:1, which implies that there was no canonical overabundance (Santilli 2014).

Whether canonically overabundant or not, the competition between forms (be they inflectional or derivational) is expected to be resolved at some point (see §2.3.3 on the resolution of competition in word formation). There are several ways in which this could happen (cf., in the main, Fernández-Alcaina 2021a: 23):

i) one of the forms may become obsolete, for example, the third person singular present *-eth* disappeared in favour of the Northern dialect variant *-es* (Aronoff 2019: 51),
ii) regional differences may emerge, for instance, *dove* is preferred as the preterite of *dive* in American English (AmE), Australian English (AusE), Canadian English (CanE), and in New Zealand English (NZE), while *dived* is preferred in British English (BrE) (Bauer et al. 2013: 572),
iii) there could be specialisation regarding domain or register of use, as in the plural forms *mouses/mice*, the former being restricted to the technological domain of computing (Palmer et al. 2002: 1590), or
iv) some semantic specialisation may emerge, such as German plural *Gesichte* 'faces'/*Gesichter* 'appearances, visions' (Mörth & Dressler 2014: 252–253).

To this, we may add a pragmatic differentiation, as in German plurals *Pizzas/Pizzen* 'pizzas', where the *-s* plural has a connotation of strangeness or foreignness (Mörth & Dressler 2014: 252).

Regarding register/domain specialisation in the formation of plural, Sweet (1891–1898: 318) claimed that:

i) the use of foreign plurals is limited to a specialised or formal register, whereas the regular *-s* plural is more frequent in everyday language (Quirk et al. 1985: 311), and
ii) there is a tendency for the foreign plural to disappear unless there is a difference in meaning.

To test this, Fernández-Alcaina & Molina-Quesada (2016) compared the distribution of foreign and regular plurals (e.g. *syllabi/syllabuses*) in the written and spoken modes using frequency data from the *Corpus of Contemporary American English* (henceforth, COCA). The results showed that, in most of the doublets analysed, there are no statistically significant differences in the use of one or the other (Fernández-Alcaina & Molina-Quesada 2016). Similarly, Aronoff & Lindsay (2014) analysed suffixal comparatives (e.g. *bigger*) as compared to periphrastic comparatives (e.g. *more interesting*). Their results go against the commonly accepted complementary distribution of comparison in English and show that competition is still in place in disyllabic forms, where the two strategies are used equally (even with those ending in *-le* and *-y*) (see also Aronoff 2016: 48–49). Further research would thus be needed to shed light on the issue, as other factors may be of relevance.

The analysis of competition in inflection may prove useful for analyses of competition in word formation. They may not only behave in similar ways but, as suggested by Fernández-Alcaina (2021a: 24), it may also allow for "the definition of inflection and derivation in terms of a continuum rather than as clear-cut categories" (see, among others, Matthews 1974; Bybee 1985: 81ff.; Booij 1993; 1996; Plank 1994; Wurzel 1992, 1996; Stump 1998; Corbett 2010; Rainer et al. 2014: ch. 1; Štekauer 2014; Hathout & Namer 2022).

2.3. Competition in word formation

Competition in word formation may emerge as a result of, for example, the coining of new words, speech errors, and reanalysis of existing words (Lindsay & Aronoff 2013), because they generate the potential for more than one word-formation process to acquire the same meaning and be applied to the same domain. Pounder (2000: 669) puts it as follows: "[…] expansion into new 'territory' creates new potential for formation and thus enhances productivity, which leads to further expansion, which leads to further synonymy and potential competitors" (see also Lieber 2004: 115). However, the main factor behind the emergence of competition in English is borrowing (Riddle 1985: 452–455; Kwon 1997; Plag 1999; Lieber 2004: 44; Bauer 2009: 189, 196; see §2.3.1). Specifically, Kaunisto (2009: 74) states:

> [t]he most significant reason for the co-existence of rival derivational elements on the one hand, and of the resulting competing words, on the other, is the historical influences that other languages have had on English, most notably, French, Latin, and Greek.

The co-existence of synonymous (and, thus, potentially competing) patterns that emerged after extensive borrowing, especially during the 17th century, resulted, for example, in the competition between native and non-native synonymous affixes, such as *-ness* (native) and *-ity* (non-native) for the derivation of nouns (Díaz-Negrillo 2017: 119). There may also be competition between processes that have always been part of the native vocabulary stock of the English language, such as *-dom*, *-hood* and *-ship* (Díaz-Negrillo 2017). These examples illustrate one level where competition may take place, that is, competition between word-formation patterns, although competition may also take place at a lexical level, that is, between individual words (e.g. *answer/reply*). Bauer (2009: 196) holds that the latter, that is, micro-level competition between forms, may have an effect on the former, that is, macro-level competition between word-formation patterns: "[i]f sufficient doublets are formed and word-formation *x* wins out the majority of cases, then word-formation process *x* will become the dominant process" (Bauer 2009: 181), unless blocking is in place (§2.3.3.6).

Competition is expected to be resolved within an indefinite period of time, but this resolution is justified in various ways. It has been claimed that competition must be resolved due to:

i) the *Principle of Linguistic Economy*, according to which "[…] a linguistic system will avoid having two forms for the same purpose" (Bauer et al. 2010: 15; cf. also Plag 2000);
ii) avoidance of synonymy (e.g. Bréal 1897: 311; Dressler 1987: 113; Lindsay 2012; Lindsay & Aronoff 2013;[9] Aronoff 2016); or
iii) the "struggle for existence", following Gause (1934) (e.g. Aronoff 2016: 39; see also MacWhinney et al. 2014: 367).

Competition is a complex concept to define, and the factors governing its resolution are also intricate. The following sections provide an overview on competition

9 See, however, Aronoff & Lindsay (2014: 71–72), where the authors acknowledge that synonymy or blocking cannot by themselves explain the complex interaction between competing affixes.

in word formation with the aim of providing a theoretical framework for the analysis carried out in this book. First, a brief account on the emergence of competition in derivation is provided, with a focus on overt affixation and zero-affixation, which are the focus of this book (§2.3.1). Then, a definition of competition is provided (§2.3.2) and the possible outcomes of competition as well as the factors at play in the resolution are presented (§2.3.3). Finally, an outline on previous research on competition in English word formation is presented, with a focus on suffixal nominalisations (§2.3.4).

2.3.1. The emergence of competition in derivation

The English language has been greatly transformed throughout history, as a result of, for example, the influence of the dialects spoken by the Germanic tribes, or of the Norman invasion in 1066, which accelerated changes already underway and caused many others.

Old English (henceforth, OE) was also influenced by Latin after the Christianisation of Britain from 597. Latin words appear in writing before the end of the OE period, many of which were assimilated. According to Baugh & Cable (2013: 52), about 85% of the OE vocabulary has been lost, and what survive are basic elements that make up a large part of any English sentence. A Germanic language, English was highly inflectional. The derivational morphology of OE is characterised by a generous use of prefixes and suffixes to form new words, some of which have largely fallen out of use (e.g. *with-*). The process of conversion also goes back to the OE period, although of the stem-/root-based type as regards the open word classes.

French became the language of communication among the upper classes in England following the Norman Conquest in 1066. The influence of French reduced English from a highly inflected language to an increasingly analytic one (Romaine 1985: 461–462; Hock & Joseph 2009: 174–178). Thousands of words were borrowed from French and thus indirectly from Latin, and about 75% of them remain in use today (Baugh & Cable 2013: 174). This had the additional effect of an extensive influence on the native morphology, such that English suffixes started to be added to Romance bases, for example, *-er* in *eraser*, and also Romance affixes to native bases, for example, *-able* in *bearable* (Hock & Joseph 2009: 174). Most importantly for this book, the co-existence of the two models led to a situation where many words appeared to duplicate each other.[10] This is

10 This duplication was resolved mainly in two main ways: i) one word was lost, or ii) both words survived, but one became specialised (e.g. *pork/veal*, *ask/question*), so they were not regarded as exact synonyms.

also the only period in which the use of nominal conversion as is often described in English is more extensive than that of verbal conversion (Biese 1941: 34). Conversion is attested in every decade until the 14th century, even if with fluctuations in the frequency of use (Biese 1941: ch. 3).

From the 14th century onwards, what is considered the counterpart to PDE gradually prevailed over French. This coincides with a steady increase in the use of conversion as a word-formation process (Biese 1941: 37). During the Renaissance, thousands of Latin-based words were introduced into English, which led again to widespread competition: "[s]ince there were no dictionaries or academies to curb the number of new words, an atmosphere favouring linguistic experiments led to redundant production, often on the basis of competing derivational patterns" (Görlach 1991: 138, cited in Kjellmer 2000: 223–224). From the 17th to the 19th century, efforts were made towards standardisation, albeit with limited success. The colonisation of the British Empire brought new borrowings from several languages. In general, no major changes take place in the morphology from the 19th century onwards, except for perhaps a "great revival" of conversion, according to Biese (1941: 48).

The changes summarised above result in what PDE is today. It evolved dramatically over time, mainly due to sustained contact with other languages, which have influenced its morphology exceptionally heavily (see Booij 2020 on the morphology of Germanic languages). The derivational morphology of English has strong isolating tendencies and, reportedly, it is taking steps towards agglutination (Hock & Joseph 2009: 178).[11] It is characterised by a wide use of compounding, affixation and conversion, the latter being one of the oldest methods of word formation. The mix of a Germanic and a Romance stock, together with other factors, has led to the existence of competing patterns of word formation that are expected to find their differentiated domain of use, or disappear. The resolution of this competition depends on various factors (§2.3.3), and also on the role played by universal forces that may be at play in language change, such as language transparency and language economy.

In word formation, as hinted above, the choice between processes could be governed by an inherent conflict between the tendency towards morphotactic transparency and the (opposite) tendency towards phonological productivity (Dressler 1985b: 250). The competition between overt affixation and zero-affixation, specifically, evidences the conflict between the transparent model (overt affixation) and

11 Hock & Joseph (2009: 178) claim that languages tend to develop in cycles, as follows: isolating → agglutinating → inflectional → isolating.

the economical model (zero-affixation).[12] In view of the above, which two forces play a major role in the competition between an overt affix and a zero-affix may be reformulated: a tendency towards iconicity (that is, morphotactic and morphosemantic transparency), and a tendency towards the use of shorter forms. The former, described by Natural Morphology (henceforth, NM) as the most natural, would be expected in overt affixation, and the latter, which is closely related to the *Principle of Least Effort*, would be behind the preference for zero-affixation. In PDE, there seems to be a clash between the two models: although NM has claimed that iconicity and, thus, transparent affixation, is expected to prevail, a language-particular system may be at play where zero-affixation would be the preferred option, given the high productivity of this process (Quirk et al. 1985: 1558; Dressler et al. 1987; Crocco Galèas 1990: 30; Štekauer 1996: 11; Gaeta 2006: 14; Plag 2016: 2421; Hengeveld & Leufkens 2018). The experimental study carried out by Körtvélyessy et al. (2015: 106) in fact demonstrated that there are significant differences when comparing preferences in terms of semantic transparency and economy of expression, "[…] suggesting that the word-formation system of the complex-word-forming language plays a crucial role in the naming process".

In sum, why these two models of word formation have coexisted for so long despite their redundancy and their apparent violation of the one-to-one preference of the two dimensions of the linguistic sign is partly explained by the evolution of English over time (see Biese 1941; Hock & Joseph 2009 and Baugh & Cable 2013), but many other factors may have also had an influence (§2.3.3).

2.3.2. Definition

Despite the growing body of research on the topic, the concept of *competition* has been ambiguously defined in the literature. Fradin's (2016) description, here taken as a starting point for the delimitation of the concept, states that two conditions must be satisfied for morphological competition to occur:

i) forms have to be morphologically correlated to the same lexical base but present distinct exponents, and
ii) the derivational exponents have to express exactly the same semantic content.

Specifically, the bases are the same if they have the same meaning and occur in the same construction or have the same distribution, and the semantic content is the same if "the overall interpretation of the derived lexemes entails the same

12 This clash could also be viewed as one between the Germanic model, where words tend to be shorter, and the Romance model, where words tend to be longer (Zipf 1949: 112).

conclusions in similar contexts" (Fradin 2016). This definition covers what seems to be the general perception of what morphological competition is, although it still raises questions, especially as regards meaning, for example, should the derivatives be absolute synonyms? The degree of synonymy required is not the same for every author: Plag (2000: 2), Pounder (2000: 669) and Koehl (2015: 56) claim that competitors need to have the *same* meaning. Other authors hold that they should have "*roughly* the same semantic content" (Hoekstra & Versloot 2016, emphasis added) or be "semantically similar" (van Marle 1985: 178). Amutio-Palacios (2013: 46) allows even more flexibility and claims that they should "[...] overlap in the expression the same or a very similar meaning [sic].". In fact, some authors do not make an explicit reference to semantics in the description of competition (e.g. Kaunisto 2009).

If the key points in the definitions of competition given in the literature are put together, competitors would:

i) have the same base ("based on the same stem" in van Marle 1985: 178; "correlated to the same lexical base" in Fradin 2016),
ii) be derived with different affixes/exponents (Plag 2000: 2; Fradin 2016),
iii) be used in the same or similar contexts or domains (Plag 1999; Fradin 2016), and
iv) bear a relation of synonymy (see Huyghe & Varvara 2023a: 3–5).

In view of the above, this book considers that, for competition[13] to obtain, forms would (Lara-Clares & Thompson 2019: 27):

i) share the same base,
ii) be derived with different affixes,
iii) take affixes that express the same semantic category(s),
iv) operate in the same domain, and
v) be free of constraints (e.g. phonological, morphological).

If all these conditions are fulfilled, then two or more forms are considered competitors. If the competition extends to more forms derived by the same process but from different bases, then it would be considered as an instance of competition between word-formation patterns. Therefore, competition at a lexical level is evidence of competition at a systemic level, that is, of a competing pattern. The focus of this book is on the latter: four competing word-formation patterns are researched by analysing groups of competing forms derived by the same process.

13 Note that this definition is restricted to the competition between affixes, as it is the focus here.

These groups will be named *clusters*, defined as "sets of synonymous derivatives morphologically related by their bases but formed with a different affix that can be grouped into doublets, triplets, etc." (Fernández-Alcaina 2017: 168).

2.3.3. The resolution of competition

An analogy has been drawn between natural languages and biology by describing competition as a *struggle for existence*, whereby no two species may coexist in the same ecological niche[14] in stable equilibrium (Lindsay 2012; Lindsay & Aronoff 2013; Aronoff 2016, 2023). Following Gause's (1934) *Competitive Exclusion Principle*, only the most efficient species will be naturally selected and thus reproduce at a higher rate. The less efficient species will become extinct or will need to find a new *ecological niche* by means of adaptive changes (see MacWhinney 2014 for a parallel interpretation, following Darwin 1859). Word-formation patterns are here analogous to species, so only the best fitting pattern will survive, and the competitors will either disappear or will need to find their own niche, that is, a domain of use where they prevail. This view of competition as a struggle for a niche illustrates some of the ways in which competition may be resolved: coming out of use or becoming specialised in some way.

In word formation, Fernández-Alcaina (2021a; 2021b) describes a series of possibilities for competition to be resolved over time. Fernández-Alcaina (2021a: 121, 169–170) divides clusters of competition into the following three groups:

i) *past competition*, where all members are classified as in disuse in the OED, for example, *quintessence*^{V}/*quintessentiate*^{V} 'extract the quintessence of or from something';
ii) *resolved competition*, where one competitor prevails over another, which eventually falls out of use, for instance, conversion prevails over *-ate* in *culture*^{V}/*culturate*^{V} 'cultivate (soil, plants)'; and
iii) *ongoing competition*, where the members are unmarked regarding their use and thus coexist for a period of time, for example, *active*^{V}/*activate*^{V} 'make active' according to the OED.

There is a fourth possibility linked to resolved competition, where each competitor remains in use but finds a specific domain of application, be it phonological (e.g. complementary distribution), stylistic (e.g. academic or informal contexts of

14 If viewed from the perspective of derivational paradigms, a niche is equivalent to a slot in the paradigm, for which forms or processes compete (Pounder 2000: 669; Bauer et al. 2013: 568).

use), or of some other kind. This situation would thus be named *ongoing competition* as long as they have not become specialised, and then *resolved competition* once their domains are differentiated, because each competitor would prevail in their domain.

However, for Pounder (2000: 322), competition needs *not* be resolved, because "equivalent formations" may coexist and "[t]here does not [...] appear to be any competition at the lexical level that would imply a low tolerance for synonymy". We would then expect forms to co-exist peacefully as long as there is not a more frequent or productive operation (Pounder 2000: 322, 669–672). This is also acknowledged by Aronoff (2016: 48): "[...] competitive states may be more normal than resolution", meaning that competition may extend itself for a long period of time when no competitor may seem to have any clear advantage over the other(s). Štekauer (2017) named this situation as one where there is an *imperfect* complementary distribution, because the scope of applicability of the rules is not settled and, thus, forms compete for the same domain. Following Fernández-Alcaina's (2021a; 2021b) classification, they are instances of ongoing competition.

The resolution of competition is governed by a series of factors that may be at play. These factors will determine the extent of use of the processes (e.g. productivity, blocking) and their domain of application (e.g. phonology, profile of the base, register distribution). However, the domain of application of derivational affixes can be defined differently for unproductive patterns and for productive patterns. In the former case, the domain can be defined only enumerating all the bases actually used (extensionally), while in productive patterns it is defined by indicating the features that any potential base (or derivational affix) should possess and any other factors that may be relevant (intensionally; Rainer 2005: 335). This book analyses only productive processes. Factors are usually described in the form of constraints or restrictions, which can be presented as base-driven or affix-driven. Whether the description is based on one or the other seems to make no actual difference (see Rainer 2005: 342–343 and 2014: 343–344 for a discussion).

The following sections describe the factors and variables that play a role in the resolution of competition according to the description of the authors whenever possible. In what follows, the review of the literature will be restricted mainly to the focus of this book, namely the competition between affixal processes. Although each factor is presented separately, they often overlap, for example, a phonetic restriction may go hand in hand with a morphological restriction.

2.3.3.1. Phonological factors

Research on phonological constraints on affixation is still scarce, even if some works (e.g. Raffelsiefen 1998; 2015; Rainer 2005; Bauer et al. 2013) provide useful insights on the topic. Rainer (2005: 344–345) classifies phonological restrictions into three types:

i) the sensitivity of a suffix to certain phonemes present in the base, for example, *-eer* shows a preference for bases ending in [t], as in *musketeer* (Adams 1973: 174–178) and *-en* is only added to bases ending in a fricative, especially those in *-t* or *-d* (Marchand 1969: 272);
ii) prosodic restrictions, such as the preference of *-eer* for bisyllabic trochaic bases, as in *profiteer/*gainer*,[15] or the constraint by which *-en* attaches only to monosyllables (Plag & Baayen 2009: 111); and
iii) the sensitivity of a suffix to the final stress of the base, whereby stress is needed, such as *-al* in *arrival*.[16]

Regarding the combination of affixes, phonological restrictions may explain why *-ity* does not attach to adjectives ending in *-less*, whereas *-ness* does: as *-less* is more easily parsable than *-ity*, it should not occur "inside" the latter (Rainer 2005: 339). This constraint was put forward by Hay (2002), and named *Complexity Based Ordering* by Plag (2002). However, it does not explain why certain combinations are unacceptable (see Hay & Plag 2004, cited in Rainer 2005: 339).

It has also been claimed that a language-specific phenomenon cuts across two types of restrictions: phonological, and regarding the origin of the affix. Latinate suffixes in English are mainly vowel-initial, whereas Germanic suffixes are mainly consonant-initial (Dressler 1987: 123). Besides, most native roots are monosyllabic or disyllabic with an unstressed second syllable (e.g. *water*), whereas most Latinate roots are polysyllabic or occur as bound morphs (e.g. *invest-*) (Plag 2003: 85). In line with this, the combination of native and non-native affixes has generally been described as follows: native affixes readily combine with non-native affixes (e.g. *-iveness*), but Latinate affixes do not tolerate native affixes (e.g. **-lessity*) (Plag 2003: 85; see also Giegerich 1999 for a revision of the theory of level ordering). The phonological behaviour of these two types of affixes is also different: affixes of Romance or Latin origin produce more phonological changes in their bases (e.g. *persuade*, *persuasive*) and they also affect stress (e.g. *atom*, *atomic*, *atomicity*), whereas native affixes are stress-neutral (e.g. *home*, *homeless*, *homelessness*) (Rainer 2005: 340).

---

15 Rainer (2005: 344) points out that this restriction could also be formulated as an output restriction according to which stress clash is avoided.

16 Malicka-Kleparska (1992: 437, cited in Rainer 2005: 344) claims, however, that the final stress may not be key in this case, but rather the fact that *-al* shows a preference for Latinate prefix-root verbs, which all happen to have final stress.

It should be noted that it is at times difficult to know whether the restriction is on the affixes or on the bases: a tendency has been described, for example, for non-native verbs to display a iambic pattern and some nominalising affixes, such as *-ment*, have shown a preference for disyllabic bases that consist of a iambic foot; whether this preference is on the affix or on the base is unknown (Bauer et al. 2013: 198).

An analysis of phonological restrictions serves to test whether apparently competing affixes may actually not be competitors, as in the case of *-ify* and *-ize*, because the former shows a preference for short (monosyllabic or disyllabic) bases, whereas the latter derives mostly from polysyllabic bases (Schneider 1987: 108; see also Lindsay 2012: 197). If there were no other domain of application in which they overlap, the identification of this restriction would then lead to the conclusion that they are not actually in competition. These suffixes, for example, are in an almost complementary distribution with respect to the type of bases they attach to, but with an overlap in trochaic bases (Plag 1999; 2003: 93–94; Kjellmer 2001: 161; Lindsay 2012: 196–198; Bauer et al. 2013: 269–274).

2.3.3.2. The profile of the base

Restrictions on word formation may also be presented as depending on the profile of the base. In the previous section, for example, a restriction regarding the length of the base was described for *-ize*/*-ify*. Another factor could be syntactic, for example, the transitivity of the base, such that transitive bases are preferred by the suffix *-able* (e.g. *observable*/**lookable*) (Bauer 2001: 133, example from Varvara 2020: 79). Plag (2004: 207) claims that exceptions can be found to this rule, because the suffix *-able* has also been attested in intransitive bases, such as *changeable* in *changeable weather*. Besides, he holds that "[…] the syntactic category of potential base words is only a by-product of the semantics of the process" (Plag 2004: 193), and that this constraint can thus be explained on purely semantic grounds.

The following sections illustrate four other types of restrictions regarding the profile of the base that have been described in the literature, that is, restrictions regarding the origin, word class or morphological structure of the base, or regarding its semantics.

2.3.3.2.1. The origin of the base

Affixes tend to agree with the base as regards their historical origin, that is, Germanic affixes tend to go with Germanic bases, and Romance affixes with Romance bases, for example, *kingly* but *royal* (Kjellmer 2000: 212; see also Kjellmer 2001: 162; Rainer 2005: 347). This was named the *Latinate Constraint*, according to which "[b]ases and affixes may combine only if their etymological features are compatible" (Plag 1996: 778). The reason why this happens has been addressed by Kjellmer (2000: 212):

> [i]f stem and affix agree in a potential word, the word will therefore conform better to the norms, however fuzzy, of the lexicon, and hence possess a higher degree of potentiality than one where this would not be the case.

Schneider (1987: 98–99) provides an example of a constraint regarding the origin of the base: the verb-forming suffix *-en* is mostly used with Germanic bases, whereas *-ify* and *-ize* (potential competitors) are mostly used with French bases, even if they may accept bases from other origins, such as German (*nazify*), Italian (*miniaturize*), Spanish (*tobacconize*), Russian (*podzolize*) or Czech (*robotize*). Anyhow, many affixes accept both types of bases (e.g. *-er*), even if most of them show a preference for one or the other. For example, for the formation of nouns, *-al* and *-ation* show a preference for non-native bases, whereas conversion shows a preference for native bases (Bauer et al. 2013: ch. 10).

2.3.3.2.2. The word class of the base

Affixes are usually classified according to the word class of their bases, that is, deverbal, denominal, deadjectival, etc. This classification implies that the syntactic category of the base plays a major role in the selection of affixes, as has been tacitly assumed in the literature. For example, Bauer et al. (2013: ch. 16) classify locative prefixes according to the word class of their bases,[17] and conclude that most prefixes attach to nouns (e.g. *ex-*, as in *ex-billionaire*), nearly all to adjectives (e.g. *inter-*, as in *interracial*), and many to verbs (e.g. *down-* as in *download*).

However, what might initially be seen as a restriction according to the word class of the base may actually be determined by the semantics of the base (Plank 1981: 43–45; Plag 1999: 237; Rainer 2005: 347–348, and references therein). Plag (2004: 214) addresses this issue and claims that the word class of the base is irrelevant, if "[…] the meaning of the pertinent bases in interaction with the meaning of the suffix satisfy the semantic restrictions on the output". It is for this reason that this book does not restrict data selection according to the word class of the base, but according to semantics; as it would be expected, however, the bases of the PDE competitors happen to all be of the same word class. For example, all the PDE competitors identified that are derived by *-ation* and by zero-affixation of the semantic category ACTION are deverbal (see Appendix 1.A).

17 Bauer et al. (2013) also classify locative prefixes according to whether they attach to: i) native/non-native bases, ii) bound bases, iii) compounds, and iv) phrases.

2.3.3.2.3. *The morphological structure of the base*

As regards the morphological structure of the base, two variables must be taken into consideration:

i) the existence of closing suffixes, and
ii) potentiation.

Closing suffixes in word formation preclude further derivation, so they limit the ability of affixes to attach to certain bases, for example, *-ism* (Manova 2015, and references therein). Specifically, a closing affix curtails the domain of a more general competing domain (Rainer 2005: 346). Closing affixes, however, do not have an effect on competition (in the sense of competition used in this book),[18] because they would not allow derivation by any of the potential competitors: a form with a closing affix could not be the base for which affixes would compete. The other variable, *potentiation*, occurs whenever an affix facilitates the attachment of another affix, for example, *en-* potentiates *-ment* in *entombment* (Williams 1981). An interesting case in this respect is the suffix *-ize*, which potentiates *-ation* and, at the same time, precludes the use of other nominal suffixes, such as *-ment*, *-al* or *-age* (Plag 2003: 63; Bauer et al. 2013: 201–202). For research on competition, an analysis of potentiation could help explain in which context one affix is preferred over another: the potentiated affix is expected to prevail, even though there might be other contexts where the non-potentiated affix prevails. An example of this situation is that of the adjective-forming suffixes *-ic* and *-ical*: *-ic* is more productive in most contexts, but *-ical* seems to prevail in bases ending in *-olog-* (Lindsay 2012: 193).

2.3.3.2.4. *The semantics of the base*

Just as the Latinate Constraint addresses a need for the compatibility of the etymological features of the base and affix, this section addresses the need for a compatibility of the semantics of the base and affix. This was named *semantic coindexation* by Soares Rodrigues (2015: 134ff.), in parallel to Lieber's (2004) concept of coindexation (see below, this section). In Spanish, for example, the relational suffix *-uno* is almost exclusively attached to nouns referring to animals, for example, *perro* 'dog' derives *perruno* 'relating to dogs' (Rainer 2005: 349).

---

18 Competition has sometimes been understood more broadly, where there is as a clash between two or more word-formation patterns independently of whether they attach to the same base (e.g. Riddle 1985; Smith 2020). In that view of competition, closing affixes may be relevant, because they have an effect on the potential combinability of the affixes in question.

In English, for example, the nominalising suffix *-ness* can take as bases both adjectives that express permanent qualities (e.g. *clever*) and states (e.g. *isolated*) (Rainer 2015: 1271). For the formation of adverbs in *-ly* a semantic restriction has been described according to which adjectival bases need to be dynamic (Kjellmer 1984).[19] The suffixes *-dom*, *-ship* and *-hood*, which form abstract nouns, all prefer nominal bases which denote persons (and sometimes animals) (Bauer et al. 2013: 248).

The examples above show that semantic restrictions on the base are mainly, as claimed by Bauer, "[...] a matter of what it makes sense to have a word for" (Bauer 2001: 134). Take the case of the prefix *step-*: as it is used to denote a relationship between two people, it only makes sense to attach it to nouns of relatives such as *mother* or *brother*.

Lieber's concept of coindexation operates with semantic and syntactic features, defined as the "binding of an affixal argument with a base argument" (Lieber 2004: 36). Coindexation could be used to ascertain whether there is any limitation in the attachment of certain affixes to certain bases and, thus, to establish whether some affixes are in competition or not. Lieber (2004: 62–71), for example, compares the coindexation of the nominal suffixes *-er*, *-ee*, *-ist* and *-ant*/*-ent*. She concludes that, even though the four affixes contribute the same semantically, "[...] their syntactic subcategorization and the co-indexation conditions of their arguments vary in small ways", for example, *-ist* has a strict requirement of volitionality, whereas *-ee* has a weaker one (Lieber 2004: 62; see also Plag 2003: 63). This could point towards a specialisation in the domain of use of the suffixes, which ultimately entails that they are not actually in competition.

2.3.3.3. Frequency and productivity

The concept of productivity was put forward by Adam Smith for economics (Dressler 2008: 458ff.). In linguistics, the notion was implicit already in the work of Sanskrit grammarians, although the first explicit reference to productivity can be found in Dietz (1838; Bauer 2001: 10–11). Since then, the concept has been used somewhat equivocally, especially because it has often been used as an equivalent to frequency (see Plag 1999: 5–35; Bauer 2001: 11–32; Gaeta & Ricca 2015 for comprehensive surveys).

This book views *productivity* as the potential of particular word-formation processes to create new words to satisfy a naming need (Plag 1999, 2006; Bauer

19 Similarly, in Italian, verbal evaluative suffixes show a preference for atelic, dynamic, and durative verbs, and are thus sensitive to the Aktionsart of the base verb (Grandi 2009: 56–57, cited in Rainer et al. 2014: 24).

2001; Gaeta & Ricca 2003a, 2003b). *Productivity* must be distinguished from *creativity*, according to how new words are created: creativity is related to analogy, whereas productivity is inherently rule-governed. Bauer believes that the two concepts, creativity and productivity, are hyponyms of innovation, so they are two different ways by which new words are coined (Bauer 2001: 64). Bauer (2001: 63–71) also points out that, when a coinage changes the rules, it is creative and, when it exploits the rules, it is productive, even if there is no clear-cut distinction between both.

The concept of *productivity* is tightly linked to that of potentiality. A potential word, as opposed to an actual word, is a word that might exist even if it does not: it would fill a lexical gap (Bauer 2001: 40). Productivity is all about potential but, as not all potentially useful words are actually created and used, we need to distinguish between the general possibility for a word to be formed (related to structural factors) and the opportunity to use the new word in actual speech (related to pragmatic factors) (Plag 2005: 125–126).

Frequency or, better, productivity, has been used to compare word-formation rules in order to:

i) determine whether a process can give rise to new forms, and
ii) measure which process gives rise (or will potentially give rise) to more new forms.

The former corresponds to *disponibilité* (availability), and the latter to *rentabilité* (profitability), using Corbin's (1987: 177) terminology (translated in Carstairs-McCarthy 1992). In this sense, productivity is not so much a factor that restricts the use of affixes, as the ones presented in the previous sections, but a way to define the extent of use of one process as compared to another. In a scenario of competition, if no other factors apply, the more productive process is expected to win out (Rainer 1988, cited in Bauer 2009: 182).

2.3.3.3.1. Availability

Availability is a discrete property that refers to the (im)possibility of a process to create new words. Although it may seem to be straightforward, the (un)availability of a process is sometimes difficult to assess. For example, the suffix *-th* was considered unavailable from the 17th century, but Walpole coined two words with that suffix in the 18th century, that is, *gloomth* and *greenth* (Bauer 2001: 206). This could be seen as proof that renewed availability can take place, that is, that an unavailable process may become available again (a possibility suggested by Bauer 2014; see also Fernández-Alcaina & Čermák 2018). However, the fact that it has only been attested as being used by one speaker and it has not been used to coin new words from the 19th century may evidence the existence of some threshold of usage above which a process is considered to be productive (see also §2.3.3.7 on analogy). Still, the spread of neologisms might work differently nowadays due to mass media and online communication, as it would make even low-frequency words available to a large community of speakers within a very short period of time.

Availability is important for competition, because it may help decide whether competition has been resolved or not: if a process becomes unavailable, it is likely to have been superseded by another (competing) process (or the naming need has disappeared; see Bauer 2009: 188). This has been largely investigated by Fernández-Alcaina (2017; 2021a; 2021b; Fernández-Alcaina & Čermák 2018), who identified c. 350 clusters of competition for the formation of verbs by affixation and conversion based on lexicographic data from the third version of the OED (OED3). The results show that the availability of forms may change over time: for example, many clusters of competition between *-en* and conversion were identified over time, which proves that the two processes were available in the past, but the suffix *-en* is considered unavailable nowadays. A look at the (un)availability of the processes over time shows that *-en* has become largely replaced by conversion for the CAUSATIVE sense, which is the most prevalent meaning in the formation of deadjectival verbs (see Fernández-Alcaina 2021b: 70). Ultimately, this stresses the need for the qualification of judgements of the resolution of competition of forms not in absolute terms, but with regard to or for specific senses.

2.3.3.3.2. Profitability

Profitability is a gradable property that refers to the extent to which available morphological processes are exploited by language users, that is, to what extent they may be used or have been used to produce new words (Bauer 2001: 49). A correlation has been described between the profitability of an affix and its range of meanings. For example, conversion into verbs is extremely productive and it "[...] exhibit[s] the widest range of meaning of all verb-deriving processes" (Plag 2000: 8). The more meanings a process has, the more likely it is to compete with other processes; at the same time, the more productive it is, the more likely it is to outlast it competitors. Productivity is, then, at the same time the cause and the consequence of the tendencies in the resolution of competition: the higher the productivity, the more likely it is to have competitors and the more likely it is to prevail over its competitors. It should be taken into account, however, that the fact of being in competition may also reduce the productivity of the process, if the other competing process is or becomes more productive.[20]

Measures of profitability have been proposed over the past 50 years in order to quantify the profitability of processes (Aronoff 1976; Baayen & Lieber 1991; Baayen 1993; 1994; 2009; Baayen & Renouf 1996; Hay 2001; Gaeta & Ricca 2003a; 2003b; Hay & Baayen 2003; Fernández-Domínguez 2013), which would allow to compare them (see, e.g., Plag 2000 for a comparison of the productivity of the verb-forming suffixes *-ize*, *-ify* and *-ate*). The profitability measures proposed so far, however, are not without problems, as they include in the computation a series of elements that lead to results that might be distorted (e.g., by the influence of lexicalised units or of typographical mistakes) and they do not seem to work well with low frequencies (see Fernández-Domínguez et al. 2007). Besides, there is, to the best of my knowledge, only one measure available that is specific to research on competition: Fernández-Domínguez's (2017) *Index of Competition* (*C*) or, in its more recent version, the *Referenced Index of Competition* (C*, Fernández-Domínguez 2024). This measure quantifies the likelihood that a morpheme will outlast its competitors. Measure *C** is based on the idea that the more units are in direct competition, the more challenging their individual survival will be. Therefore, the more competitors there are in a cluster, the lower measure *C** will be, because the very presence of other units means the existence of rivals, and then each unit has fewer chances of success. There are three main advantages in the use of this measure for the assessment of profitability in competition:

i) the competitive status of a form is not assessed through an isolated numerical value, but it is in the context of the cluster in question through several variables,
ii) it allows for an analysis at the level of the senses (see §3.3.2.2.3 for the application of this measure in this book), and
iii) it allows for cross-cluster comparison, which is especially useful to analyse patterns of competition.

2.3.3.4. Register distribution

Traditional models for measuring morphological productivity did not make a distinction between the productivity of certain word-formation processes according to type of discourse. For this reason, Plag, Dalton-Puffer & Baayen (1999) examine

20 Dressler (2008: 461) puts it as follows: "[a] productive rule without a productive competition is more productive than a rule that competes with another in the same domain of applications".

how morphological productivity varies across three different types of discourse: written language, context-governed language, and everyday conversations. This paper relies on BNC data for 15 suffixes classified into different categories. It uses Baayen's "productivity in the strict sense" formula, defined as "the quotient of the number of hapax legomena *n1* with a given affix and the total number of tokens *N* of all words with that affix" (Plag et al. 1999: 216). The findings are that derivation is much less productive in spoken language than in written language, and that productivity is higher in context-governed speech than in everyday conversations. This may be because derivational morphology is the main source for vocabulary growth, and written language is lexically richer than spoken language (Plag et al. 1999: 218). The results also show that some suffixes are widely used in written language but hardly ever in spoken language, as is the case of *-type*, *-like* and *-free*. The only counterexample here is the suffix *-wise*, which is more productive in spoken than in written language. Other affixes, such as *-able* (partitive), *-ful*, *-ion*, *-ist*, *-ity* and *-less*, show a significant variation (Plag et al. 1999: 223–224). Structural factors cannot explain this variation and the authors justify these differences from a functional point of view: the referential function of derivational morphology, as well as the labelling function, are frequently needed in written language, whereas orality has other means of maintaining reference (establishing common ground, paralinguistic possibilities, prosody, deixis; Plag et al. 1999: 225-226). This study set the ground for later research on register variation (see, e.g., Efthymiou et al. 2012; Laws & Ryder 2018), but the lack of a semantic classification of affixes makes it difficult to use their results for an analysis of competition.[21] Furthermore, as the focus is on the general productivity of affixes and not on competition, the forms under study do not (necessarily) derive from the same base(s).

Most studies on productivity across registers have excluded zero-affixation for the methodological difficulties in its computation, one exception being the study by Benítez-Castro & Valera (2010). They analyse morphological complexity in the written academic register based on data from the BNC sampler and show that affixation is the most frequent process, followed by conversion. This tendency holds also when only nouns are analysed: affixation shows the highest type frequency, followed by conversion and compounding. Similarly, research on which affixes are more frequently used in scientific English than in general English shows that abstract noun-forming suffixes (e.g. *-ity*, *-ion* and *-ness*) are more

21 Bauer et al. (2013) describe affixes in terms of their productivity and their meaning. However, they do not specify how they measured productivity, apart from the fact that they assessed productivity "[...] based on noticing the extent to which neologisms formed by a particular process can be found".

frequent in scientific registers than in the BNC (Montero-Fleta 2011). Similarly, Guz (2009) concludes that *-ness* is preferred in fiction, whereas *-ity* is preferred in the academic register.

2.3.3.5. Non-structural factors

The first non-structural factor to consider is of a pragmatic kind. Pragmatic effects deal with the way in which words are used or the nature of the real-world referent of the word (Bauer 2001: 134). This kind of constraint is thus related to non-structural factors that "[…] make certain elements desirable to use and therefore productive" (Plag 2005: 126). Three main pragmatic constraints have been listed in the literature in this regard:

i) there has to be a need, or the form would be redundant for language use,
ii) the object denoted must be nameable, that is, something we can think of when we hear the word, and
iii) the object of the label needs to exist (in the real world or in fiction), that is, hypostatisation.

Pragmatics is usually behind output conditions, such as the context of use. The French suffixes *-age*, *-ion* and *-ment* have been considered to be roughly synonymous, but a distinction has been made based on the degree of technicality of the action denoted, for example, *-age* nominals tend to be more technical than *-ion* ones (Wauquier et al. 2020b). Restrictions could also be described according to the input: learned affixes, for example, are often limited to learned bases and, if they are applied to ordinary bases, there will be a jocular effect (Rainer 2005: 349).

Also associated with pragmatic constraints are fashion or aesthetics (Fernández-Domínguez et al. 2007: 32). Take the example of prefixes like *mega-*, *giga-* or *mini-*, which have been used irregularly, depending on the fashion of the period (Plag 2003: 60).

Another non-structural factor that has been described in the literature is gender-based variation. Säily (2011) analysed the use of *-ity* and *-ness* and showed that *-ity* is used less productively by women than by men (regarding *-ness* no gender difference was found). This might be justified by the fact that borrowed suffixes were initially only available to educated individuals, who were mostly men (Romaine 1985: 461–462), a situation which may have led to a stylistic difference in the use of one suffix or the other: *-ity* in the higher variety, and *-ness* in the lower one (Säily 2011: 120; see §2.3.4.1.1 on the competition between *-ity* and *-ness*).

The constraints described so far are generalisations on the speakers' choice for one or another word-formation process. However, individual differences must be taken into account too. These differences are rooted in the speakers' creative approach to word formation, that is, the *Principle of Creativity within Productivity Constraints* (Štekauer 2005). This principle dictates that it is the language user that decides which of the options available will be used in the particular act of naming. This selection will be affected by factors such as the ones cited above, as well as by a series of sociolinguistic or psycholinguistic factors. This is because a naming strategy is in place, which is "[…] the preference of a language speaker to coin semantically transparent or formally economical complex words" (Körtvélyessy et al. 2015: 99). The naming strategy speakers use will depend on their age group, education, profession, and verbal or non-verbal abilities (Körtvélyessy et al. 2015: 99). Two groups of language users were identified based on their tendencies in the naming acts in English (Štekauer et al. 2005: 28, 32):

i) higher educated users show a preference for more explicit morphological types or rules (interpretation friendly), and
ii) lower educated users show a preference for brevity of expression by using simpler and more general naming units.

The comparison of native and non-native users is a different matter, and it has been shown in several realms that the non-native group lays greater emphasis on accuracy and, thus, on explicitness (Štekauer et al. 2005: 36).

2.3.3.6. Blocking: type and token

One mechanism that may limit the productivity of word-formation processes is blocking or preemption. The term was defined by Aronoff (1976: 43) as "the non-occurrence of one form due to the simple existence of another". Rainer (1988) made a distinction between two types of blocking (cf. also Plag 2005: 126):

i) token blocking, that is, "the impossibility of forming a potential regular form due to an already existing synonymous word" (e.g. *arrival* blocks **arrivement*), and
ii) type blocking, that is, "the impossibility of applying one rule if there is another pertinent rule" (*-ation* blocks zero-affixation in the formation of nouns ending in *-ify* or *-ize*).

Token blocking applies especially to rare words (token-infrequent), in the face of more common synonymous words (more token-frequent) (Bauer 2009: 188). This could be due to a matter of processing because a speaker might, for example, produce a word such as **arrivement* when they momentarily fail to retrieve the standard term (Rainer 2005: 337; see also Plag 2003: 66). Type blocking is based on the principle that each suffix has a domain of application which is exclusive to them. When competition arises, it is usually claimed that the (more) special case blocks the more general case (Plag 2000: 2).

The concept of *blocking* has always been subject to criticism (see, e.g., van Marle 1985; Bauer 2001; Rainer 2005; Bauer et al. 2013: 575–578), and the definition has been revised multiple times. For example, (token) blocking is "[...] the failure of a particular word to become established in a community due to the fact that a word with the same base and the same meaning is already established in that community" (Bauer et al. 2013: 34). Following this definition, the very existence of competitors would be impossible, and yet many counterexamples can be found. The same could be applied to word-formation processes: one could claim that words or processes are not blocked as such, but rather that their use is restricted to, for example, a pragmatic domain (e.g. *rooster* replacing *cock*, for the sexual sense of the latter).

Aronoff & Lindsay (2014) admit that Aronoff's initial definition was too simplistic, and that competing forms or processes are deflected, rather than simply blocked. This is illustrated as follows: the suffixes *-ness*, *-ce* and *-cy* are competitors, because they all form abstract nouns from adjectives (e.g. *pleasantness*, *elegance* and *buoyancy*). The former suffix, *-ness*, is the default nominaliser in adjectival bases, and the other two are more productive in specific domains: *-cy* is favoured in words ending in *-ate* (e.g. *piracy*) and *-ce* is favoured in words ending in *-ent* and *-ant* (e.g. *resistance*, *dependence*). However, the competing suffixes are not always completely blocked, but rather either there is a difference in meaning or one of the members or the pair becomes more specialised (especially *-ncy* forms) (Aronoff & Lindsay 2014: 70–71). The conclusion is as follows (Aronoff & Lindsay 2014: 71):

> [...] the idea that a given word bearing one of these three suffixes simply blocks its rivals does not begin to do justice to the complex interaction both among the suffixes and within individual pairs of words.

In view of the above, blocking would not prevent the formation of a word, but its institutionalisation, and it does not require just a relation of synonymy, but also stylistic equivalence (Bauer 1983: 88; Bauer et al. 2013: 577). This stresses why an analysis of the register of use (e.g. based on BNC data) and any other stylistic or regional difference (e.g. based on OED data) are necessary for research on competition.

2.3.3.7. Analogy

The role of analogy in word formation has been debated extensively in the literature, often to point to the difficulty in its assessment, because it "[...] is neither a static nor a homogeneous concept" (Mattiello 2017: 50; see also Moder 1992; Plag 1999: 17–22; Bauer et al. 2013: 519–530, 633–635, and references therein). An analogical form has been defined as "a new formation clearly modelled on one already existing lexeme, and not giving rise to a productive series" (Bauer 1983: 96). Analogy has thus been used to explain the derivation of forms that could not have been formed by the application of a productive rule, but rather due to the influence of paradigmatic relationships (Moder 1992: 180). See the example given above for the formation of *greenth*. If derivation by *-th* was not available, then Walpole could have derived that word by means of analogy (see Plag 2006: 122). To give another example, the word *morpheme* itself appears to have been formed on the analogy of *phoneme*, *grapheme* or *lexeme* (Mattiello 2017: 38).

It is commonly assumed that instances of analogy may develop into rules if their use becomes extensive enough (see Lehrer 1996: 67; Bauer 2001: 75–97). There is thus a gradient in analogy, just as there was in profitability, and there is a point where the repetitive formation via analogy becomes a rule; how to tell that point is, however, unclear. The same happens, by extension, with the distinction between creative and productive formations (see discussion in Mattiello 2017: 50). Mattiello (2017) proposes a model of analogy where it is seen as a gradual concept. At one end of the scale is surface analogy, that is, analogy based on a unique exemplar (e.g. the coinage of *software* after *hardware*), and at the other end is analogy via schema, based on several prototypes (*software*, *firmware*, *adware* and *spyware* become prototypes for the creation of later *malware*, *bloatware*, etc.).

In research on competition, both blocking and local analogy are expected to play a role (see, e.g., Plag 2000), but exactly how they do so is unclear. Kaunisto (2007: 38), for example, analyses the competition between *-ic* and *-ical* for the formation of adjectives, and claims that "[…] the significance of this factor [i.e. analogy] remains a mere theoretical possibility, as its effect is difficult to verify with absolute certainty".

Analogy can also be modelled computationally. Analogical algorithms can account for rule-like behaviours (or analogy via schema), as well as local analogies, but they have so far been restricted to small sets of data. Arndt-Lappe (2014), for example, analyses the competition between *-ity* and *-ness* using an analogical model, and concludes that the variability of use of these affixes decreases over time in some types of bases, so the system might be regularising without an underlying rule. The results show that *-ness* is the default nominaliser, but *-ity* prevails in some domains as compared to its competitor. An overview on research on this pair of competitors is provided in §2.3.4.1.1.

2.3.4. Research on competition in English affixation

Previous research on competition can be grouped according to the word class of the derived form and, within the same word class, according to the competing patterns analysed. The following list provides some of the main references that deal, more or less directly, with each group of competitors:

i) Nominal competition: three references that provide a comprehensive overview on the competition between nominalising patterns are Lieber (2004; 2016) and Bauer et al. (2013). References about specific patterns are:[22]
   a. *-ation*/zero-affixation: Lara-Clares (2017);
   b. *-ity*/*-ness*: Aronoff (1976); Aronoff & Anshen (1981); Riddle (1985); Romaine (1985); Anshen & Aronoff (1988); Guz (2009); Säily (2011; 2018); Baeskow (2012); Lindsay (2012); Arndt-Lappe (2014) and Rainer (2015);
   c. *-ing*/conversion: Lieber & Plag (2022);
   d. *-ness*/zero-affixation: Lara-Clares & Thompson (2019);
   e. *-ship*/*-dom*/*-hood*: Aronoff & Cho (2001); Trips (2009); Baeskow (2010); Lieber (2010); Amutio-Palacios (2013); Lehrer (2003) and Díaz-Negrillo (2017);
   f. *-ster*/*-ette*/*-ess*: Adams (1973) and Bauer (2009);
   g. zero-affixation[23]/suffixation: Cetnarowska (1993); Renner (2020) and Iordăchioaia (2022);
   h. actional nominalisation (Fernández-Domínguez 2024); and
   i. diminutives: Bauer (2009) and Lehrer (2003).

ii) Verbal competition: six references that provide comprehensive overviews are Plag (1999), Kjellmer (2001), Gottfurcht (2008), Bauer et al. (2013) and Fernández-Alcaina (2021a; 2021b). References about specific patterns are:
   a. *-en*/conversion: Bauer et al. (2010);

22 A difference has been described between competition between processes (e.g. suffixation vs. periphrastic expressions in the formation of comparative and superlative) and between word-formation patterns (e.g. *-ity* vs. *-ness* in nominalisations) (Fernández-Alcaina 2021b: 22). As this book deals with affixal processes, the competition described is both between processes and patterns, although the latter term will be of preference for its higher specificity.

23 Cetnarowska names this process *bare nominalisation* and Renner names it *morphostasis*.

b. *-en*/*-ify*/*-ize*/*-ate*/conversion:[24] Schneider (1987); Raffelsiefen (1998); Plag (2000); Lindsay (2012) and Lindsay & Aronoff (2013);
c. *-ize*/conversion: Fernández-Alcaina (2017);
d. zero-affixation[25]/suffixation: Fernández-Alcaina (2021a, 2021b); Debouzi (2024); and
e. negative prefixes: Bauer (2009).

iii) Adjectival competition: two comprehensive references are Hamawand (2007) and Bauer et al. (2013). References about specific patterns are:
a. *-ed*/*-y*: Nagano (2022);
b. *-ic*/*-ical*: Gries (2001, 2003); Kaunisto (2007); Lindsay (2012) and Aronoff & Lindsay (2014);
c. *-ish*/*-y*: Malkiel (1977);
d. *-ive*/*-ory*: Kaunisto (2009); and
e. *-some*/*-able*: Smith (2020).

iv) Adverbial competition: an overview can be found in Bauer et al. (2013), where they deal, for example, with the competition between *-ward* and *-ways*.

The list above might give the impression that competition has been researched in depth for most word classes, especially for nouns and verbs. However, the variability in how the phenomenon is dealt with makes it difficult to assess and compare results from one study to another, and there are also substantial differences in the very concept of competition (i), in the number of patterns (ii), and in the factors under study (iii):

i) Some authors view competition as cases where two forms or processes mean the same (or roughly the same), independently of whether they compete for the same bases (e.g. Riddle 1985) or, for that matter, any study on affix productivity deal indirectly with competition (e.g. Bauer 2001 and Romaine 2004, among others). Other authors take a narrower view on competition, where forms or processes need to be synonymous and be applied on the same bases (e.g. Bauer et al. 2010; Fernández-Alcaina 2017, 2021a, 2021b on English; Fradin 2019 on French; Radimský & Štichauer 2021 on Italian). This divergence may impact the results greatly, as a wider consideration of competition needs a more in-depth analysis of constraints. For example, in Lara-Clares's (2017) analysis of *-ation* vs. zero-affixation for the expression

24 Please note that not all references deal with the five processes, but with at least three of them. Plag (2000), for example, addresses the competition between *-ify*, *-ize*, *-ate* and conversion.

25 Cetnarowska names this process *bare nominalisation* and Renner names it *morphostasis*.

of ACTION, all the bases analysed are simple and verbal. However, if these processes were compared on any base they may apply in, the possible influence of the word class and of the morphological structure of the base would also come into play. This book takes the narrower approach to competition, as described in §2.3.2.

ii) There is considerable variation in the number of patterns analysed and, thus, on the size of the clusters. For example, Bauer et al. (2013) deal with every affix available for the expression of certain meanings, whereas Kaunisto (2009) looks at the competition between two affixes. Furthermore, some authors stress the importance to consider not only the competing affixes in question, but also the whole derivational paradigm (see Pounder 2000 and Fernández-Alcaina & Čermák 2018). A balance should be found between the number of processes analysed and the degree of detail to be attained.

iii) Regarding the factors that may play a role in the resolution of competition, the attention paid to some is uneven: Guz (2009) and Säily (2011), for example, focus on differences of use of *-ity* and *-ness* (the former on register, the latter on gender), whereas others analyse a wider variety of factors, even if results are often inconclusive. Bauer et al. (2010), for example, address the competition between *-en* and conversion and test whether variables such as phonological makeup or semantic class play a role in its resolution. Their conclusion is that no uniform pattern of resolution can be identified, even if the phonological variable seems to be more influential than others.

The various approaches to competition in the literature may therefore give a blurred image of its actual extent. In fact, it has been claimed that competition may not be as pervasive as previously thought (see, e.g., Fernández-Alcaina 2021a: 33), mainly because some differences can usually be found on the use of one or the other process(es), so that they are actually not in competition. Besides, most research focus on suffixal processes,[26] so it is yet to be seen whether there are different profiles (or not) regarding prefixation or any other word-formation process.

2.3.4.1. Competing patterns in nominalisation

The competition between nominal affixal word-formation processes has been analysed by several authors since the 70's. However, most research focuses on

26 This comes as no surprise, because suffixation is more pervasive than prefixation, as proved for example by Štekauer et al. (2012: 308ff) and Antoniová & Štekauer (2015: 74), who claim that derivational paradigms are constituted by means of suffixation much more frequently than by prefixation.

two competing patterns: *-ity/-ness* and *-ship/-dom/-hood*, and the conclusions provided by the authors are at times contradictory. Still, their analysis provides useful insight on the phenomenon. By way of illustration, the following two sections show how competition in nominal word formation, be it class-changing or class-maintaining, has been approached in the literature. The first provides a chronological overview on previous research on the competition between *-ity* and *-ness*, and the second between *-ship*, *-dom* and *-hood*.

2.3.4.1.1. Class-changing: -ity/-ness

The term *rivalry* was, to the best of my knowledge, first used by Aronoff (1976) to refer to the competition between *-ity* and *-ness*. Aronoff claimed that these suffixes clash for bases ending in *-ous*, even though *-ness* would dominate in that context. Since then, Aronoff has used a variety of techniques to analyse these processes (see, among others, Aronoff & Anshen 1981; Anshen & Aronoff 1988). The results show that *-ness* is the default nominaliser, while *-ity* is preferred in some contexts,[27] namely bases ending in *-al*, *-able/-ible* and *-ic* (e.g. *duality* is preferred to *dualness*) (Aronoff 2019: 57; see also Bauer 1997: 248). Lindsay (2012: 195–196) also adds adjectival bases ending in *-ous* and *-ar*. There are other niches where the preference is less robust, but there is still some specialisation, as in adjectival bases ending in *-ive* (*expressivity/expressiveness*). The conclusion is that there is no general productivity, but only productivity of affix/niche pairs (Aronoff 2019: 60).

Riddle (1985) holds that, although the suffixes are mostly semantically distinct, the distinction is not realised on all bases. It is as follows: *-ness* tends to denote an embodied attribute or trait, and *-ity* tends to denote an abstract or concrete entity.

Guz (2009) compared the context of use of the two affixes and concludes that *-ness* is preferred in more informal contexts (fiction), whereas *-ity* is preferred in more formal ones (academic). Guz (2009: 454) justifies this in two ways:

i) *-ness* derivatives are more transparent (in terms of decomposability and predictability) than *-ity* derivatives, so derivation with *-ness* is a safer option when little processing time is available, and
ii) the bases to which *-ness* attaches denote personal qualities or feelings, which are not common in a technical or scientific domain.

However, the results obtained by Guz may not parallel those obtained by other authors because Guz (2009) does not compare the two processes as applied to

27 Aronoff (2019: 60) named *distributional niches* the phonological or morphological contexts where an affix is potentiated.

the same bases. This variability, therefore, may not be found if the competition between *-ity* and *-ness* was analysed from a narrow perspective.

Saïlly (2011) in turn compared the two affixes according to the prevalence of use by men and women and concludes that *-ity* is used less productively by women than by men, while no difference was found in the use of *-ness*. Both differences could be explained on historical grounds: *-ity* corresponded to the higher variety because of its French (ultimately, Latin) origin, whereas *-ness* corresponded to the lower one (Riddle 1985: 445-6; Romaine 1985: 461–462; Säily 2011: 120; see also Säily 2018 and Rodríguez-Puente et al. 2020 for the diachronic development of the productivity of *-ity* and *-ness*).

Baeskow (2012: 34), in line with Riddle's (1985) embodied trait, argues that there is a semantic difference between the two affixes that is dependent on the base: "[t]he suffix *-ness* is sensitive to the scalar structure of its adjectival bases and tends to select relatively high degrees of the properties they denote" (Baeskow 2012: 34). The suffix *-ity*, on the other hand, usually has a generic interpretation, matching Riddle's abstract entity. It "[...] nominalizes properties in the abstract" and is indifferent as to the scalar structure of the gradable adjectives it selects (Baeskow 2012: 34).

Arndt-Lappe (2014: 498) confirms the preference of *-ity* for certain bases but claims that the distribution of the two affixes is "neither complementary nor fully random". Arndt-Lappe's analysis of the productivity of the two affixes supports the idea of affix/niche pairs mentioned above: *-ness* is globally productive, while *-ity* is more restricted in its productivity but, in the domains where *-ity* is productive, *-ness* is restricted (Arndt-Lappe 2014: 502–503; see also Plag 2003: 92; Bauer et al. 2013: 245–248). Regarding the factors that may cause the different productivity, Arndt-Lappe (2014: 506) holds that semantics does not play a role, against Riddle's claim, because the affixes are synonymous, and that the only convincing parameter is the morphological category of adjectival bases.

Last, Rainer (2015: 1279) points to a difference according to the origin of the base: *-ity* is mostly confined to Latinate bases, while *-ness*, which is Germanic in origin, is used mostly in Germanic bases, although it has extended its reach to some Latinate base types (see also Lindsay 2012: 195; Bauer et al. 2013: 248; Arndt-Lappe 2014: 498, 501).

This overview shows how much research is needed to examine some competing patterns: *-ity* and *-ness* seem to be differentiated mainly according to the origin and morphological structure of the base, but other differences, such as their semantics, need further research. The conclusion would be that these affixes are close to being in complementary distribution, but there are domains in which they are still in ongoing competition. This supports the claim that competition is gradable, that is, there are different levels at which processes may compete, depending, for example, on the degree of semantic overlap between the affixes (Huyghe & Wauquier 2021; Huyghe & Varvara 2023a).

2.3.4.1.2. Class-maintaining: -ship/-dom/-hood

The competition between the suffixes *-ship/-dom/-hood* has focused mainly on their semantics because, formally, they are currently very similar: as they always belonged to the native stock of English, the language of origin does not play a role in the choice of one or another affix. Regarding the profile of the base, they all preferably attach to concrete nominal bases, and mostly to those denoting persons or animals (Bauer et al. 2013: 248; Díaz-Negrillo 2017: 121). In the Middle Ages, however, they would interchangeably attach to adjectives, but the suffix *-ness* consolidated as the primary suffix forming nouns from adjectives, and each of the three competitors then found a niche in nominal bases (Riddle 1985: 450).

The three suffixes thus derive nouns from nominal bases, even though they may occasionally attach to verbs and adjectives, and they express an abstract or collective meaning (see, e.g., Lehrer 2003 and Lieber 2016: 70–71). In order to try to predict the resolution of this competition, attempts have been made to find a difference in meaning between the three affixes. Aronoff & Cho (2001) and Aronoff (2019: 54–57) show that *-ship* attaches to stage-level predicates that do not denote permanent conditions, whereas *-hood* attaches to individual-level predicates. The suffix *-dom* has become specialised and is the preferred option for DOMAIN or REALM. Trips (2009: 206) goes further and claims that "[…] they never meant exactly the same" and, as frequency increases, these affixes may attach to bases that do not mean persons only, but also abstract entities. Later research by Lieber (2010) proves, however, that in certain contexts they may be used completely interchangeably. The conclusion, then, is that for the most part semantically equivalent doublets or triplets are the norm rather than the exception, and that differences in individual forms should be attributed to lexicalisation (Lieber 2016: 134–136).

Díaz-Negrillo (2017), in contrast, addresses the competition between the three affixes considering their polysemy. Her analysis, based on senses, reveals different profiles of competition in each semantic domain. For example, the suffix *-dom* dominates in REALM, and the suffix *-ship* in SKILL (Díaz-Negrillo 2017: 153). At the same time, there is an overlap between the competitors in some domains and some clusters are identified where the three suffixes are attested on the same base (e.g. *sheriff*) and with the same core meaning (here, POSITION), although some differences are found that explain why the three suffixes remain in use: the sense POSITION is classified as *obsolete* in the OED in *sheriffhood*, while *sheriffdom* denotes, in addition to POSITION, also TERRITORY, REALM and COLLECTIVITY (Díaz-Negrillo 2017: 154). Some specialisation for each affix seems to apply: a diachronic analysis of their semantics reveals that each suffix may have acquired different nuances within the same sense, for example, for the sense POSITION, *-dom* tends to denote 'authority' and 'dignity', *-hood* social position, and *-ship* 'occupations' and titles of respects (Díaz-Negrillo 2017: 155). Therefore, it seems that a certain degree of semantic specialisation is in process, so one may expect that they end in semantic complementary distribution.

2.4. Summary

Competition emerged in English mainly due to the influence of other languages (primarily Latin and French), which led to massive borrowing. As a result, the derivational morphology of English is characterised by the clash between a Germanic and a Romance model. This clash could be resolved in favour of more iconic forms, which would be the most natural according to NM, or in favour of shorter forms, which would be preferred according to the Principle of Least Effort. The former would predict a prevalence of overt affixation, and the latter would be behind the preference for zero-affixation. In English, however, there could be a language-particular system at play where zero-affixation could be the preferred option. This book thus sets out to investigate if one or the other process is preferred in a situation of competition.

The concept of *competition* dates as far back as the 5th century BCE, when it was noticed by Sanskrit grammarians, and it has of late received increasing attention. However, the concept has been defined rather heterogeneously in the literature. *Competition* has been described as the situation where two or more forms fill one slot in the paradigm, be it inflectional or derivational. In word formation, there is a general agreement that competitors need to be synonymous, although some authors allow flexibility and would describe near-synonyms as competing. Regarding the base for derivation, there is also some variability, but the most restrictive approach indicates that competitors have to be derived from the same bases (e.g. *fluidize*, *fluidify*).

The situation of competition is expected to come to an end after some time, either by means of the obsolescence of one of the competitors or by means of specialisation (e.g. semantic, pragmatic or dialectal). Previous research on competition in word formation has focused on which factors may guide the choice of one process over another. Most research has focused on suffixation, and most studies deal with the competition between doublets for the formation of verbs, nouns, or adjectives. For example, a phonological factor guides the choice of *-ify* and *-ize* for the derivation of verbs: the former shows a preference for monosyllabic or disyllabic bases, whereas the latter derives mainly from polysyllabic bases (Schneider 1987: 108). Regarding the formation of nouns, most research has focused on the competition between *-ity* and *-ness*. Several factors have been described that may guide the selection of each affix. For example, *-ity* is preferred in bases ending in *-able*/*-ible* and *-ic* (Aronoff 2019: 57) and is confined mainly to Latinate bases, while *-ness* is less restricted regarding the morphological structure of the base and it is used mainly in Germanic bases (although it can extend to Latinate bases) (Rainer 2015: 1279). The influence of some other factors, such as semantics, is still unclear. Therefore, it seems that these affixes are still in competition, but *-ity* may be undergoing a process of specialisation. Another factor that is key to any study of competition is productivity, but most studies dealing with this do not restrict their data to forms derived from the same base nor do they compute frequencies considering semantics. This is the gap that the volume aims to fill, by analysing competitors that derive from the same base and are of the same semantic category, so that the influence of factors that may guide the choice of overt affixation or of zero-affixation becomes clearer.

3. Method

3.1. Introduction

This chapter[28] is a description of the method used for the collection and analysis of affixes in competition for the formation of English nouns. The chapter is divided into two sections:

i) §3.2 focuses on the selection of a data source for sample extraction, both of a corpus and of a dictionary; and
ii) §3.3 describes the process followed for the extraction and analysis of two samples. Within this section, a further separation can be made:
    a. §3.3.1 describes the collection and analysis of *Sample1* from the complete frequency list of the BNC, further analysed using OED data; and
    b. §3.3.2 describes the extraction of *Sample2* exclusively from the OED, further analysed using both OED and BNC data.

3.2. Data source selection: corpus and dictionary data

This book used both corpus and dictionary data for the study of competition. Corpus data was used:

i) for the retrieval of a first sample for an overview of competition, ultimately aiming at the selection of competing patterns to be analysed in this book, and
ii) for attestation of senses of competing forms.

Dictionary data was used for collection of lexicographic information such as number of senses of a form, earliest or latest attestation, and the identification of potential competitors. Dictionary data was also used to extract a second sample of competing forms as explained in §3.3.2.

3.2.1. Corpus selection

For the selection of the corpus, manageability and representativeness of modes, registers and domain play a crucial role, since they are key aspects for the analysis

---

28 Some sections of this chapter are in line with the methodological standpoints in Lara-Clares (2016), Fernández-Domínguez (2017), Lara-Clares (2017) and Lara-Clares & Thompson (2019).

of competition. Taking this into consideration, two corpora that could fit our purposes are:

i) the COCA, and
ii) the BNC.

The former is halfway between a monitor corpus and a sample corpus, as it grows in number of lemmas (over 25 million words per year), while keeping a similar distribution of text-types. The latter is a sample or reference corpus, which is balanced for registers[29] but has not been updated since 1994.

A comparison of the results for a study of competition resulting from the use of one or the other corpus is available in Fernández-Domínguez (2017: 69–75): where the same forms are attested in both corpora, COCA token frequencies tend to be higher, as could be expected due to the bigger size of the corpus. However, differences cannot always be attributed to the size of the corpus, and that "[...] raises questions on the actual status of presumed competitors in specific language varieties" (Fernández-Domínguez 2017: 71). Besides, the sample contained forms that were attested in one corpus and not in the other, for example, 30 nouns fewer in the BNC (92) than in the COCA (124). The lower attestation in the BNC reduces the size of the competing clusters and the range of meanings attested (10 in the BNC and 13 in the COCA). Although this description may seem to prove that the COCA is the best option for an analysis of competition, it should be noted that, where forms are lacking in the BNC, they are wrongly tagged in the COCA in nearly all cases (e.g. adjectives tagged as nouns), or they are typos, recorded as *obsolete* in the OED, not in English (e.g. *extremite*), or they did not attest the competing meaning, which leads to the conclusion that "[...] the main patterns [of competition] are still found regardless of the data source" (Fernández-Domínguez 2017: 75; see also Kaunisto 2009: 85 and Fernández-Alcaina & Čermák 2018: 88 for a discussion on the limitations of corpora for research on competition).

For this book, the BNC was chosen over the COCA because:

i) it is more manageable, as it is five times smaller than the COCA, and
ii) it has a static character, as the updates of the COCA would entail variation in the results during the development of this piece of research and afterwards.

The BNC corpus consists of approximately 100 million words of written and spoken British English dating mainly from the 1970s to 1994. It is a synchronic,

29 The term *register* is used here to refer simply to discourse occurring in particular contexts (as in Hunston 2002: 160).

general corpus in that it is not restricted to a particular field or register and includes a wide range of text types.

The written section of the corpus amounts to approximately 90% of the corpus and includes newspapers, periodicals, journals, academic books, popular fiction, letters, and essays, among others. Corpus texts contain a maximum of 45,000 words due to copyright limitations. Shorter texts, such as magazines or newspapers, are in full. The spoken part amounts to approximately 10% of the corpus and consists of formal and informal transcribed speech, classified as *demographic* or *context-governed*. The former contains conversational English by 130 speakers who tape-recorded themselves over a period of two to seven days. The speakers were from all age groups, of both sexes and of the four social classes considered in the corpus classification. As they recorded conversations with other people, the total number of participants was above a thousand. The latter, the context-government part, is divided into four contextually-based categories: educational, business, public/institutional, and leisure. They are 60% dialogues and 40% monologues, all sampled within three geographic regions. This part of the corpus consists of 757 texts which are classified into the following types:

i) educational and informative (lectures, talks, classroom interaction, etc.),
ii) business (company talks and interviews, sales demonstrations, consultations, etc.),
iii) public or institutional (political speeches, sermons, legal proceedings, parliamentary proceedings, etc.), and
iv) leisure (speeches, club meetings, talks to clubs, etc.).[30]

3.2.2. Dictionary selection

For the selection of a source of lexicographic data, a choice was made between a synchronic or a diachronic dictionary. The latter was chosen, because a diachronic overview of competition may cast light on current patterns. The dictionary selected had to contain, at least:

i) a description of senses over time,
ii) the earliest and latest attestation date of each sense of the entries,
iii) the etymology of the entries, and, ideally,
iv) an accessible list of derivatives.

30 http://www.natcorp.ox.ac.uk/docs/URG/BNCdes.html#spodes

To the best of my knowledge, the only (or, at least, most comprehensive) dictionary containing that information is the OED, which is available online. The OED contains approximately 600,000 entries and over 3.5 million quotations. It was first published in 1884 and is continuously under revision (see Simpson 2004).[31] The OED is, undoubtedly, a matchless dictionary in terms of size or scholarly authority (Kastovsky 2000; Spencer 2019: 9; Baugh & Cable 2013: 334–335; Ogilvie 2015: 2) and it has been shown to include a considerable number of neologisms (Plag 1999: 99). It was selected for the purposes of this book accordingly.

3.3. Samples

The data sources described in §3.2 were used for data extraction and analysis in two stages, here named *Sample1* and *Sample2*. Sample1 consisted in the main in the analysis of a sample from a frequency list (§3.3.1; see Lara-Clares 2016 for a description of the tests carried out regarding the sampling method). This sample supplied a list of competing patterns in PDE affixation. From these, four patterns were selected for further analysis in a second stage of data extraction and analysis (Sample2, §3.3.2).

3.3.1. Sample1: the frequency list

The source chosen for extraction of Sample1 data was the complete BNC frequency list, which amounts to approximately 615,000 types. The list is lemmatised and ordered by frequency; where frequency is the same, it is ordered alphabetically. If only entries tagged as nouns (the focus of the present study) are considered, which are the focus of the present study, the list consists of more than 345,000 types. A frequency list was chosen at this stage over the web interface of the corpus for easier extraction of a sample using a number of filters, in view of the amount of data contained in the whole corpus. A tool was created for this purpose: *Scáthach* (Lara-Clares 2016; see also Lara-Clares & Lara-Clares 2016).

3.3.1.1. Sample extraction

The software *Scáthach* allows sampling according to a series of filters such as word class, frequency, or sequences of letters that entries contain or do *not* contain.

Forms containing a hyphen (e.g. *self-government*) were excluded, because compounding as a word-formation process falls outside the scope of this study, which focuses on affixation. Entries containing numbers or symbols (e.g. the entry

31 https://public.oed.com/about/

o[sep]dell/resident) were also filtered out using this software. The extraction of sequences of letters was used to select only affixed forms. This selection of affixed forms is justified by the fact that affixed forms may compete with other affixed or zero-affixed[32] forms, but zero-affixed forms cannot compete with each other. This is because forms, to be competitors, need to have originated from the same base and be derived by a different process (see §3.3.1.2 for the characteristics of competitors), but any other word-formation process is not relevant here. Thus, the extraction of affixed forms ensured that only potentially competing patterns were extracted. This entailed discarding the following at a later stage, in which every unit in the sample was analysed manually (see §3.3.1.3):

i) solid compounds (e.g. *shareholder*),
ii) forms tagged wrongly (e.g. *ultrahigh* in "an ultrahigh vacuum", tagged as noun),
iii) typos (e.g. **agremeent*),
iv) proper names (e.g. *Didier*), and
v) foreign forms (e.g. *vraie* from French, *comraind* from Middle Irish).

Allomorphic and orthographical variants (e.g. *organization* and *organisation*) were searched in the possible forms and their frequencies were added up.

The filters which where to be used in *Scáthach* as well as the sampling size were selected in three steps. For extraction of Sample1, "SUBST" (i.e. noun) was selected as the word class in the first step, and entries containing numbers and symbols were excluded by ticking the relevant boxes.

The second step is designed for selection of strings of characters to be filtered out or included. Here, hyphens are excluded and, as an example, words containing the suffixes *-er* and *-ment*, and the prefix *un-* are included. As the software does not distinguish affixes from character sequences that are formally identical to affixes, they needed to be classified manually at a later stage (e.g. forms such as *water* or *power* are irrelevant for an analysis of competing affixes, even if they contain the sequence "-er").

The third step is used for the extraction of a sample of a specific size. This step is described farther below (this section), where the size of the samples used for this book is shown.

32 Forms are a priori considered to be zero-affixed when there is another attested word which is formally identical but of a different word class (see below, this section). Zero-affixation, which cannot be extracted automatically using this software, is attested (or discarded) according to the results obtained from the OED, as described in §3.3.1.2.

From the sample of affixed forms, only their base form was used for further analysis using the OED (e.g. from *instrumentation* and *instrumental*, the base *instrument* would be extracted; see §3.3.1.2). The affixes introduced in the software were taken from two sources: Quirk et al. (1985: 1540–1552) and Stockwell & Minkova (2001: 89–94). While some of the units on the resulting list, such as *crypto-* or *-ocracy*, may not be considered affixes but combining forms (Quirk et al. 1985: 1545; Díaz-Negrillo 2020; see also Mattiello 2022), sampling is intended to be as inclusive as possible in the first stages of data collection. Any unwanted element was discarded after manual analysis at a later stage.

Sample1 was extracted and analysed in three stages for manageability reasons. The size of the sample for each stage was calculated using a tool for the calculation of the sample size of a population (Raosoft Inc. 2014). The margin of error was set at 5%, the confidence level at 95% and the distribution at 50%, all of which are default values. The result, according to the abovementioned Raosoft tool, is that a representative sample of affixed nouns should consist of at least 380 forms.

In each stage, therefore, c. 380 nominal forms were extracted,[33] amounting to a total of 1,147 nouns. Sampling was done using the third step in *Scáthach*, which allows extraction of one out of every *x* number of entries, starting at a different point of the original list in each stage. This avoids repetition of data in the various stages. To calculate the skip with which forms were to be extracted, the following calculation was made:

$$\text{skip} = \frac{\text{size of the corpus}}{\text{sample size needed}}$$

The list of non-hyphenated affixed nouns amounts to a total of 103,476 entries. As the sample size aimed at was 380, the skip had to be 1/270. For the first sampling stage, sampling started from entry number 1, so entries number 1, 271, 541, etc. were extracted. For the second stage, it started from entry number 5. For the third, it did from number 7.

3.3.1.2. *The analysis of Sample1*

For forms to be considered as in competition and, thus, as part of a competing cluster (as the one in Table 3.1), the conditions are (Lara-Clares & Thompson 2019):

i) to share the same base (*bother*^{V}),
ii) to be derived with different affixes (*-ation*, *-er* and zero),

33 That is, 384 forms in stage 1, 382 forms in stage 2, and 381 forms in stage 3.

iii) to take affixes that express the same semantic category(s) (INSTRUMENT),
iv) to operate in the same domain (they are not classified as *dialectal* or pertaining to any register or domain in the OED), and
v) to be free of constraints (e.g. phonological or morphological; a priori, inasmuch as the forms are attested, it is expected that no constraints apply, but that is verified at a later stage).

Following this, forms extracted from Sample1 (and, later, also Sample2) were analysed with OED data and classified into clusters using a template (Table 3.1). The simplified version of the template consists of seven columns:

i) competing forms,
ii) their competing sense in the OED,
iii) the word class of the base,
iv) the meaning of the competitors: first the semantic category, following Bagasheva's (2017) classification, and the gloss in the OED,
v) the number of senses of each form in the OED, classified as *in use*, *obsolete/dated*, *dialectal* and *register/domain* (in light green, the state of the competing sense),
vi) the absolute frequencies of forms in the BNC, and
vii) a timeline of each competing sense: first, the earliest attestation date and then, the latest attestation date, in the second column if classified as *in use* and in the third (†),[34] if classified as *obsolete* or *rare*.

Competitors were identified using the list of entries on the right-hand side of the OED web interface. For example, in the BNC sample, the derivative *botheration* was extracted. It was then searched in the OED, where potential competitors could be identified using the entry list. In this example, *bother* and *botherer* as nouns have a sense that is apparently synonymous to that of *botheration* and, thus, they qualify as potential competitors.

The complete template consists of four extra columns, as follows:

i) the OED online version of the entry (e.g. for *bother*^{N}, OED3, last updated in 2016);
ii) comments on any extra information that could be relevant at some point (e.g. if a sense is classified as *in use* and the other as *obsolete* but both compete);

34 Note that, whenever it is the (sub)sense of a form that is in competition, the attestation date is taken from that sense, and not from the whole form, for example, the earliest attestation date of *botheration* is 1797, but the date of its second sense, that is, the one in competition, is 1801 (see Table 3.1).

iii) notes regarding the directionality (e.g. verb>noun or verb<noun) using dictionary data, in order to discard cases in which a nominalisation seems very unlikely; and

iv) the OED's description of the etymology of the word, to check whether the entry has been categorised as derivation in English (e.g. for *bother* it reads "formed within English, by conversion") or whether it may have been borrowed (e.g. the etymology for *aliment*^{N} reads "either (i) a borrowing from French. Or (ii) a borrowing from Latin", in which case the potential competitor is marked as *dubious* and may be excluded at a later stage).[35]

The semantic category of the affixes was identified based on the gloss in the OED. Following Plank (2010), the category was here identified at sense level, that is, not for the word but considering each of its senses, so the actual use of the particular competing sense of that form was tested. BNC concordances were used for that purpose (see below, this section). By way of an example, in the cluster *bother/botheration/botherer* above, the gloss in the OED of the three entries include "thing which" (Table 3.1), so it would seem that the three entries may have an instrumental meaning. Whether the actual sense is INSTRUMENT, AGENTIVE or any other is tested at a later stage (see §3.3.2.2). In this case, the analysis of concordances of all the forms derived by *-ation* and zero-affixation identified in the OED as potentially competing for the sense INSTRUMENT showed that that sense is actually not attested in the BNC for any of the forms. For this reason, this competing pattern was discarded for further analysis.

35 Forms were only analysed further if they are synchronically analysable as complex. Therefore, data is restricted to *Wortbildung*, as opposed to *Wortgebildetheit*, following Dokulil (1964, 1968).

Table 3.1: Simplified version of a competing cluster in the template with the base bother^{V}

Compet-ing forms	Sense	W-class base	Meaning		Senses (OED)				Freq.	Timeline		
			Sem. category	Def. (OED)	In use	Obs./ Dated	Dial.	Reg./ Dom.	BNC	Ear-liest	Latest	†
botheration	2	V	INSTRUMENT	A person who or thing which causes annoyance, irritation, or vexation; a nuisance.	2				2	1801	2014	
bother	1c	V	INSTRUMENT	A person who or thing which causes annoyance, trouble, or difficulty; a nuisance.	1	1			201	1866	2012	
botherer	1	V	INSTRUMENT	A person who or thing which bothers, annoys, or harasses someone.	2				0	1815	2010	

This book focuses on PDE competition, so only forms attested in the BNC were selected for further analysis. This means that Sample1 is used for the creation of a database of competing patterns over time using the template above, which then becomes the evidence for the selection of a number of patterns that are analysed synchronically (§4.2). In the example in Table 3.1, *botherer* was discarded, because it is not attested in the BNC, while *botheration* and *bother*^{N} were selected. It should be noted that lexicographic and corpus data do not agree on whether *botherer* is in use or not. It is not attested in the *iWeb* corpus either, even though it is attested once in the COCA.[36] As the use of various corpus sources would likely lead to conflict, it was decided to rely on the BNC for attestation of the current use of competing forms. Besides, Sample1 is an overview of competition between affixes, that is, it includes affixation vs. affixation. For Sample2 the scope of analysis was narrowed down from affixal competition over time to synchronic competition of zero-affixation vs. overt suffixation.

3.3.1.3. Methodological decisions

The method followed in this book is gradually restrictive, so that, if one form seemed to be opaque from a synchronic perspective, it was first considered as a derivative and searched in the OED for potential competitors. However, if the lexicographic information supports the analysis as an opaque form, it was left aside for further morphological analysis (that is, following Rainer et al. 2014: 11–12 on lexicalisation). Data collection thus also involved data selection, as OED data collection for potential competitors was simultaneous with manual deletion of irrelevant entries (e.g. typos, as described above), which are approximately 70% of the sample.

As hinted above, the distinction between base and derivative by zero-affixation was not without problem, as the directionality of this process is not always clear and it is difficult to determine whether a presumable zero-derivative really is a derivative. For that reason, when a word may have been derived by zero-affixation (determined by the existence of the same form but of a different word class) it was considered a derivative. However, as some very dubious cases of verb-to-noun derivation were identified, the criterion of semantic dependency as in Marchand (1963, 1964) was applied (see Cetnarowska 1993: 24–39, Plag 2003: 108–111, Bauer & Valera 2015: 11–12, Bram 2011; see also Ruz & Cetnarowska 2023 for the applicability of this criterion to affixation).

---

36 *And at the time, that was known as a God* ***botherer****, and they didn't play it on the radio* (SPOK: NPR_ATC).

Finally, because the OED is updated regularly, some data in this book, especially regarding etymology, classification of senses and timelines, might not agree with the current data of the online version of the OED3 (2023). Changes in the above data were detected after the update, showing the caution with which this kind of information should be taken.

3.3.1.4. An illustration of data analysis of Sample1

By way of illustration of the method explained so far, see Table 3.2 showing 20 entries from the third list of Sample1.

The OED was used to search for the base form of each of these entries. Whenever they were attested in the dictionary, the list of derivatives in the web interface was searched for potential competitors. If competitors were found, they were classified into the template.

Of the 20 entries above, 11 are not attested in the OED (*higby, neumeier, prodger, sello, teethgrinder, zassoursky, arithmeticae, beskydy, cozumel, dubilier, houlder*) and were thus discarded. Other entries were also discarded because they are:

i) borrowings (*epiphysis*),
ii) derived by a combining form (*cholecystostomy*), or
iii) compounds (*metalworker*) (see §3.3.1).

Table 3.2: A list of 20 rows of Sample1 of the BNC, showing the row number of the complete frequency list, the entry and the absolute frequency

Row number	Entry	Absolute frequency
134329	*crankiness*	5
135422	*epiphysis*	5
137121	*higby*	5
138494	*legalist*	5
140041	*neumeier*	5
141655	*prodger*	5
142850	*sello*	5
144128	*teethgrinder*	5
145949	*zassoursky*	5
148720	*aliment*	4
149242	*arithmeticae*	4

(*Continued*)

Table 3.2: (Continued)

Row number	Entry	Absolute frequency
150027	*beskydy*	4
151578	*cholecystostomy*	4
152321	*cozumel*	4
153569	*dubilier*	4
155095	*fraternization*	4
156869	*houlder*	4
158004	*kettler*	4
159845	*metalworkers*	4
161782	*overplus*	4

Three forms do not have any potential competitor in the OED list of derivatives (*crankiness*, *fraternization*, *overplus*). The other two forms have potential competitors, as follows:

i) For the base *legal*^{Adj}, five nominal forms may be potential competitors (*legalese*, *legalism*, *legalist*, *legality*, *legalness*). The last two forms compete for the sense STATE and are thus classified into the template. However, they are not further analysed because none of them has a sense in common with *legal*^{N}. Therefore, it is an example of the competition between *-ity* and *-ness*, but not between zero-affixation and other suffixes. Also, there is the derivative *legalization*^{N}: according to the OED, it is not derived from *legal*^{Adj} but from *legalize*.
ii) For the base *aliment*^{V}, the zero-affixed derivative *aliment*^{N} does compete for the sense ACTION with *alimentation*, and for the sense INSTRUMENT with *alimentation* and *alimenter*. The second of these clusters is fully analysed in this book.

Therefore, from the 20 entries above, only one instance of the competition between an overt affix and a zero affix is found: the one with the base *aliment*^{V}. That may illustrate why, from a list of more than a thousand entries from the BNC, only 36 clusters of the competition between affixes in PDE were identified, 29 of which represent the competition between any overt affix and zero-affixation (see §4.2 for an overview).

3.3.1.5. The selection of competing patterns

Once the database of nominal competition based on Sample1 had been designed, four of the competing patterns identified were selected for further analysis by using OED data to enlarge the sample (Sample2).

The patterns selected, in the chronological order in which they were analysed, are:

i) *-ation* vs. zero-affixation with the sense ACTION,[37] selected because it was the second most frequent pattern in the sample,[38]
ii) *-ness* vs. zero-affixation with the sense STATE,[39] which served to analyse derivatives which would mostly have an adjectival base, as the other competing patterns have verbal bases. Even though other patterns with adjectival bases were more frequent, *-ness* was expected to be more germane in PDE than others (e.g. *-al*) due to its higher productivity (Bauer 2001: 129; Baeskow 2012),
iii) *-er* vs. zero-affixation with the sense AGENTIVE, and
iv) *-er* vs. zero-affixation with the sense INSTRUMENT, selected alongside pattern iii) in order to compare results when forms derived by the same affix but of a different sense are in competition.

All patterns have zero-affixation as a competitor in common, as the aim of this book is, ultimately, to test whether economy or transparency of expression prevail when in competition.

3.3.2. Sample2

After analysing the first sample, a number of competing patterns were selected (§3.3.1.5) for further analysis.

3.3.2.1. Sample extraction

For each competing pattern, a second sample (Sample2) was extracted using the OED advanced search facility, as in previous studies on competition (Arndt-Lappe 2014; Fernández-Alcaina 2017; 2021a; Lara-Clares 2017; Lara-Clares & Thompson 2019). Data was at this stage extracted from the OED instead of from a corpus such as the BNC, because it allows:

i) straightforward extraction of zero-affixed competing forms. Previous studies have excluded this process for methodological difficulties for extraction from corpora (Plag 1999; Kjellmer 2001), and
ii) a restricted search that facilitates the extraction of specific competing patterns.

---

37 Partial results published in Lara-Clares (2017).

38 The most frequent was zero-affixation vs. *-ing* with the sense ACTION, which was discarded due to the difficulty to tell PDE *-ing* forms that come from OE *-ung* forms from those that date back to *-ing* forms, and because a high number of *-ing* forms were expected to be wrongly tagged as verbs.

39 Partial results published in Lara-Clares & Thompson (2019).

By way of illustration, for the competing pattern *-er* vs. zero-affixation with the semantic category AGENTIVE, the search was as follows:

i) Language of origin: English (i.e. to avoid borrowings).
ii) Word class: noun.
iii) Sequence of letters: *er.
iv) Keywords in the definition: 'person that/who', 'one that/who'.

This search returned more than 5,000 hits, which were analysed in search for additional competing clusters of the said pattern, following the same procedure as for Sample1 (see §3.3.1):

i) the derivatives list was used to identify zero-affixed nominal forms with the same base (e.g. *cram*^{N} when analysing the entry *crammer*),
ii) if there was an affix counterpart, senses of both the zero-affixed form and the *-er* form were compared in search for a competing sense (e.g. AGENTIVE), and
iii) if potential competition was identified, then the competitors were introduced into the template and other competitors with the same base were also searched for in the derivatives list and, when applicable, added to the cluster in the template (e.g. *crammer/cram/crammist*).

The OED was used for the above instead of the BNC, because it allows identification of competing clusters over time, independently of their current state of use. In the example above, 55 new competing clusters were identified and classified into the template for the competition between *-er* and zero-affixation for the sense AGENTIVE, 19 of which are attested in the BNC (see §3.3.1).

A different search in the OED was used for each word-formation pattern. Table 3.3 shows the search for each pattern analysed in this book and the number of hits resulting from the search.

Table 3.3: Filters in the OED advanced search

	-ation: **ACTION**	*-er*: **AGENTIVE**	*-er*: **INSTRUMENT**	*-ness*: **STATE**
Language of origin	English	English	English	English
Word class	noun	noun	noun	noun
Sequence of letters	*ation	*er	*er	*ness
Keywords in definition	'action' 'act'	'person that/who' 'one that/who'	'that which' 'thing which', 'device for' 'used for'	'state' 'condition'
N hits	1,042	5,505	1,367	1,670

Nearly 10,000 dictionary entries were thus looked up in search for zero-affixed potential competitors. The search resulted in the identification of 144 clusters in diachrony (c. 1.5% of the OED entries) and 60 clusters in PDE (c. 0.6% of the entries). Some of these clusters are made up of two competitors (doublet) and other of three of more competitors.

3.3.2.2. *The analysis of Sample2*

After competing clusters were identified and classified into the template, those in current competition were selected, that is, the clusters where at least two forms are attested in the BNC were selected for further analysis. The analysis carried out consisted of:

i) manual concordance analysis, to quantify the attestation of the sense in competition,
ii) the computation of the Referenced Index of Competition (C*) of the competitors, for clues on the outcome of resolution, and
iii) an analysis of the register distribution of the competitors, to test whether there is any difference in their use.

Additionally, some clusters of competition were further analysed by looking for possible differences in the meaning or use of the competitors, by means of:

i) an examination of the definitions and any other information provided by some of the main PDE dictionaries, and
ii) an analysis of the cooccurrences of the competitors, to test whether there are differences in the domains of use or as regards the collocates of each keyword.

3.3.2.2.1. *Semantic concordance analysis*

Once all the hits in the OED had been analysed and classified into the template, each competitor was analysed using the concordances in the BNC. The aim was to count how many concordances actually are of the competing sense and in which registers.

Concordance analysis is key to this book, because while most research on competition does acknowledge the fact that most competing forms are polysemous, the frequency of use of each individual sense is not considered separately (see, e.g., Lara-Clares 2017 for a comparison of the results obtained in a study of competition with and without sense classification). This allows for an analysis of the frequency of specific competing senses rather than of the forms, following Plank (2010; see also Givón 1970: 835; Koehl 2015).

The semantic classification of affixes is based on the principle that affixes not only determine the word class of the derivative, but they also convey semantic information. There are several approaches to this aspect of meaning in morphology (see Booij 2007). However, there is still not a comprehensive semantic theory that allows an unequivocal computation of the meaning of affixes, and it is "highly improbable" that it will be available anytime soon (Bagasheva 2017: 36ff., and references therein). A decision was taken, then, to use a theory-neutral semantic classification that would partly simplify the issue. The semantic classification in this book is thus based on Bagasheva's (2017) list of 51 cross-linguistic semantic categories. It was chosen over other options because:

i) the categories are unspecified for word class, so they can be used for an analysis of competition independently of the word class of the base or the derivative,
ii) they are descriptive categories which can be used both for language-specific research and for cross-linguistic research, so they would allow extension of the analysis to other languages and to other affixal word-formation processes within English (see also Štekauer et al. 2012), and
iii) they are flexible in the sense that they can be combined to account for the polysemy of affixes.

The majority of concordances were manually classified. In broad terms, the classification was into two categories: as being of the semantic category under study, or of a non-competing semantic category. This analysis is, however, rather complex, either because some concordances can be interpreted in several ways or because slight differences in meaning could be identified within the semantic category under study (see Riddle 1985; Aronoff & Cho 2001; Baeskow 2012; Díaz-Negrillo 2017 for the difficulty of applying general semantic definitions in order to capture differences in meaning between affixes). For this reason, the analysis carried out was further checked by an additional informant. Still, it was decided to also do a further test for the automatic classification of concordances, which would allow a more fine-grained classification. This was done in one doublet, as described in §3.3.2.2.1.5.

The total number of concordances manually analysed in this book is 74,536, as detailed in Table 3.4:

Table 3.4: Number of concordances analysed by competing pattern

	-ation/ **zero-affix.: ACTION**	*-er*/ **zero-affix.: AGENTIVE**	*-er*/ **zero-affix.: INSTRUMENT**	*-ness*/ **zero-affix.: STATE**
N concordances	27,997	21,104	16,828	8,607

The following sections describe the semantic categories of the competing patterns as analysed in this book (ACTION, AGENTIVE, INSTRUMENT and STATE) and §3.3.2.2.1.5 describes how the automatic semantic annotation was carried out.

3.3.2.2.1.1. Manual semantic annotation: ACTION

The semantic category ACTION is described in Bagasheva (2017: 53) as "performing of an activity". Therefore, all entries described in the OED as "action of" or "act of" would a priori be included within this category. It must however be differentiated from two other semantic categories: CUMULATIVE and PROCESS. The former is described as "performing an action to achieve a considerable amount of something", whereas the latter is a "natural, non-volitional unfolding of a change of state". Therefore, forms that would fit into any of these two categories were left out of the analysis.

The semantic classification of concordances proved complex, as it was often not possible to tell whether the form referred to the action being carried out or rather to its result. For this reason, the classification allowed for an "unclear" tag for those concordances in which no clear meaning could be captured from context. Example (1) is an illustration of a keyword classified as ACTION. Example (2) is unclear, because it could be both the action (preventing the action of disputing) and the result (preventing the dispute that emerges from the action of disputing). Example (3) corresponds to the category PROCESS.

(1) *The question is whether the prohibition on alienating the land followed by the* ***exhortation*** *to keep it for descendants amounts to a trust.*[40]
(2) [...] *you felt the the procedures were worked out so finely that they in fact prevented* ***disputes*** *because they were so long and drawn out perhaps or er it took the fire out of disputes if you like?*
(3) *Jesus's resurrection onward is referred to as to the, as the state of* ***exhortation****, now what does that term mean, well as Jesus according to his divine nature has always been* [...].

3.3.2.2.1.2. Manual semantic annotation: AGENTIVE

Bagasheva (2017: 53) describes the category AGENTIVE as "performer of an activity/ Name of a profession, job, title or permanent activity". It thus includes both performers and occupations. In this book, the category AGENTIVE is restricted to the former, unless the occupation could either be a professional job or a voluntary

40 Unless otherwise indicated, all examples are taken from the BNC (Davies 2004).

act. For example, *aider* and *aid*^{N} are described in the OED as "a person who provides assistance or support". There is a third competitor in the cluster (*aidant*) that is described as "a helper, an assistant". Because being an assistant could be either a job or just a temporary role, it was included in the cluster with the sense AGENTIVE.

In the analysis of concordances, the category AGENTIVE was restricted to volitional[41] performers of temporary activities, as in (4). The keyword in some concordances showed a meaning different from AGENTIVE (e.g. ACTION in (5) or INSTRUMENT in (6)). Finally, the tag "unclear" was used when meaning could not be assessed from context, as in (7):

(4) *You could even be right, head, the little* ***cheat*** *almost had me believing in blood-spitting puppets.*
(5) *By conventional standards, it is true, the inconclusive ending is a* ***cheat****, but it is the right ending nonetheless.*
(6) *These include fitting cars with catalytic convertors, installing cleaning devices, such as gas* ***scrubbers*** *in power stations, and introducing nitrogen oxide controls.*
(7) *Weights crush power* ***lifter*** *# A FITNESS fanatic died when 26 stone of weights fell on him as he exercised.*

3.3.2.2.1.3. Manual semantic annotation: INSTRUMENT

The category INSTRUMENT must be differentiated from that of ENTITY. The former refers to an "object specifically used for a specialised activity" and the latter to an "object that has real existence, material expression entity" (Bagasheva 2017: 54). Therefore, a key distinguishing feature between the two categories is whether the object is used for performing a specialised activity, or not. For example, *muffler* is defined in the OED as "wrap or scarf (frequently of wool or silk) worn round the neck or throat for warmth" and it is thus classified as INSTRUMENT, as in (8). The form *preserve*^{N} is also classified as INSTRUMENT and it is defined in the OED as "goggles used to protect the eyes from dust, bright light, etc.", but no instance of this meaning in *preserve* was found in the BNC: the concordances either showed other meanings (9) or were verbs wrongly tagged as nouns (10).

---

41 The need for agents to be animate or volitional has long been debated in the literature (see, e.g., Cruse 1973; Jackendoff 1987; Huyghe & Wauquier 2021). In order to be on the safer side, this book restricts the category to animate volitional performers in order to delimit the range of meanings that would be considered as in competition.

(8) *Even Sir Henry came out of his chill library to stand for a time, wrapped in greatcoat and **muffler** [...]*
(9) *Gardening is sometimes considered the **preserve** of the middle aged and elderly.*
(10) *I have discussed old lines with various people and a common view seems to be '**preserve** what you can, without being silly about it'.*

3.3.2.2.1.4. Manual semantic annotation: STATE

The category STATE is described by Bagasheva (2017: 56) as a "particular condition of being, be in a state". This category comprises both temporary states, that is, states that remain for a period of time, and more permanent states. The suffix *-ness* can be found in both categories: *cleverness* as a permanent quality, and *drunkenness* as a temporary state (Rainer 2015: 1269–1271). In the sample, competing derivatives showed both readings, so a decision was taken to classify as STATE in this book only the concordances which reflect a temporary or non-permanent sense (11), as opposed to a permanent one (12).

(11) *The only dealers who remain in their jobs are those who can sustain **alertness** during their long working hours.*
(12) *Occupation is unquestionably one of the most important factors in preserving mental **alertness** and bodily health.*

The classification also allowed for a tag "unclear" and some concordances were classified as non-STATE, because they were part of a set phrase (e.g. *to have the hots for someone*) or because they were (part of) a proper name (e.g. *Heart of Darkness*).

3.3.2.2.1.5. Automatic semantic annotation: a test

For the automatic semantic annotation, a test was performed using a large language model (LLM), specifically, GPT-4o, using an API (Lara-Clares & Fernández-Alcaina 2024). Previous research on LLMS for the annotation of syntactic, semantic or pragma-discursive data (Gilardi et al. 2023; Yu et al. 2023; Imamovic et al. 2024) proved that prompt engineering techniques play a crucial role in the results obtained. For this reason, the prompt to be used was carefully designed and tested on the doublet wrap vs. wrapper, in order to get an even more fine-grained semantic classification of this doublet.

The analysis was at the level of the sense, with very specific labels created based on information for the OED and PDE reference dictionaries (Cambridge, Longman, Merriam-Webster and Wiktionary). For example, both competitors share the label "material", "blanket", and "loose_clothing". The classification was done manually by both authors and also by the LLM. Example (13) serves as an illustration of a concordance which was classified as "indoor_garment" by both humans, a label used for concordances reflecting the meaning: 'A loose piece of clothing that is worn in the house, sometimes over other clothes'.

(13) *Starting to feel a little frazzled round the edges, she went and had a bath, donned a nightdress and cotton* ***wrap****, and brushed out her hair. It was too early to go to bed yet - though she'd an idea that while this worry was on her mind she*

Once concordances had been classified by both humans and the GPT, Krippendorff's alpha (1970, 2012) was computed for interrater agreement both between human1 and human2 and between humans and GPT4o for the interpretation of the results.

3.3.2.2.2. Profile of the affixes: constraints and Naturalness

The semantic categories described in the previous section are generally linked to particular word classes of the base. For example, ACTION nouns are typically derived from verbs, and STATE nouns are typically derived from adjectives. There may be exceptions in this regard, and they may, together with other constraints, play a role on the competition between affixes.

Constraints on word formation have mostly been researched on different bases (see §2.3.3), but Romaine (2004: 1638) argues that it would be more "instructive to compare word formation processes which compete for the same bases" because "[i]n such cases the factors constraining productivity become clearer".

This section provides a general description regarding:

i) the constraints that may be at play on the competing affixes analysed in this book, that is, *-ation*, *-er*, *-ness*, and zero-affixation, and
ii) the rank in the scales of Naturalness of the competitors under study.

This section is restricted to the clusters in PDE competition analysed in this book, that is, to those clusters in which:

i) at least a zero-affixed and a suffixed form compete according to OED data, and
ii) they are both attested in the BNC.

It should be noted, however, that the fact that the forms are attested means that the constraints may hinder the derivation of certain forms, but it does not necessarily prevent it.

This section is intended as an overview on the profile of the competing patterns. For a more thorough review of these affixes see, for example, Raffelsiefen (1998; 2004); Giegerich (1999); Lieber (2004); Bauer et al. (2013).

3.3.2.2.2.1. *-ation*

The *-ation* competitors analysed in this book are all deverbal (see Appendix 1.A), as is expected because the semantic category with which they compete is ACTION. The competitors are all derived from non-native bases, so they follow the general tendency for non-native affixes to be attached to non-native bases.

As regards morphotactic transparency (see Dressler 1985a; Kilani-Schoch 1988: 118; Crocco Galèas 1998: 37), all *-ation* competitors are instances of agglutinative affixation, but they undergo at least one phonetic change in derivation, stress shift, as they carry their main stress on the penultimate syllable, for example, *transportation*. Some competitors undergo more modifications, as in *registration*, where the second vowel mutates from /ɪ/ to /ə/ when affixed, so it would be an example of vowel change, and more specifically, vowel laxing, and thus ranked in level II on the scale of morphotactic transparency (Dressler 1985a: 316–317; adapted in Crocco Galèas 1998: 38–40). Despite the phonological changes, all forms suffixed by *-ation* rank higher on the scale of morphotactic transparency than their zero-affixed counterparts. In the scale of morphosemantic transparency (see Dressler 1985a, adapted in Crocco Galèas 1998: 58–60), the *-ation* forms rank second level (as opposed to the zero-affixed competitors, which rank sixth).

3.3.2.2.2.2. *-er*

Competitors in *-er* are analysed in this book associated with the sense AGENTIVE and with the sense INSTRUMENT. In both cases, nearly all the bases are verbal and mostly of a native origin (e.g. *clip*^{V}, the base of *clipper*), with some exceptions (e.g. *bolt*^{V}, the base of *bolter*, is of Romance origin according to the OED).

The base is phonologically fully recoverable from the derivative in nearly all *-er* forms. Most bases end in a consonant, which does not undergo any kind of modification in derivation. Stress is not affected in most forms. One exception is *adulterer*, where there is stress shift and vowel strengthening, so it would rank level II on the scale of morphotactic transparency. On the scale of morphosemantic transparency, all *-er* forms rank second level of the scale.

3.3.2.2.2.3. *-ness*

The forms in *-ness* researched in this book are all deadjectival, as is expected, because the sense for which they compete is STATE. The bases for derivation are both native (e.g. *dry*^{Adj}) and non-native (e.g. *savage*^{Adj}).

As regards their phonology, competitors in *-ness* do not undergo any stress shift. Most derivatives bear stress on the first syllable, with the exception of *alertness*, which keeps the stress on the second syllable (as in the base form *alert*^{V}).

Most bases end in a consonant, with two exceptions, which end in diphthongs (*dry* and *low*), and none of them undergo a phonological change. Therefore, the suffix *-ness* does not affect the stress pattern or the segmental phonology of the bases to which it attaches (see also Bauer et al. 2013: 245–248). All forms are thus morphotactically transparent, so they rank first on the scale. As regards morphosemantic transparency, the competitors in *-ness* are in the second level of the scale.

3.3.2.2.2.4. Zero-affixation

Zero-affixation is researched in this book when associated with four different semantic categories: ACTION, AGENTIVE, INSTRUMENT and STATE. As regards the first three, the bases of the competitors identified are verbal, with very few exceptions (e.g. $down^{N}$, derived from $down^{Adv}$). As for the last category, STATE, the bases are adjectival. Bases are mostly Germanic (e.g. $cram^{V}$, as the base for *crammer*) although the number of non-native bases is not negligible (e.g. $faint^{Adj}$ as the base for *faintness*). This was to be expected, because nearly all native verbs have a nominal zero-affixed counterpart, although the process has been fully productive in non-native bases (Bauer et al. 2013: 203–204).

Regarding the transparency scale, zero-affixation ranks very low, because the affixal exponent is maximally opaque. On the scale of morphotactic transparency, it is level VI (i.e. lack of compositionality), whereas on the scale of morphosemantic transparency, it is level X (i.e. suppletion + no transparent affix). The base form, however, is transparent, and it typically undergoes either stress shift or no phonological change.

3.3.2.2.3. Productivity: the Referenced Index of Competition

After the semantic classification of concordances, the Referenced Index of Competition (*C**, Fernández-Domínguez 2024) is calculated. This index is based on a previous measure of the same, named Index of Competition (*C*, Fernández-Domínguez 2017). *C** is calculated using the following formula:

$$C^{*} = \frac{N/Nc}{Vc} / \, Rc \, ,$$

where N is the token frequency of a competing form, Nc is the joint token frequency of all forms in the cluster, and Vc is the number of forms in current competition. Rc, in turn, modulates the resultant value based on how many rivals are in competition. The maximum value of Rc is 1, where only one of the competitors in the cluster is attested in the corpus, that is, in cases of resolved competition. The more competitors in the clusters, the lower this value: the value of Rc is 0.5 if there are two competitors in the clusters, 0.33 if there are three, etc.

Measure C* posits that the more units are in direct competition, the more challenging their individual survival will be. Under this assumption, the more competitors there are in a cluster, the lower the reference C* because the mere presence of other units means the existence of rivals and, in principle, then each unit stands fewer chances of success.

Table 3.5 illustrates the computation of the C* value with the competing cluster *coolness/cool/coolth*. Absolute frequencies (N) are those of the sense STATE. As there are three members in the cluster, the Rc is 0.33. In the example, the C* value of *coolness* is the highest, so it is the most likely to survive, whereas *coolth* is expected to decay.

Table 3.5: Computation of the C value of the cluster coolness/cool/coolth *with the sense* STATE

		C value			
	N	*Nc*	*Vc*	*Rc*	*C**
coolness	82	122	3	0.33	**0.68**
cool	39	122	3	0.33	**0.32**
coolth	1	122	3	0.33	**0.01**

In this book, C* is calculated using not the frequencies of the competitors as a whole, but the frequencies of the sense in competition, following the semantic classification of concordances. This allows for a more fine-grained analysis inasmuch as concordances that are not actually in competition are not included in the count. However, this also limits the size of the clusters: only doublets were semantically analysed, so the other potential competitors in the clusters (if any) were left out.

3.3.2.2.4. Register distribution

The register distribution of competitors was then analysed to test whether there is any specialisation in the use of any competing patterns. This book tests whether the realisation of one process as opposed to the other may depend on use (specifically, mode or register), that is, whether one context may favour one linguistic variant, and another context another variant. For this reason, a linguistic feature design is used, which allows to investigate factors that may play a role in the use of competitors (see Brezina 2018: 22). The first step was to manually classify all the occurrences of the competing patterns:

i) by mode (i.e. spoken vs. written), and
ii) by register, following the BNC classification of registers (i.e. spoken, written fiction, written magazine, written newspaper, written non-academic, written academic, and written miscellaneous).

In order to analyse their distribution, cross-tabulation tables (contingency tables) were used, which allow examination of the relationship between two categorical variables (see Brezina 2018: 108ff.). In cross-tabulation tables, one linguistic variable and one or more explanatory variables are cross-plotted. The most basic one is a 2×2 table, which was used here for the analysis of mode, containing one linguistic variable and one explanatory variable, of two categories each. For register analyses, the tables are 2×7 (see, e.g., Table 3.6).

Table 3.6: Absolute frequencies of -ation/*zero-affixation competitors with the sense* ACTION *by register*

	Spoken	**W_fict**	**W_magaz**	**W_newsp**	**W_non-acad**	**W_acad**	**W_misc**
-ation	136	91	160	213	598	877	920
zero-affix.	280	167	422	1395	2055	1118	2638

In this book, the linguistic variable is the competing pattern, which can take on two possible values that are encoded as two categories (e.g. *-ation* suffixation with the sense ACTION and zero-affixation with the sense ACTION). The explanatory variable is either "mode" or "register": the former has two categories (spoken and written) and the latter has seven categories (listed above). Conventionally, linguistic variables are presented as columns and explanatory variables as rows but, as the analysis of registers contains many more categories within the latter, this book presents them as follows:

i) rows show the linguistic variable, that is, the competing pattern, and
ii) columns show the explanatory variable, that is, mode or register.

The analysis of the relationship between these variables was done in two ways:

i) by means of a comparison of the normalised frequencies of the competitors across corpus parts, and
ii) by means of statistical tests to compare both the frequencies of the spoken vs. the written mode and the frequencies across registers.

The method used to this end is illustrated here with the competing patterns *-ation*/zero-suffixation when associated with the sense ACTION for an analysis of mode distribution.

In order to quantify the proportion to which one pattern prevails in one mode, percentages are calculated from column total using normalised frequencies.[42] For example, the normalised frequency of *-ation* with the sense ACTION in the spoken mode is 14.62, and that of zero-affixation is 30.11. The sum of both is 44.73. The proportion to which *-ation* prevails in that mode is calculated as follows:

$$\text{Probability columns } (\%) = \frac{\text{freq. of WFP1 in one mode (e.g. 14.62)}}{\text{freq. of WFP1+WFP2 in same mode (e.g. 44.73)}}$$

The result is 32.7%. Zero-affixation in turn prevails in the spoken mode to 67.3%.

The distribution is also analysed by rows, which serves to illustrate the distribution of each competing pattern. For example, the normalised frequency of *-ation* with the sense ACTION in the spoken mode is 14.62 and in the written one it is 33.27, so the total is 47.89. In order to calculate, out of all the occurrences of *-ation*, which percentage occurs in the spoken mode, the following formula is used:

$$\text{Probability rows } (\%) = \frac{\text{freq. of WFP1 in one mode (e.g. 14.62)}}{\text{freq. of WFP1 in the both modes (e.g. 47.89)}}$$

The result is that 31% occurs in the spoken mode, and thus 69% in the written mode.

The percentages described above are presented as figures for easier comparison. In the percentages by rows, the size of each register/mode is also illustrated for easier comparison. This is because affixes are expected to occur more or less frequently according to the size of the corpus part, that is, if a corpus part is larger, affixes would be expected to occur more often in that part than in smaller ones. However, that is not always the case, and variations in this respect could point towards specialisation of use.

The percentage analyses are thus used to:

i) identify the proportion to which each competing pattern may prevail in each register(s)/mode(s), and
ii) examine the distribution of the patterns with respect to the size of each corpus part.

---

42 Normalised frequencies are calculated with respect to the size of each corpus part per million. For example, the raw frequency of *-ation* with the sense ACTION in 'Spoken' is 136. The size of that register is 9,300,606 units. The normalised frequency is calculated as follows: (136/9,300,606)*1,000,000. The result is 14.62.

Statistical significance is tested, in order to evaluate whether there is evidence against the null hypothesis. The null hypothesis (H_0) states that there is no difference as regards register/mode for the two competing patterns (and the reverse is the alternative hypothesis (H_1)). Statistical tests are calculated using a script in R.[43]

Pearson's chi-square test was computed after checking that the data satisfies the assumptions of this test (see Brezina 2018: 112–113):

i) Independence of observations, for example, that the linguistic features in one text are assumed not to be influenced by the linguistic features in another. This assumption needs to be relaxed in corpora, because a corpus cannot be a random sample of linguistic words/features: they are text samples which combine interconnected words/features. Otherwise, the violation of this principle may increase the number of falsely significant results.
ii) Expected frequencies need to be larger than 5 (in tables larger than 2×2, at least 80% of the values need to be larger than 5). If this assumption is not met, other tests should be used instead of the chi-square test.

The results of the test provide three values: the degrees of freedom (hereafter, df), the test statistic and the p-value. The last one is the probability value that the observed values are due to chance alone and it is used to decide whether to reject the null hypothesis or not. If the p-value is lower than 0.05, which is the conventional cut-off point, the null hypothesis is rejected, concluding that the observed difference is unlikely to be due to chance and thus the result is statistically significant. This means that the difference observed in the corpus is likely to be a difference in all language use. If the p-value is higher than 0.05, the conclusion would be that there is not enough evidence in the corpus to reject the null hypothesis. P-values are associated with test values, and they are dependent on the degrees of freedom. In a 2×2 table (df=1), the 0.05 significance critical value is 3.84: any chi-square test value higher than 3.84 is here considered significant.

Taking as an example the competition between *-ation* and zero-affixation for the expression of ACTION by mode, that is, in spoken vs. written speech, the chi-square value is 6.96, meaning that the p-value is lower that 0.001 ($\chi2$ (1) = 6.96, p < .001), so the null hypothesis is rejected. Based on this, it is established that the two competing patterns differ as regards mode. In order to establish how

43 The script is based on Gries (2013: 367–371) in the main, except that it has been adapted to adjust it to the data of this book.

large that difference is, an effect size measure is used: Cramer's *V*.[44] The result is interpreted according to the degrees of freedom. In the example, the result is 0.025, which, for a 2×2 table, means that the overall effect is very weak.

If the chi-square value shows that there is a significant difference in the use of the competing patterns, then it would be relevant to see in which cells there is a (significant) difference. This could be done by manually comparing observed and expected frequencies but, when the table contains many categories, it may be difficult to interpret the results. For this reason, it is more appropriate to use Pearson's residuals, which are computed for each cell in the table. Residuals are positive when the cell frequency is higher than expected, and negative when it is lower than expected. In this book, the *standardised* residuals are used for their easier interpretation: by convention, if the standardised residual is larger than 2 (or, more specifically, 1.96), it would indicate that the frequency in that cell is significantly larger than expected, if the null hypothesis were true. If it were lower than –2, then the observed frequencies are significantly smaller than expected. In 2×2 cross-tabulation tables, all the standardised residuals will have the same value, but two will be negative. In the example, the standardised residuals are shown in Table 3.7.

Table 3.7: Standardised residuals of the chi-square test for -ation *and zero-affixation for the sense* ACTION *in the spoken and written modes (BNC)*

	Spoken	**Written**
-ation	2.64	–2.64
zero-affixation	–2.64	2.64

A graphical representation of the deviation from the expected frequencies is provided by association plots (see example in Figure 3.1). Boxes above the line represent cell frequencies higher than expected, and boxes below represent cell frequencies lower than expected. The heights of the boxes are proportional to the residuals, and the widths are proportional to the square roots of the expected frequencies (Gries 2013: 370).

44 This book uses Cramer's *V* instead of Phi (φ), because tables larger than 2×2 are used for the analysis of registers.

Figure 3.1: The association plot of the relation between the competing pattern (-ation/zero-affixation with the sense ACTION*) and mode (spoken/written). Black represents higher frequencies than expected, and grey lower than expected.*

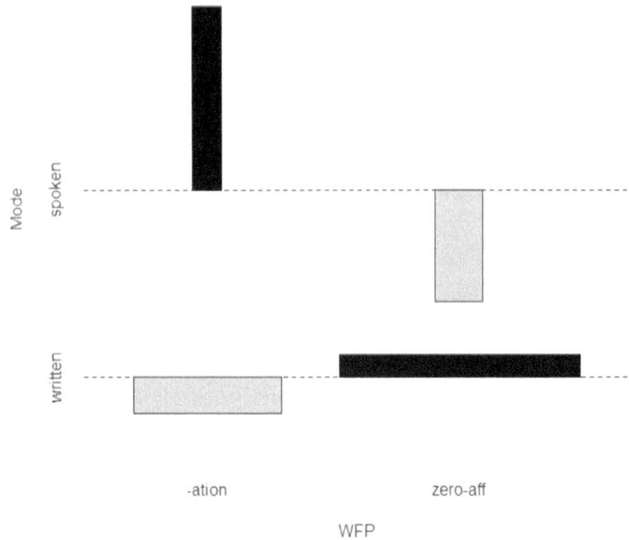

3.3.2.2.5. Cooccurrences

The statistical tests described above establish whether there is a difference between the competing patterns as regards register or mode. If a significant difference is identified, then it is expected that the context of use and, thus, the co-text of the competitors, will not be the same. This is explored by means of the cooccurrences of the competitors. The rationale behind the analysis of cooccurrence to compare the use of forms is in line with the hypothesis of distributional semantics that forms that are semantically similar are also similarly distributed in corpora. For this reason, the nearest neighbours of words, which are the most similar distributionally, are expected to be the most semantically similar (Huyghe & Wauquier 2021: 362; see also Wauquier et al. 2020a and Guzmán Naranjo & Bonami 2023 for an analysis of competitors using Distributional Semantic Models). For this reason, some doublets among the ones with the highest frequencies were chosen at random for further analysis. Low frequency doublets were not chosen, because a cooccurrence analysis is done on the basis of sentences where the keywords occur, and a low count of sentences may give equivocal results.

Cooccurrences were examined in two ways:

i) by means of the list of collocates[45] of the competitors extracted from BNC and COCA, and
ii) by means of the representation in the form of graphs of the words cooccurring with the competitors in the BNC concordances showing the competing sense.

The former was done by setting a window of four before and after the keyword and by leaving the rest of the options as default. This includes setting the minimum A mutual information score at three, in order to remove high frequency noise words, such as *the*, *with*, etc. This search provides a list of collocates, sorted by frequency. However, these searches, even though they can provide hints of differences between the competitors, are based on all the occurrences of the competitors in each corpus and are thus not specific to the competing sense. For this reason, software was developed (*Aífe*, Lara-Clares 2023) to allow an examination of the cooccurrences of competitors based only on the concordances from the BNC classified as showing the competing sense.

The software was written in Python 3.6, using the Networkx[46] library, and analysed using Gephi,[47] which allows the visualisation and analysis of networks. The aim was to create weighted non-directed[48] graphs which consist of nodes (i.e. the cooccurring forms) and edges, which represent the frequency of cooccurrence of the forms. The thicker the edge, the higher the cooccurrence frequency (see example in Figure 3.2). In order to process the concordances which had already been semantically classified, a preprocessing stage was necessary:

i) the text was converted into lower-case,
ii) unwanted characters, such as asterisks, were eliminated (this is known as 'char filtering'),
iii) forms of less than two characters were discarded, and
iv) the remaining text was tokenised using the NLTK toolkit,[49] which allows one to:

---

45 The term "collocate" follows the BNC/COCA terminology, even if this book does not explore whether they are actually collocates or just cooccurring forms.
46 https://networkx.org
47 https://gephi.org/
48 *Non-directed* means that the order of occurrence is not taken into account. Thus, if "believe firmly" appears five times in the sample, and "firmly believe" occurs three times, then the weight would be eight, independently of word order.
49 https://www.nltk.org

a. to discard stop words (using the Gensim library[50]) as they would introduce noise into the results, and
b. obtain a list of words ordered by appearance in the sentence.

After that, the cooccurrence graph is created with a window of four words before and after the keyword. There are two conditions that nodes must fulfil in order to be represented in the graphs:

i) to have a minimum weight of 6, so that only high-frequency cooccurrences are shown, and
ii) to cooccur with at least one of the two competitors.

The graphs created using this software were analysed and represented using Gephi. A visualisation method named Force Atlas 2[51] was applied, which allows showing the graph depending on particular characteristics, such as the number of vertices of the nodes. This method allows the differentiation of the two key nodes, that is, differentiation of the competitors. It thus allows the representation of the cooccurrences of the doublets so that one image shows both the cooccurrences in common between the two competitors, and the cooccurrences that are unique to each keyword (see example in Figure 3.2).

Colours are used in the edges to represent whether they are cooccurrences of zero-affixation (dark blue) or of the overt suffix (light blue). It also allows interaction by selecting specific nodes, which highlights the ones that are connected to that node (in the example, *prevent* is selected). The graph of cooccurrences is available in Appendix 1.B for *importation* and in Appendix 1.C for *import*^{N} for easier visualisation.

Note that all graphs are based on doublets and not on the competing patterns as a whole. They are used to compare, for example, *importation* and *import* with the sense ACTION, but not to compare *-ation* and zero-affixation. This is because the graphs created with the competing processes were too complex to interpret due to the large amount of cooccurrences, so no clear conclusions could be drawn from them. A view of doublets, however, did provide some hints as to differentiated fields or contexts of use of the pairs of competitors (see Chapter 4). If forms show similar patterns of cooccurrence, it could be a hint that the competition is still not resolved.

---

50 https://pypi.org/project/gensim/
51 https://journals.plos.org/plosone/article?id=10.1371/journal.pone.0098679

Figure 3.2: Graph of the cooccurrences of importation and import for the sense ACTION.

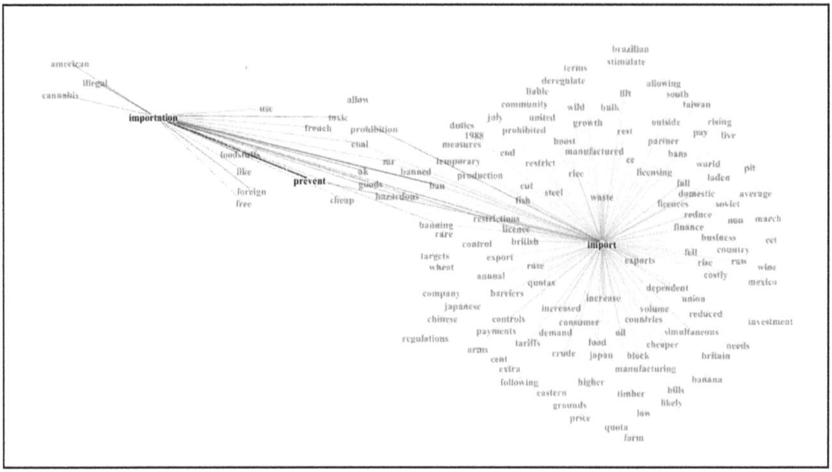

3.4. Summary

This chapter describes the method followed for the extraction and analysis of nominal competition in PDE. The data has been extracted in the main from a corpus source, the BNC, and a lexicographic source, the OED. Data processing was done in two differentiated stages:

i) extraction and analysis of Sample1, which was based on the complete frequency list of the BNC and served to identify approx. 40 competing patterns for the formation of nouns in PDE, and
ii) extraction and analysis of Sample2, which was done by means of an advanced search in the OED in order to identify all the competitors of four competing patterns selected from Sample1, which were then analysed by manually classifying all the concordances of the competitors in order to assess their context of use.

Within each stage, the method followed were from less to more strict on conditions, such that data is first extracted in an inclusive way, with the aim of being comprehensive, but becomes gradually restrictive.

4. The competition between overt affixation and zero-affixation

4.1. Introduction

This book investigates the competition between nouns derived from the same base by zero-affixation and overt affixation for the expression of four different semantic categories: ACTION, AGENTIVE, INSTRUMENT and STATE. More specifically, it aims to address four research questions and also discusses how the methodological decisions taken for this piece of research may have affected the results obtained. The research questions, as outlined in Chapter 1, are the following:

i) RQ1: Is there any historical tendency in the resolution of the competition for the patterns under study? If so, does it agree with PDE corpus data?
ii) RQ2: Does synchronic data point to any of the possibilities of resolution of competition for the patterns under study? Specifically, is any pattern expected to fall out of use or to become specialised?
iii) RQ3: If a resolution tendency is identified for any given pattern, does each competition cluster follow that tendency?
iv) RQ4: Does the data analysed reflect a preference for transparency or for economy in cases of competition? If so, is it dependent on the context of use?

This chapter addresses each research question individually and, when necessary, it presents the results by morphosemantic pattern. Besides, each section ends with a discussion of the results obtained. The chapter is structured as follows: the first section, §4.2, outlines the results obtained from Sample1, that is, it provides an overview of competition for the formation of nouns in PDE. From the patterns identified in that sample, four patterns of competition were selected for further analysis. The results thus obtained serve to identify some historical tendencies in the resolution of competition (§4.3), and also in PDE (§4.4). Then, the analysis is performed at a lexical level, that is, by competitor instead of by pattern (§4.5). The next section, §4.6, discusses the clash between an economic model, which would favour zero-affixation, and a transparent model, which would favour overt affixation, in view of the results obtained. Finally, §4.7 deals with the effect that the methodological decisions taken might have on the results. The chapter ends with a summary.

4.2. Overview: competing patterns in PDE

The analysis of Sample1 identified 36 clusters of affixal competition in PDE, that is, c. 3% of the entries in the BNC frequency list are in competition (see Table 4.1). The clusters are classified according to the semantic category for which they are attested to compete, that is, ABSTRACTION, ACTION, AGENTIVE, AUGMENTATIVE. ENTITY, INSTRUMENT, PATIENT, PROCESS, RESULTATIVE and STATE.

The classification by the frequency of the semantic categories recorded is as follows:

i) The semantic category that contains most clusters is ACTION (14 clusters),
ii) a second group of categories by frequency features:
  a. INSTRUMENT (five clusters),
  b. STATE and AGENTIVE (four clusters),
  c. RESULTATIVE (three clusters), and
  d. PATIENT, and
iii) the rest of categories contain one cluster each.

The classification by the frequency of the word-formation processes recorded is as follows:

i) zero-affixation is the prevailing word-formation process: it competes in 30 clusters and is recorded in nearly all semantic categories,
ii) *-ing* suffixation is the second most frequent process: it competes in 22 clusters, but is recorded only in four semantic categories,
iii) *-ation* suffixation is the third most frequent process recorded as in competition (13 clusters),
iv) *-ment* and *-er* suffixation compete in eight clusters, and
v) some processes are attested only once in competition in the sample: *-ster*, *-ety*, and *over-*.

This summary shows that some processes can compete for virtually any semantic category (e.g. zero-affixation), whereas others are very restrictive semantically (e.g. *-ee*). Also, suffixation was found to be much more pervasive in competition than prefixation. This may be for the higher productivity of suffixation in general, but it may also be partly because prefixed forms are often not listed in dictionaries such as the OED. Therefore, conclusions on the comparison of suffixation and prefixation are not made in this regard.

The processes selected for further analysis are among the top six more pervasive ones in the sample, and the semantic categories selected are the ones which contained the highest number of clusters. The following sections describe and discuss the results obtained from the analysis of Sample2 both by pattern and by competitor, over time and in PDE.

The template with the information about each pattern extracted from the OED for the PDE competitors is available in Appendices 1.A, 2.A, 3.A and 4.A.

Table 4.1: Competing patterns identified from Sample1 by semantic category (PDE)

Action			Agentive			Instrument			Resultative			State		
Patterns		**N clusters**	**Patterns**		**N clusters**	**Patterns**		**N clusters**	**Patterns**		**N clusters**	**Patterns**		**N clusters**
Ø	*-ing*	9	Ø	*-er*	1	Ø	*-er*	2	Ø	*-ing*	1	*-ity*	*-ness*	2
-ation	*-ing*	5	*-er*	*-ster*	1	*-ment*	*-er*	1	Ø	*-ance*	1	*-ity*	*-ism*	2
Ø	*-ation*	4	*-er*	*-ant*	1	*-ation*	*-or*	1	Ø	*-ment*	1	Ø	*-ness*	1
Ø	*-al*	2	*-ment*	*-ist*	1	*-ment*	*-ion*	1				*-ety*	*-ness*	1
-ing	*-al*	2				Ø	*-ation*	1						
Ø	*-ery*	1												
-ery	*-ing*	1												
Ø	*-y*	1												
-ation	*-y*	1												
Ø	*-age*	1												
-ing	*-age*	1												
-age	*-al*	1												
-ing	*-ment*	1												
Ø	*-ment*	1												
Abstraction			Augmentative			Entity			Patient			Process		
Patterns		N clusters	Patterns		N clusters	Patterns		N clusters	Patterns		N clusters	Patterns		N clusters
-ness	*-ing*	1	*sur-*	*over-*	1	Ø	*-y*	1	Ø	*-ee*	1	*-ing*	*-ment*	1
									-ation	*-ee*	1			

4.3. Historical tendencies

4.3.1. Introduction

Once the four competing patterns were selected, further analysis was carried out to explore possible tendencies in the resolution of competition. To this end, a search was made in the OED for each pattern to identify the historical evolution of the clusters that make up each of the patterns.

Specifically, the book aims to classify clusters according to their profiles of competition or resolution (see §2.3.3 for a description of the terminology used):

i) incidental competition, that is, at least one member is short-lived,[52]
ii) past competition, that is, all forms come out of use,
iii) resolved competition, that is, one member is attested as in use but the other(s) fall(s) out of use, and
iv) ongoing competition, that is, at least two forms remain in use.

The results are presented by competing pattern in the following sections.

4.3.2. *-ation* vs. zero-affixation: ACTION

This section describes the results obtained from the analysis of the historical tendencies identified in the competition between *-ation* and zero-affixation for the expression of ACTION.

The OED search for the potential competitors of *-ation*/zero-affixation for the sense ACTION identified 16 clusters of potential competition over time:

i) seven clusters are made up of two forms (doublets),
ii) seven are made up of three (triplets), and
iii) two are made up of five forms.

Figure 4.1 shows the all the main profiles of competition or of resolution:

i) incidental competition (e.g. for the bases *assassine*, *exorcize*),
ii) past competition (e.g. for the bases *dispute*, *transport*),
iii) resolved competition (e.g. for the bases *cure*, *experiment*), and
iv) ongoing competition (e.g. for the bases *aliment*, *register*).

In some cases, the members of the cluster are attested at different points in time, that is, one is recorded to have come into existence after the other has fallen out

52 See Fernández-Alcaina (2021a: 203–204) for a discussion on whether one-time attestations should actually be considered as competing or not.

of use, so the dates do not attest actual competition (e.g. *fidget*). In others, some forms are attested only for a short period of time in which they are in competition with other forms, while the competitor remains in use, although it may eventually fall out of use (e.g. *exhort*, *interlope*, both instances of past competition). As regards the base *float*, the *-ation* form seems to have superseded the zero-affixed form, but they were never in competition, or they were only for a short period of time (*float*^{N} was latest attested in 1817 and *floatation* was earliest attested in 1806). Where competition between zero-affixation and *-ation* remained for some time and is resolved, it is in favour of *-ation* in three clusters (*assassin*, *float* and *scatter*) and in favour of zero-affixation in one (*experiment*). Three triplets (*import*, *puncture* and *register*) and one doublet remain in competition (*aliment*).

This overview illustrates the heterogeneous profile of this pattern of competition over time. No clear resolution pattern is found in favour or one or the other form. Corpus data is thus used to check whether additional evidence may tell how the competition might resolve in the clusters where the two forms are attested in the BNC[53] (§4.4.2).

Figure 4.1: Timeline of potentially competing clusters by suffix obtained from the sample for the expression of ACTION *in the period 500–2020, where zero-affixation is represented by a continuous dark blue line and diamond ends, and* -er *is represented by a light blue discontinuous line and arrow ends.*

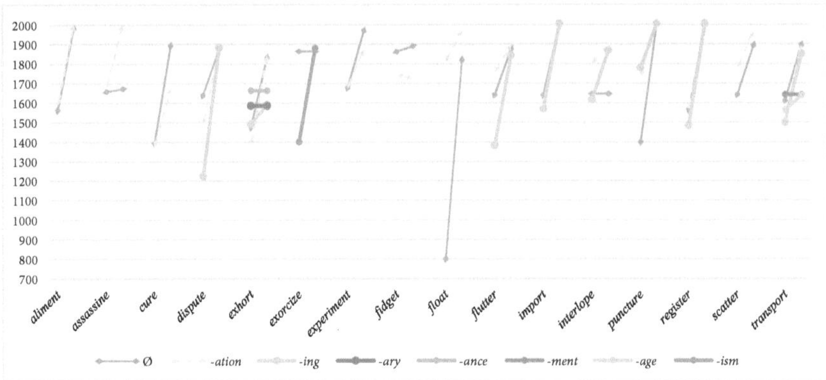

53 Note that some clusters may appear as resolved competition, but they are classified as in ongoing competition based on corpus data. This is because some forms are not attested for the competing sense in the OED in the last century, even if evidence of attestation of the whole form can be found in corpora (BNC attestation of the competing sense is checked at a later stage).

4.3.3. *-er* vs. zero-affixation: AGENTIVE

The search in the OED for potential competitors over time resulted in the identification of 56 clusters of competition: four are triplets, and the rest are doublets.

Figure 4.2 shows the earliest and latest attestation of the competing sense for each competitor, from which the following profiles of competition or resolution can be identified:

i) incidental competition (e.g. *chouse*, *nim*),
ii) past competition (e.g. *cater*, *fawn*, *scrub*),
iii) resolved competition (e.g. *judge*, *prog*), and
iv) ongoing competition (e.g. *aid*, *bother*).

Figure 4.2: Timeline of potentially competing clusters by suffix obtained from the sample for the expression of AGENTIVE *in the period 500–2020, where zero-affixation is represented by a continuous dark blue line and diamond ends, and* -er *is represented by a light blue discontinuous line and arrow ends.*

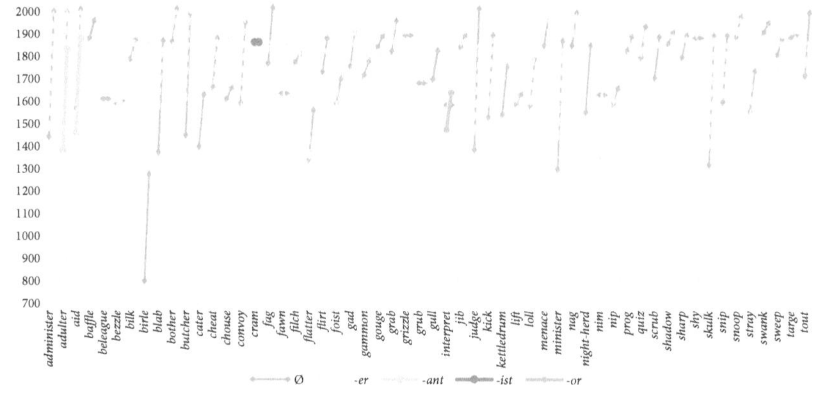

Where competition between zero-affixation and *-er* for the expression of AGENTIVE remained for some time and is now resolved, it is in favour of zero-affixation in five clusters, and in favour of *-er* also in five clusters. There are 10 clusters of ongoing competition.

Regarding triplets, one of them (competing for the base *cram*^{V}) shows that all competitors fall out of use in the 19th century, and two of the competitors are attested only once in the OED. In the cluster competing for the base *interpret*^{V}, the *-er* form is the only one to remain in use, and it was the one attested earliest (in the 15th century) too. In the two remaining triplets, competing for the base *adulter*^{V}

and *aid*^{V}, the *-ant* form fell out of use in the 19th century, and zero-affixation and *-er* remain in competition.

This overview shows that all competitors have fallen out of use in most cases. Where one of the forms has remained in use, there is no clear preference for *-er* or for zero-affixation. For this reason, corpus data is used to try to find hints on the resolution of competition in those clusters where the two forms are attested in the BNC (4.4.3).

4.3.4. *-er* vs. zero-affixation: INSTRUMENT

The search in the OED for the potential competitors of *-er*/zero-affixation for the sense INSTRUMENT identified 35 clusters of competition over time. All clusters but one are made up of two forms, and the remaining one is a triplet (*cumberer*, *cumber*^{N}, *cumberment*). Figure 4.3 shows different profiles of competition or resolution:

i) incidental competition, that is, at least one member is short-lived (e.g. *cumber*, *sweep*),
ii) past competition, that is, all forms come out of use (e.g. *bolt*, *clack*, *preserve*),
iii) resolved competition, that is, one member is attested as in use but the other(s) fall(s) out of use (e.g. *conserve*, *twitch*), and
iv) ongoing competition, that is, at least two forms remain in use (e.g. *down*, *hack*).

Figure 4.3: Timeline of potentially competing clusters by suffix obtained from the sample for the expression of INSTRUMENT *in the period 500–2020, where zero-affixation is represented by a continuous dark blue line and diamond ends, and* -er *is represented by a light blue discontinuous line and arrow ends.*

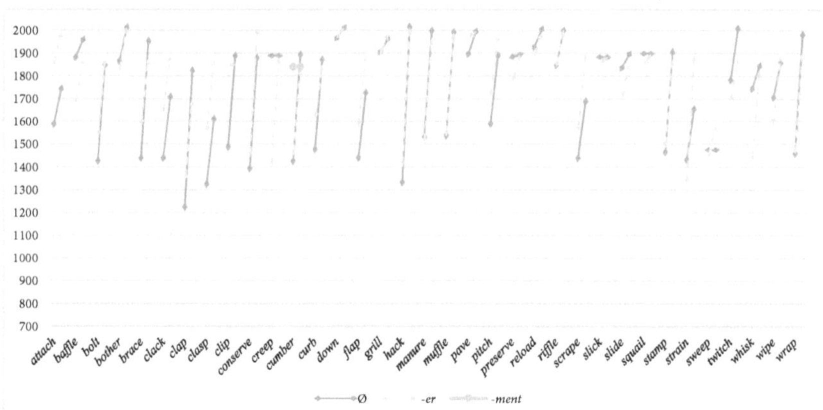

In the competition for the base *attach*^{V}, the competitors of the cluster are attested at different points in time, that is, *attacher* comes into existence after *attach*^{N} has fallen out of use, so they never actually compete. In other cases, the overlap in time is small, and one form seems to have quickly superseded the other (e.g. *clasp*). Where competition between zero-affixation and *-er* remains for some time and is eventually resolved, it is in favour of zero-affixation in five clusters, and in favour of *-er* in three clusters. As regards past competition, in some clusters the latest attestation dates of both competitors are close to each other (e.g. 1859 vs. 1890 for the base *whisk*), so an assessment of the resolution in favour of one or the other competitor is not possible. Rather, one would expect that another form has superseded these competitors or there is no need to express that meaning anymore. Nine clusters remain in competition.

This overview shows that competition may be resolved in some clusters, but there is some heterogeneity in the profile of resolution. For this reason, corpus data is searched for hints regarding the resolution of competition in those clusters where the two forms are attested in the BNC (§4.4.4).

4.3.5. *-ness* vs. zero-affixation: STATE

The OED search resulted in the identification of 27 clusters of the competing pattern *-ness*/zero-affixation for the sense STATE. Four of those clusters are made up of three forms (triplets), and one is made up of four forms; the rest are doublets. A timeline of the earliest and latest attestation date of the forms is shown in Figure 4.4, and it serves to identify the following profiles of competition:

i) incidental competition, that is, at least one member is short-lived (e.g. *savage*, *doleful*),
ii) past competition, that is, all forms fall out of use (e.g. *calm*, *grim*),
iii) resolved competition, that is, one member is attested as in use but the other(s) come(s) out of use (e.g. *altogether*, *ripe*, *watertight*), and
iv) ongoing competition, that is, at least two forms remain in use (e.g. *alert*, *dark*, *soft*).

According to OED data, however, three clusters were never really in competition: in the pair *watertight*/*watertightness*, the two forms never coexisted, because the sense STATE is attested in *watertight*^{N} only once (1539) and in *watertightness* it comes into use in 1826. Similarly, for the bases *lame* and *laxative*, the *-ness* form is earliest attested after the zero-affixed form has fallen out of use. In the clusters where there was coexistence but competition is resolved, the zero-affixed form decays when in competition with *-ness* in five clusters. In two of them, *-ness* stays in competition with other affixes (*-th* for the base *cool*, and *-ery* and *-ism* for the base *savage*). In contrast, the *-ness* form falls out of use in two clusters and the zero-affixed counterpart remains in use (in *dry/dryness* and *rot/rotness*), although in the former cluster, the latest attestation dates of both members are close to each other (1968 for *dry* and 1944 for *dryness*). In 11 clusters there is ongoing competition between *-ness* and zero-affixation, whereas in nine both competitors become obsolete (i.e. they are instances of past competition).

Lexicographic data thus points to a possible resolution of competition in which *-ness* would supersede zero-affixation, but it could be the case that one or both processes stay in use but become specialised.

For this reason, corpus data is used to explore whether there is any difference as regards their use in PDE (§4.4.5).

Figure 4.4: Timeline of potentially competing clusters by suffix obtained from the sample for the expression of STATE *in the period 500–2020, where zero-affixation is represented by a continuous dark blue line and diamond ends, and* -ness *is represented by a light blue discontinuous line and arrow ends.*

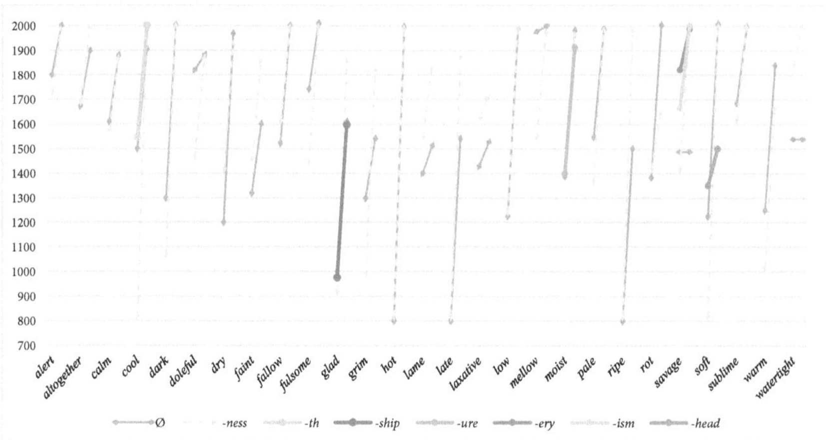

4.3.6. Discussion

The first research question deals with historical tendencies on the resolution of competition. From a diachronic point of view, three main resolution patterns can be identified (see §2.3.3):

i) past competition, where all members are tagged as in disuse in the OED,
ii) resolved competition, where one competitor prevails over another, which eventually falls out of use, and
iii) ongoing competition, where the members are unmarked regarding their use and are therefore assumed to be in coexistence for a period of time.

Resolution tendencies are analysed in this book by exploring the earliest and latest attestation dates of the competing sense of competitors, which may cast light on the availability of the processes and, thus, on the resolution of competition, as in Bauer et al. (2010) and Fernández-Alcaina (2021a, 2021b) for verbal competition, or Díaz-Negrillo (2017) for nominal competition, among others.

This book focuses on four patterns of competition for the formation of nouns. The OED data of the earliest and latest attestation of the competing sense shows that competition is often resolved by the decay of both competitors (past competition), either because a third competitor superseded them both, or because the naming need has disappeared (see Bauer 2009: 188) (Table 4.2). In three patterns, approximately half of the clusters are classified as past competition, but in the competition between *-ness* and zero-affixation for the expression of STATE, the percentage is lower (33%).

Table 4.2: Diachronic profiles of resolution of the competing patterns according to OED data

	Past competition	**Resolved competition**		**Ongoing competition**
		Zero-affixation prevails	**Overt affixation prevails**	
-ation vs. zero-affixation ACTION	50% (8 clusters)	6% (1 cluster)	19% (3 clusters)	25% (1 cluster)
-er vs. zero-affixation AGENTIVE	64% (36 clusters)	9% (5 clusters)	9% (5 clusters)	18% (10 clusters)
-er vs. zero-affixation INSTRUMENT	51% (18 clusters)	14% (5 clusters)	9% (3 clusters)	26% (9 clusters)
-ness vs. zero-affixation STATE	33% (9 clusters)	7% (2 clusters)	19% (5 clusters)	41% (11 clusters)

As regards resolved competition, the results are unequal for each pattern: for the expression of ACTION and STATE, overt suffixation prevails in nearly 20% of the clusters (vs. 6–7% of clusters where zero-affixation prevails). For the expression of INSTRUMENT, the opposite resolution is found: zero-affixation prevails in nearly 15% of clusters, as opposed to 9% of clusters where overt suffixation prevails. For the expression of AGENTIVE, the results are inconclusive: both processes prevail in 9% of clusters. The proportion of clusters remaining in competition is similar for three patterns (between 18% and 26%), while c. 40% of clusters are classified as ongoing for the expression of STATE.

The similarities found between the three deverbal patterns (for the expression of ACTION, AGENTIVE and INSTRUMENT) as opposed to the deadjectival pattern (for the expression of STATE) raises the question whether the resolution profile may be affected by the word class of the base. While this book does not explore this component for want of a wider number of competing patterns, previous research approached this point, with results that are, again, not entirely conclusive (see discussion in §2.3.3.2.2).

The results presented in this book, as in Table 4.2, focus on pairs of competitors. However, as stated above, it could be the case that there are more competing forms at play. The data collected did not identify any affixal competitor in use aside from the two processes under study, that is, aside from the specific overt suffix explored in each case and zero. For example, in the competition between *interpret*^{N}*/interpreter/interpretor*, both the *-or* and the zero-affixed form fall out of use for the expression of the semantic category AGENTIVE, and only the *-er* form remains in use. Still, this book identifies cases where one of the two main competing forms falls out of use (i.e. *-ation*, *-er*, *-ness* or zero-affixation) and the other competing form plus some other competitor(s) remain in use (i.e. partial competition according to Fernández-Alcaina 2021a: 142–143). One such example can be found in derivation from the base *savage*^{Adj}, where four competitors are available in the OED for the expression of STATE: *savage*^{N}, *savageness*, *savagery* and *savagism*. However, dictionary and corpus data evidence uneven earliest attestation dates and uneven corpus attestation data. The final profile is one where zero has decayed and overt affixation remains in use for this base and this semantic category (see §4.7.2).

4.4. Resolution of competition in PDE

4.4.1. Introduction

Once the PDE competitors were identified, concordances were extracted from the BNC, which were classified semantically in order to compute the frequency of the sense in competition. Based on this, a number of analyses were carried out:

i) comparison of frequencies before and after sense classification,
ii) computation of the referenced index of competition (C*), and
iii) analysis of mode and register distribution.

The following sections present the results by competing pattern, and then discusses them.

4.4.2. *-ation* vs. zero-affixation: ACTION

The semantic classification of concordances of the competitors in *-ation* or zero-affixation for the expression of ACTION show that 1% of keywords are wrongly tagged, and nearly 7% were classified as *unclear*. Otherwise, the sense ACTION is attested in nearly 40% of concordances. Forms derived by *-ation* suffixation attest the competing sense in a lower percentage than forms derived by zero-affixation (c. 27% for *-ation*, c. 73% for zero-affixation). Even if concordances classified as *unclear* were included in the count, *-ation* would still attest the competing sense twice as many times as zero-affixation.

The *Referenced Index of Competition* allows the computation of the likelihood that one form (and, thus, one affix) may prevail in a cluster. Table 4.3 presents the C^* value of each competitor.

Table 4.3: C^* values of the competitors from the sample for the sense ACTION

Derivative	**C***	**Expected to prevail**
alimentation	-	
aliment	-	
curation	0	
cure	1	✓
disputation	0.004	
dispute	0.996	✓
exhortation	1	✓
exhort	0	
experimentation	0.694	✓
experiment	0.306	
importation	0.096	
import	0.904	✓
registration	0.968	✓
register	0.032	
transportation	0.06	
transport	0.942	✓

The results show that zero-affixation is expected to prevail in four clusters (*cure*, *dispute*, *import* and *transport*) and *-ation* in three (*exhort*, *experiment*, *register*). One cluster, *aliment/alimentation* cannot be computed because the competing sense is not attested in the BNC for that base.

Two clusters could be interpreted as resolved competition, because one member of the doublet is not attested for the competing sense: *exhortation* supersedes *exhort*, and *cure* supersedes *curation*. Outcomes are thus opposite with respect to the word-formation process, in that the *-ation* derivative prevails in the former and the zero-affixed form does in the latter. The rest of the clusters are *a priori* instances of ongoing competition, but only if they are used equally in the same contexts. This will be explored by examining their distribution first by mode and then by register.

The use of the competing pattern (*-ation*/zero-affixation for the sense ACTION) in the spoken and the written mode are first viewed in percentages. This allows comparison in terms of:

i) the proportion of use of each affix in each mode, and
ii) the distribution of the two modes (Figure 4.5).

In order to see the proportion to which each competing pattern prevails in each mode, the percentage of the occurrence of *-ation*/zero-affixation for the sense ACTION with respect to the total normalised frequency of each mode is used. The results show that zero-affixation is preferred in both modes: zero-affixation occurs at 67% in the spoken mode, and at 73% in the written mode, as opposed to *-ation*, which occurs at 33% in the spoken more and 27% in the written.

As regards their distribution (Figure 4.5), c. 70% of all the instances of *-ation* suffixation are in the written mode (and c. 30% in the spoken mode). The zero affix shows a similar distribution: c. 75% of occurrences are in the written mode, and c. 25% in the spoken mode. A comparison of their distribution to that of the size of the corpus parts (spoken vs. written) shows that these competing patterns are used to a comparatively bigger proportion in the spoken mode (and a smaller in the written) than could be expected.

Figure 4.5: Distribution in terms of mode of -ation *(blue) and zero-affixation (patterned blue) for the sense* ACTION. *The size of each mode in the BNC is presented in dotted yellow for easier comparison.*

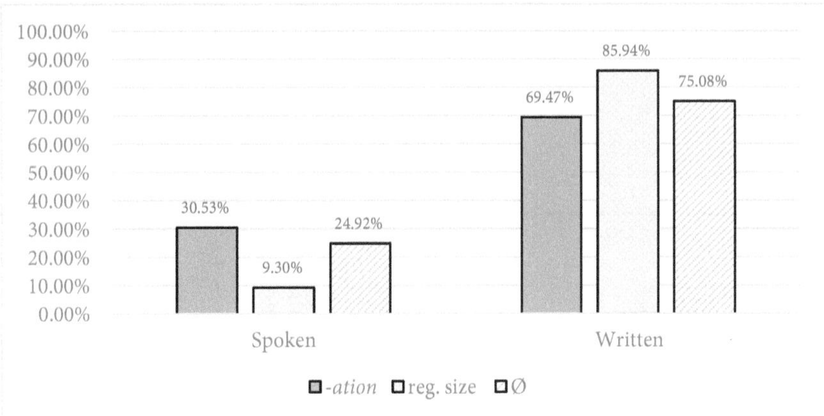

For a statistical comparison of the use of the two competing patterns in the spoken and the written mode, the following hypotheses are formulated:

i) H_0: There is no difference as regards mode for zero-affixation and *-ation* for the sense ACTION; mode distribution$_{\text{zero-aff.ACTION}}$ = mode distribution$_{\textit{-ation}\text{.ACTION}}$.
ii) H_1: Zero-affixation and *-ation* differ as regards mode for the sense action; mode distribution$_{\text{zero-aff.ACTION}}$ ≠ mode distribution$_{\textit{-ation}\text{.ACTION}}$.

The results show that there is a significant association between mode and competing pattern ($\chi 2$ (1) = 6.96, $p < .001$), so the null hypothesis is rejected. The overall effect, however, is very weak (Cramer's $V = 0.025$), that is, the word-formation process and mode are only weakly associated. The standardised residuals show that the frequency of *-ation* is significantly higher than expected in the spoken mode and lower than expected in the written mode (2.64 in the spoken mode and -2.64 in the written mode).

In what follows, data will be presented by registers. The percentages of use of each competing pattern shows that zero-affixation prevails in all registers, as expected from the data presented above, but the proportion to which one or the other pattern is preferred seems uneven. For example, zero-affixation prevails in 'W_newspaper' (89.7%), because the normalised frequency of this process is 6.5 times higher than that of *-ation* in that register. In 'W_academic', in contrast, both percentages are close to 50%, although *-ation* seems slightly dispreferred (c. 44%). Based on the data presented above, it would be expected that the competing patterns are not evenly used across registers. This is illustrated in Figure 4.6.

Figure 4.6: Register distribution of -ation *(blue) and zero-affixation (patterned blue) for the sense* ACTION*. The size of each register in the BNC is presented in dotted yellow for easier comparison.*

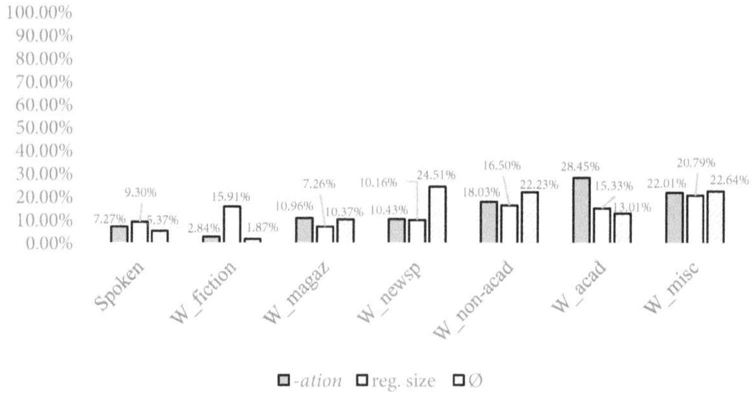

The register distribution of *-ation* shows that c. 28.5% of all the occurrences of this process for the sense ACTION in the BNC occur in 'W_academic' and c. 22% in 'W_miscellaneous'. In contrast, only 2.8% occur in 'W_fiction', even if it is one of the most represented registers of the BNC (nearly 16% of the corpus). Zero-affixation also occurs infrequently in that register (c. 1.9%) and most instances of this pattern are found in 'W_newspaper'.

Considering the data presented above, it seems that zero-affixation and *-ation* are not equally distributed across registers and that the former is expected to prevail in all. A statistical test of significance and effect size measures thus need to be performed. For that, the following hypotheses are formulated:

i) H_0: There is no difference as regards register for zero-affixation and *-ation* for the sense ACTION; register distribution$_{\text{zero-aff.ACTION}}$ = register distribution$_{\textit{-ation}\text{.ACTION}}$.
ii) H_1: Zero-affixation and *-ation* differ as regards register for the sense ACTION; register distribution$_{\text{zero-aff.ACTION}}$ ≠ register distribution$_{\textit{-ation}\text{.ACTION}}$.

In order to test the hypotheses above, Pearson's chi-square test was performed. The result of chi-square test by register rejects the null hypothesis ($\chi2$ (6) = 489.81, $p < .001$). This result is supported by Cramer's *V*, which reveals a very strong association between the variables (Cramer's $V = 0.21$). It can be concluded, then, that there is a strong association between word-formation pattern and register and, thus, the observed difference regarding register in the two competing patterns is statistically significant.

Figure 4.7: Association plot of the relation between the competing pattern (-ation*/zero-affixation) and register, where black represents higher frequencies than expected, and grey represents lower frequencies than expected.*

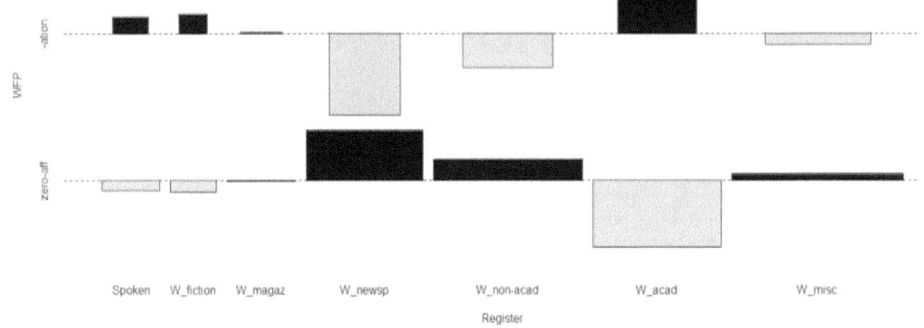

Specifically, the association plot (Figure 4.7) shows that frequencies are higher than expected for *-ation* in 'Spoken', 'W_fiction' and 'W_academic', and in 'W_newspaper' and 'W_non-academic' for zero-affixation. This is confirmed by the computation of Pearson's standardised residuals. The standardised residuals also reveal that the deviations from the expected values in 'W_magazine' and 'W_miscellaneous' are not statistically significant, since they are not within the ±1.96 threshold.

The results thus show that there is no clear resolution pattern over time and that, in PDE, there is a specialisation as regards register.

4.4.3. *-er* vs. zero-affixation AGENTIVE

This section describes the results obtained from the analysis of the competition between *-er* and zero-affixation for the expression of AGENTIVE in PDE.

Sample2 reveals 19 doublets in competition in PDE. A little over 21,100 concordances were analysed in order to identify which attest the competing sense AGENTIVE, and to test whether there are differences in meaning or use between the competitors.

The results show that the sense AGENTIVE is attested only in 2.4% of concordances: 1.7% in *-er* forms and 0.7% in zero-affixed forms. The tag 'unclear' was given to c. 26% of concordances, and less than 1% of the concordances correspond to tagging errors. If these results are viewed for each process separately, c. 61% of the *-er* concordances were classified as AGENTIVE, nearly 7% as unclear, and the rest (c. 32%) do not show the sense AGENTIVE. As regards zero-affixation, c. 0.7% of the concordances show the competing sense, c. 26% are unclear, nearly 1% are tagging errors, and c. 72% show a sense different from AGENTIVE.

The computation of the C* value shows a clear preference for the suffix *-er* for the expression of AGENTIVE: of the 19 clusters, *-er* is expected to prevail in 15, zero-affixation in three, and one cannot be computed because none of the competitors show the sense AGENTIVE. Besides, total prevalence of *-er* is attested in 10 clusters, because the competing sense is not recorded for the zero-affixed counterpart (Table 4.4).

Table 4.4: C values of the competitors from the sample for the sense AGENTIVE*

Derivative	C	Expected to prevail
adulterer	0.98	✓
adulter	0.02	
aider	0.88	✓
aid	0.12	

Derivative	***C***	**Expected to prevail**
bilker	1	✓
bilk	0	
cheater	0.08	
cheat	0.92	✓
crammer	1	✓
cram	0	
gouger	1	✓
gouge	0	
grabber	1	✓
grab	0	
grubber	1	✓
grub	0	
kicker	1	✓
kick	0	
lifter	1	✓
lift	0	
nagger	0.66	✓
nag	0.34	
nipper	–	–
nip	–	–
scrubber	1	✓
scrub	0	
shadower	0.28	
shadow	0.72	✓
skulker	1	✓
skulk	0	
snipper	1	✓
snip	0	
snooper	0.92	✓
snoop	0.08	
swanker	0.34	
swank	0.66	✓
sweeper	0.9	✓
sweep	0.1	

Although there is a clear preference for *-er* for the expression of the competing sense, the use of both affixes will be compared in order to see whether one of them has fallen to a *niche* where it is dominant.

The proportion to which each affix is used in the spoken and in the written mode shows that *-er* prevails over zero-affixation in both modes. Specifically, the overt suffix is used at c. 85% in the spoken mode (zero-affixation at c. 14%) and at c. 70% in the written mode (zero-affixation at c. 30%).

The distribution of the competing processes (Figure 4.8) shows that *-er* affixation is used nearly as often in the spoken mode (c. 51%) as in the written mode (c. 49%). With respect to the size of the corpus parts, *-er* affixation is used more frequently than it would be expected in the spoken mode (28%) and less frequently than expected in the written mode (72%).

Figure 4.8: Distribution in terms of mode of -er *(blue) and zero-affixation (patterned blue) for the sense* AGENTIVE. *The size of each mode in the BNC is presented in dotted yellow for easier comparison.*

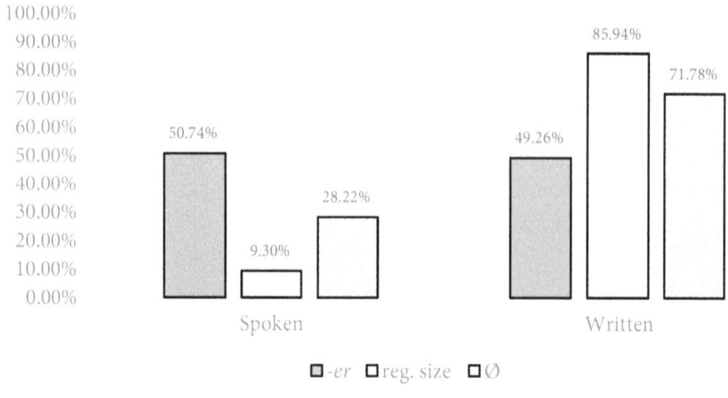

For a statistical comparison of the use of the two processes in the spoken and written mode, the following hypotheses are formulated:

i) H_0: There is no difference as regards mode for zero-affixation and *-er* for the sense AGENTIVE; mode distribution$_{\text{zero-aff}^{\text{'}}\text{AGENTIVE}}$ = mode distribution$_{\textit{-er}.\text{AGENTIVE}}$.
ii) H_1: zero-affixation and *-er* differ as regards mode for the sense AGENTIVE; mode distribution$_{\text{zero-aff.AGENTIVE}}$ ≠ mode distribution$_{\textit{-er}.\text{AGENTIVE}}$.

Pearson's chi-square test reveals that there is a significant difference between the two patterns as regards mode ($\chi 2$ (1) = 4.85, $p < .05$), so the null hypothesis is rejected. The overall effect is, however, very weak (Cramer's $V = 0.098$). The association plot shows that the suffix *-er* is used more frequently than expected in the spoken mode and less in the written, and the opposite in the case of zero-affixation. The computation of the standardised residuals shows that the difference is significant (±2.6).

A comparison by register shows that *-er* prevails in all registers, and the smallest difference in use is found in 'W_fiction'. Regarding the distribution of the processes, both are skewed towards 'W_newspaper' (c. 35% in the case of *-er* and c. 45% in zero-affixation). The overt suffix has a distribution similar to that of the corpus in 'Spoken', 'W_fiction' and 'W_academic' and it is attested less frequently than it would be expected in 'W_non-academic' and 'W_miscellaneous'. In 'W_magazine', its frequency is higher than that of the corpus part. Zero-affixation, similarly, is attested less frequently than it would be expected in 'W_non-academic', 'W_academic' and 'W_miscellaneous'. In 'Spoken', its frequency is similar to that of the corpus, and in 'W_fiction' and 'W_magazine' it is attested more frequently than it would be expected (Figure 4.9).

Figure 4.9: Register distribution of -er *(blue) and zero-affixation (patterned blue) for the sense* AGENTIVE. *The size of each register in the BNC is presented in dotted yelow for easier comparison.*

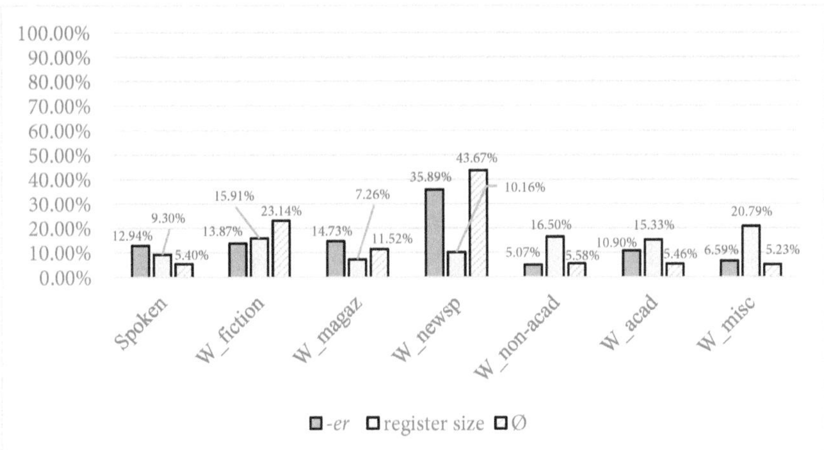

In order to test whether there is a significant difference between the two competing processes as regards register, two hypotheses are formulated:

i) H_0: There is no difference as regards register for zero-affixation and *-er* for the sense AGENTIVE; register distribution$_{\text{zero-aff.AGENTIVE}}$ = register distribution$_{\text{-er.AGENTIVE}}$.
ii) H_1: Zero-affixation and *-er* differ as regards register for the sense AGENTIVE; register distribution$_{\text{zero-aff.AGENTIVE}}$ ≠ register distribution$_{\text{-er.AGENTIVE}}$.

These hypotheses were tested using Pearson's chi-square test, and the result indicates that the difference is significant ($\chi 2$ (6) = 17.609, $p < .01$), so the null hypothesis is rejected. The overall effect is medium (Cramer's $V = 0.19$). The computation of the standardised residuals indicates that the difference between the processes is significant in 'Spoken', 'W_fiction' and 'W_academic'. The suffix *-er* is used significantly more frequently than it would be expected in 'Spoken' and 'W_academic', and zero-affixation in 'W_fiction'.

The results described in this section show that there is no clear preference over time for one or the other process for the expression of AGENTIVE. In PDE, the proportion to which this sense is attested for the competing forms is very low, and there seems to be a preference for *-er* suffixation. Still, there might be a specialisation as regards register, where *-er* prevails in the spoken register and zero-affixation in written fiction.

4.4.4. *-er* vs. zero-affixation: INSTRUMENT

This section describes the results obtained from the analysis of the competition between *-er* and zero-affixation for the expression of INSTRUMENT in PDE.

The search in the OED served to identify 24 doublets in competition in PDE. Approximately 16,800 concordances were semantically classified in order to quantify the frequency of occurrence of the sense INSTRUMENT in these competitors.

The results show that the competing sense is attested only in c. 11% of concordances (c. 3.4% in *-er* forms, c. 7.5% in zero-affixed forms). Nearly 5% of concordances were classified as unclear, and c. 1.5% were tagged wrongly. Therefore, nearly 87% of the total number of concordances did not show the competing sense. If these results are viewed separately for each word-formation process, c. 33% of the concordances of the *-er* forms were classified as instrumental, c. 4% as unclear and c. 0.5% were tagging errors. Regarding zero-affixation, c. 8% of the concordances of the zero-affixed forms show an instrumental meaning, c. 1% were classified as unclear, and c. 1% were tagging errors.

The computation of the C* value shows that zero-affixation is expected to prevail in 11 clusters, whereas *-er* is expected to prevail in eight. In nearly all of these clusters, competition could be considered resolved, because only one of the forms in the doublet is attested for the competing sense (e.g. *brace*, *downer*) or one of the forms is attested to a comparatively much lower frequency (e.g. *muffle* is attested for the competing sense four times more than *muffler*). The only exceptions are the doublets *stamp/stamper* and *wrap/wrapper*: in the former, zero-affixation is expected to prevail; in the latter, *-er* affixation is expected to prevail. The C* value could not be computed for five clusters because none of the forms is attested for the sense INSTRUMENT (Table 4.5).

Table 4.5: C values of the competitors from the sample for the sense* INSTRUMENT

Derivative	C	Expected to prevail
bolt	0.98	✓
bolter	0.02	
brace	1	✓
bracer	0	
clap	–	–
clapper	–	–
clasp	0.9	✓
clasper	0.1	
clip	0.9	✓
clipper	0.1	
creep	–	–
creeper	–	–
curb	1	✓
curber	0	
down	0	
downer	1	✓
flap	–	–
flapper	–	–
grill	1	✓
griller	0	
hack	1	✓
hacker	0	
muffle	0.06	
muffler	0.96	✓
pitch	0	

(*Continued*)

Table 4.5: (Continued)

Derivative	**C**	**Expected to prevail**
pitcher	1	✓
preserve	–	–
preserver	–	–
scrape	0	
scraper	1	✓
slick	–	–
slicker	–	–
slide	0.9	✓
slider	0.1	
stamp	0.76	✓
stamper	0.26	
strain	0	
strainer	1	✓
sweep	0	
sweeper	1	✓
twitch	1	✓
twitcher	0	
whisk	1	✓
whisker	0	
wipe	0.12	
wiper	0.88	✓
wrap	0.4	
wrapper	0.6	✓

Considering the results presented so far, it seems that the competition between zero-affixation and *-er* for the expression of INSTRUMENT may have been resolved, but it could be so in terms of their use (e.g. one process being used more frequently in one register and the other in a different one), or it could be resolved in a by-competitor basis (i.e. each competitor showing a different profile of resolution). For this reason, the use of this competing pattern is compared next, and the results of the analysis of the individual doublets are presented in the following section (§4.5.4).

The use of each affix in the spoken and in the written mode shows that zero-affixation prevails over *-er* in both modes. Specifically, the overt suffix is used at c. 41% in the spoken mode (zero-affixation at c. 59%) and at c. 30% in the written mode (zero-affixation at c. 70%).

The distribution of the competing processes (Figure 4.10) shows that *-er* is used more frequently in the spoken mode (c. 66%) than in the written mode (c. 34%). With respect to the size of the corpus parts, *-er* is used more frequently than expected in the former, and less frequently than expected in the latter. Zero-affixation is similarly distributed: it is also used more frequently in the spoken mode (c. 54%) than in the written mode (c. 46%).

Figure 4.10: Distribution in terms of mode of -er *(blue) and zero-affixation (patterned blue) for the sense* INSTRUMENT. *The size of each mode in the BNC is presented in dotted yellow for easier comparison.*

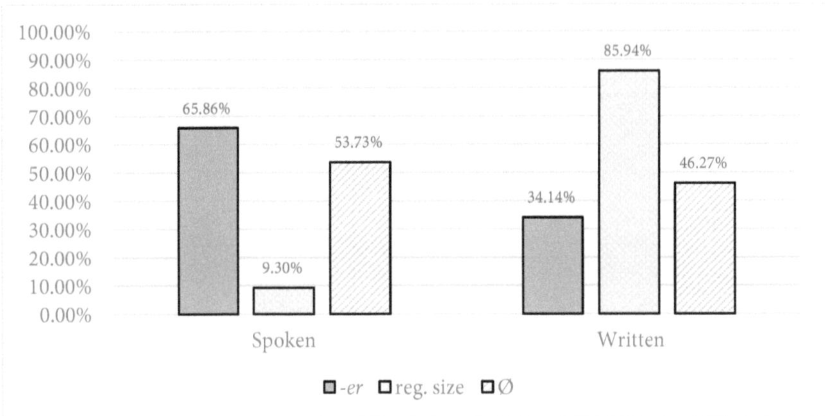

For a statistical comparison of the use of the two processes in both modes, the following hypotheses are formulated:

i) H_0: There is no difference as regards mode for zero-affixation and *-er* for the sense INSTRUMENT; mode distribution$_{\text{zero-aff.INSTRUMENT}}$ = mode distribution$_{\text{-er.INSTRUMENT}}$.
ii) H_1: Zero-affixation and *-er* differ as regards mode for the sense INSTRUMENT; mode distribution$_{\text{zero-aff.INSTRUMENT}}$ ≠ mode distribution$_{\text{-er.INSTRUMENT}}$.

The result of Pearson's chi-square test shows that there is a significant difference as regards mode ($\chi 2$ (1) = 13.021, $p < .001$). The null hypothesis is thus rejected. The overall effect is however very weak (Cramer's $V = 0.084$). The association plot shows the differences in use with respect to the expected values. It shows that *-er* is used more frequently than expected in the spoken mode and less frequently than expected in the written one (and the opposite for zero-affixation). The computation of the standardised residuals indicate that the difference is significant (±3.6).

In a comparison by register, the percentages of use of each competing pattern show that zero-affixation prevails in all registers, although the use of *-er* is close to 50% of the total of the register in 'Spoken' and 'W_non-academic'. A look at the distribution of the competitors reveals that the frequency of both affixes for the competing sense is higher than the register size in 'Spoken', 'W_fiction' and 'W_magazine'. In the latter, the frequency of both processes is more than three times higher than it would be expected with respect to the register size. In the rest of the registers the frequency of both affixes is lower than expected (see Figure 4.11).

Figure 4.11: Register distribution of -er *(blue) and zero-affixation (patterned blue) for the sense* INSTRUMENT. *The size of each register in the BNC is presented in dotted yelow for easier comparison.*

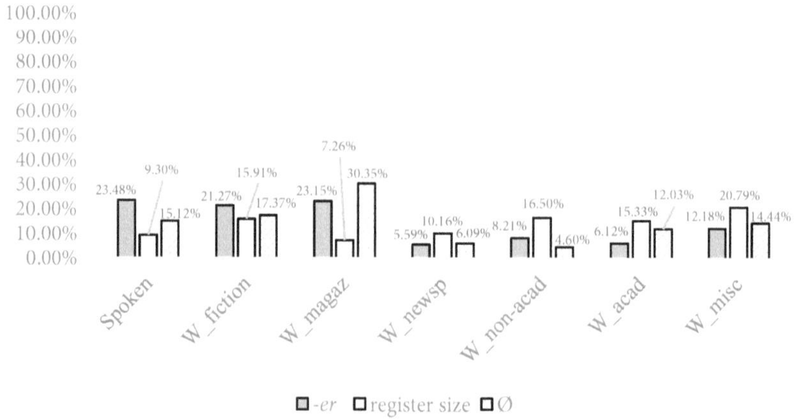

Two hypotheses are formulated in order to test whether there is a significant difference between the two competing processes as regards register:

i) H_0: There is no difference as regards register for zero-affixation and *-er* for the sense INSTRUMENT; register distribution$_{\text{zero-aff.INSTRUMENT}}$ = register distribution$_{\text{-er.INSTRUMENT}}$.
ii) H_1: Zero-affixation and *-er* differ as regards register for the sense INSTRUMENT; register distribution$_{\text{zero-aff.INSTRUMENT}}$ ≠ register distribution$_{\text{-er.INSTRUMENT}}$.

Pearson's chi-square test was performed to test these hypotheses, and it indicates that the difference is significant ($\chi 2$ (6) = 50.67, p < .001), so the null hypothesis is rejected. The overall effect, however, is weak (Cramer's V = 0.17). In order to identify in which registers the difference is significant, Pearson's standardised residuals were computed (Table 4.6), and it revealed that it is not in two registers: 'W_newspaper' and 'W_miscellaneous'. In three registers, the frequency of *-er* is significantly higher than expected ('Spoken', 'W_fiction' and 'W_non-academic') and in two it is lower than expected ('W_magazine', 'W_academic'). The opposite holds for zero-affixation.

Table 4.6: Standardised residuals of the chi-square test for -er *and zero-affixation for the sense* INSTRUMENT *across registers in the BNC*

	Spoken	W_fict	W_magaz	W_newsp	W_non-acad	W_acad	W_misc
-er	3.61	2.28	−2.27	−0.39	3.55	−4.37	−1.80
zero-affix.	−3.61	−2.28	2.27	0.39	−3.55	4.37	1.80

The results show that the competition between *-er* and zero-affixation for the expression of INSTRUMENT in PDE may be partly resolved. Zero-affixation seems to prevail in more clusters than *-er*, but there might be a specialisation as regards register, in which *-er* would prevail in more informal contexts.

4.4.5. *-ness* vs. zero-affixation: STATE

This section describes the results obtained from the analysis of the competition between *-ness* and zero-affixation for the expression of STATE in PDE.

The semantic analysis of the PDE English competitors shows that only c. 27% of the *-ness* concordances and c. 9% of the zero-affixed ones convey the sense STATE. In both processes, nearly 2% of the concordances were classified as unclear, whereas all the tagging errors were identified in the zero-affixed forms (nearly 30% of concordances). The remaining 52% was classified as conveying a sense other than STATE (see examples (14) and (15)).

(14) *She gazed into the* ***darkness****, eyes dry and burning.*

(15) *Crews with breathing apparatus searched the block after the* ***alert*** *was raised at 5.45 pm yesterday.*

In order to assess the competition by cluster, the *Referenced Index of Competition* was computed. The results (Table 4.7) show that the *-ness* forms have a higher C* value than their competitors in eight out of nine clusters. The zero affix is thus expected to prevail only in one cluster (*lowness/low*).

Table 4.7: C values of the competitors from the sample for the sense* STATE

Derivative	**C**	**Expected to prevail**
alertness	0.68	✓
alert	0.32	
coolness	0.68	✓
cool	0.32	
darkness	0.72	✓
dark	0.28	
dryness	1	✓
dry	0	
faintness	0.74	✓
faint	0.26	
hotness	1	✓
hot	0	
lowness	0.02	
low	0.98	✓
savageness	1	✓
savage	0	
warmness	1	✓
warm	0	

Four clusters may be interpreted as instances of resolved competition, because only the *-ness* form is attested in the corpus for the competing sense. In the *lowness/low* cluster, the profile is the opposite, even if *lowness* for the sense STATE is attested in the BNC. All in all, these results support the trend identified from lexicographic data: there seems to be a clear preference for the suffix *-ness* for the expression of STATE. Still, it could be the case that the zero affix is (becoming) restricted to a certain domain of use where it would prevail over the overt counterpart. This is explored by analysing the use of both processes by mode and by register.

The percentages of use of each competing pattern shows that zero-affixation occurs at c. 64% in the spoken mode, and at c. 27% in the written mode, and *-ness* suffixation occurs at c. 36% in the spoken mode and c. 73% in the written one. These figures illustrate the proportion to which each word-formation process prevails in each mode: the suffix *-ness* prevails in the written mode, whereas the zero-affix prevails in the spoken mode.

A look at the distribution of these affixes (Figure 4.12) reveals that c. 80% of all instances of the suffix *-ness* are in the written mode (and c. 20% in the spoken). The zero suffix, in contrast, is more evenly distributed: c. 57% of all instances of the suffix are in the spoken mode, and c. 43% in the written mode. A comparison of their distribution with the size of the corpus parts shows that both suffixes are used more frequently than expected in the spoken mode (and less in the written).

Figure 4.12: Distribution in terms of mode of -ness *(blue) and zero-affixation (patterned blue) for the sense* STATE. *The size of each mode in the BNC is presented in dotted yellow for easier comparison.*

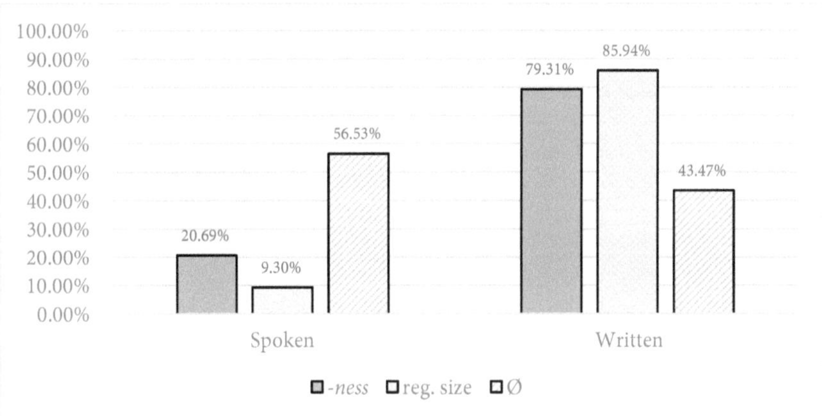

For a statistical comparison of the use of the two processes in the spoken and the written mode, the following hypotheses are formulated:

i) H_0: There is no difference as regards mode for zero-affixation and *-ness* for the sense STATE; mode distribution$_{\text{zero-aff.STATE}}$ = mode distribution$_{\text{-ness.STATE}}$.
ii) H_1: Zero-affixation and *-ness* differ as regards mode for the sense STATE; mode distribution$_{\text{zero-aff.STATE}}$ ≠ mode distribution$_{\text{-ness.STATE}}$.

The result of the computation of Pearson's chi-square test determines that there is an association between competing pattern and mode ($\chi2$ (1) = 48.104, $p < .001$), so the null hypothesis is rejected. The overall effect is weak (Cramer's $V = 0.19$). In order to identify in which mode the frequency of each affix is higher or lower than expected, Pearson's standardised residuals show that the frequency of the zero affix is significantly higher than expected in the spoken mode and lower in the written one (and the opposite in the overt suffix). The results by mode thus indicate that there is a specialisation for each affix. A look at their register distribution may show whether there is also some specialisation at the level of register.

Regarding registers, zero-affixation prevails in 'Spoken' and 'W_newspaper'. In the former, it is used nearly twice as frequently as *-ness*. The suffix *-ness* prevails in the rest of the registers. In three registers, the proportion of use of *-ness* with respect to zero-affixation is 80/20 and in two it is 70/30.

Based on the results presented so far, an uneven distribution across registers is expected. Figure 4.13 shows that the suffix *-ness* is attested less frequently than it would be expected with respect to the size of the corpus parts in all but two registers: 'W_fiction' and 'W_magazine'. The former register displays nearly 45% of the concordances of this process for the sense STATE. Zero-affixation, in contrast, is attested more frequently than would be expected in four of the seven registers ('Spoken', 'W_fiction', 'W_magazine' and W_newspaper'). The register 'W_fiction' displays over 40% of the attestations of this process.

Figure 4.13: Register distribution of -ness *(blue) and zero-affixation (patterned blue) for the sense* STATE. *The size of each register in the BNC is presented in dotted yelow for easier comparison.*

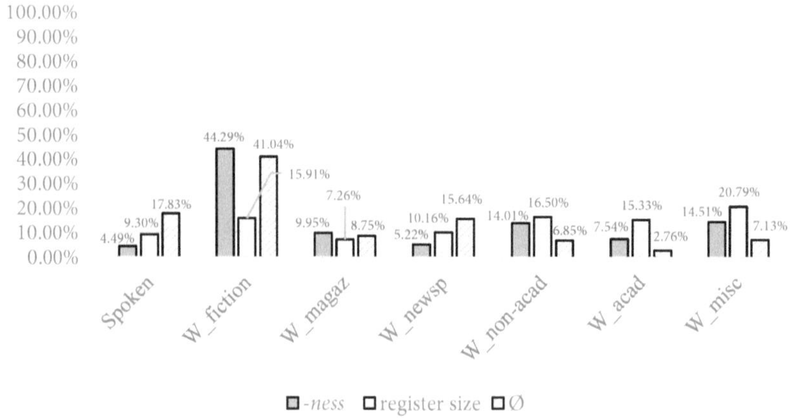

The data presented above suggests that there may be a difference as regards register in the use of the two competing processes. Two hypotheses are thus formulated, which are statistically tested:

i) H_0: There is no difference as regards register for zero-affixation and *-ness* for the sense STATE; register distribution$_{\text{zero-aff.STATE}}$ = register distribution$_{\text{-ness.STATE}}$.
ii) H_1: Zero-affixation and *-ness* differ as regards register for the sense STATE; register distribution$_{\text{zero-aff.STATE}}$ ≠ register distribution$_{\text{-ness.STATE}}$.

The result of the chi-square test confirms that there is an association between register and competing pattern ($\chi 2$ (6) = 108.05, $p < .001$). The null hypothesis is thus rejected. This is supported by Cramer's *V*, according to which the effect is very strong (Cramer's $V = 0.29$). There is, then, a significant difference as regards register for the competing pattern *-ness*/zero-affixation for the expression of STATE.

Table 4.8: Standardised residuals of the chi-square test for -ness *and zero-affixation for the sense* STATE *across registers in the BNC*

	Spoken	W_fict	W_magaz	W_newsp	W_non-acad	W_acad	W_misc
-ness	–6.93	–0.73	0.02	–5.84	3.31	3.02	3.85
zero-affix.	6.93	0.73	–0.02	5.84	–3.31	–3.02	–3.85

The standardised residuals (Table 4.8) show that the observed difference is not significant in 'W_fiction' nor 'W_magazine', but it is in the rest of registers. Specifically, the frequency of zero-affixation is higher than expected in 'Spoken' and 'W_newspaper', and it is the opposite for the suffix *-ness*.

The results over time show that zero-affixation is expected to fall out of use when in competition with -ness for the expression of STATE, which is partly supported by PDE data, but there may be specialisation as regards register and mode.

4.4.6. Discussion

The second research question deals with the information synchronic data provides as regards the resolution of competition. There are three main possibilities of resolution, as described above (past competition, resolved competition and ongoing competition). When a competing cluster is classified as in ongoing competition (i.e. both forms are attested as in use in PDE), there are three main ways in which this co-existence may be resolved (see §2.2), that is, as a result of:

i) regional differences,
ii) register specialisation, or
iii) semantic specialisation.

There is also a fourth possibility: competition is not resolved yet. In this case, no differences can be identified, and the forms are then expected to remain in use without any differentiating mark for some time, even if resolution is expected (see discussion in §2.1 and §2.3.3).

The first possibility of resolution, that is, regional differences, is not explored in detail in this book for two reasons:

i) the main corpus used for the analysis is a general corpus of British English. Still, this book assumes that the BNC is representative enough of the use of the competing patterns in PDE (see Fernández-Domínguez 2017: 69–75), and
ii) nearly none of the competing senses of the competitors analysed in this book were tagged as pertaining to a specific dialect in the OED. Specifically, of the 120 forms classified as in PDE competition, only two were classified as such in their competing sense in the OED: *pitch*^{N} and *pitcher*, in competition for the expression of the semantic category INSTRUMENT. The competing sense in both forms is classified as 'British regional' in the OED, and both forms are attested in the BNC, although only *pitcher* actually attests the instrumental meaning.

However, it could be the case that some clusters behave differently according to regional variety, but such analysis is outside the scope of this book and is left for further research (see Bauer 2009: 191 for a discussion of the difficulties of such analysis).

The second possibility for the resolution of PDE competition is specialisation regarding register. This book identifies 60 doublets of competition where both members are attested in the BNC. Of the 120 competitors, 11 are classified as specific to a register or domain in the OED (see Table 4.9):

i) two members are classified as being restricted to (Scottish) Law (i.e. *aliment/alimentation*), and
ii) nine belong to a more informal register, that is, they are tagged as 'slang' or 'colloquial' (e.g. *swank/swanker*, within the AGENTIVE category, and *wipe* within the INSTRUMENT one).

All competitors within the STATE category are tagged as either *in use* or *obsolete/rare*, without any sense being *dialectal* or of a specific register/domain.

Table 4.9: Forms in PDE competition classified as pertaining to a specific register or domain in the OED

	Ongoing competition (OED)	**Sense classified as of register/ domain (OED)**	**Register/ domain**
-*ation* vs. zero-affixation ACTION	16	2	(Scottish) Law
-*er* vs. zero-affixation AGENTIVE	38	7	Slang; colloquial
-*er* vs. zero-affixation INSTRUMENT	48	2	Slang
-*ness* vs. zero-affixation STATE	18	0	–

This book explores register based on the concordances classified as attesting the competing sense, whose frequencies were grouped using the BNC classification of registers. The aim is to identify whether any process is preferred in any given register, meaning that the choice of the process used for derivation would be according to the context of use. For this, a statistical analysis is performed to tell whether the association between word-formation process and register is significant or not. Table 4.10 summarises the results obtained for each competing pattern from the statistical analysis:

i) in the second column, whether the chi-square test for the association between word-formation process and register is significant, or not,
ii) in the third column, the effect size (calculated using Cramer's *V*), and
iii) in the fourth column, the results of the standardised residuals, to see in which registers the difference between the observed and the expected frequencies is significant.

The fourth column thus shows the registers where the overt affix is used significantly more or less than expected. In these registers, opposite results would correspond to the zero affix. For example, for the expression of AGENTIVE, the overt affix is used significantly *less* than expected in 'W_fiction', and the zero affix is used significantly *more* than expected in that register.

Table 4.10: Results from the statistical analysis of the competing patterns as regards register

	Chi-square	**Effect size**	**Residuals (overt affix)**	
			> expected	**< expected**
-*ation* vs. zero-affixation ACTION	Significant	Very strong	Spoken; W_fiction; W_academic	W_newspaper; W_non-academic
-*er* vs. zero-affixation AGENTIVE	Significant	Medium	Spoken; W_academic	W_fiction
-*er* vs. zero-affixation INSTRUMENT	Significant	Weak	Spoken; W_fiction; W_non-academic	W_magazine; W_academic
-*ness* vs. zero-affixation STATE	Significant	Very strong	W_academic; W_non-academic; W_miscellaneous	Spoken; W_newspaper

The results presented in Table 4.10 show that the association between word-formation process and register is significant in the four patterns, so the observed register differences are not due to chance. The effect size is then measured to calculate how strong that association is. The calculation of Cramer's *V* shows that, in two patterns, for the expression of ACTION and STATE, the association is very strong, so there is an association between the process and the register where it is used. In another pattern, for the expression of AGENTIVE, the effect size is medium, so there is some association between the variables, even if it is not a perfect one. In one pattern, for the expression of INSTRUMENT, the effect is weak: there is only a small association between the variables. The choice of one word-formation process over its competitor may be concluded to be dependent on the register where the derivative is used, but to a variable degree. Besides, the meaning to be expressed is key: the association between register and process is not the same, for example, for the expression of AGENTIVE and of INSTRUMENT, even though the processes used for derivation are formally the same: -*er* and zero-affixation.

Even if differences can be identified regarding register for each of the competing patterns, the analysis of register distribution reveals registers where both competing processes within each pattern are used more frequently than in the rest of the registers. Specifically,

i) for the expression of ACTION, most instances of -*ation* occur in 'W_academic', whereas most instances of zero-affixation do in 'W_newspaper' (around 25% of their attestations),

ii) for the expression of AGENTIVE, both *-er* and zero-affixation are skewed towards 'W_newspaper' (c. 40% of their attestations),
iii) for the expression of INSTRUMENT, both processes are skewed towards 'W_magazine' (c. 30% of their attestations), 'Spoken' (c. 20% of their attestations) and 'W_fiction' (c. 20% of their attestations), and
iv) for the expression of STATE, both processes are heavily skewed towards 'W_fiction', where over c. 40% of their attestations occur.

These results are to be expected for the kind of information that is typically presented in each register:

i) newspapers typically depict agents and the actions they perform,
ii) academic texts usually include descriptions of the actions carried out,
iii) fiction texts frequently describe the states of the characters, and
iv) instruments are described in a wider variety of texts, including popular magazines, fiction texts and in the spoken mode.

Therefore, it may be concluded that:

i) certain semantic categories are more frequent in certain registers, and
ii) the word-formation process used to express that meaning will vary according to register.

These results are in line with previous research, where associations between word-formation processes and the degree or formality or technicality of the context were found (Plag et al. 1999; Guz 2009; Montero-Fleta 2011; Wauquier et el. 2020b).

The third possibility for the resolution of competition in PDE is semantic specialisation, which is closely related to register and domain specialisation: if a form is restricted to a specific field and its competitor becomes restricted to a different field, then they would have become specialised as regards register, therefore also partly as regards semantics. If there is no more overlap in their use, then competition would have been resolved. If there is still some overlap, there is partial competition. Rifón Sánchez (2011: 253) explains the process of specialisation as follows:

> The arrival of another [noun] implies competition and- thanks to the push of the new noun – can cause the already existing noun to move to other areas of meaning, or it can be the new noun that moves when faced with the resistance of the older one, thus sharing out the meanings. It can also occur that the push of the new one or resistance of the old one completely eliminates the other, making it disappear. This tug of war and movement involves, at least, two elements: time and frequency. The former is necessary for the motion of derived words or the possible disappearance of one of them. The

frequency affects the strength with which one derived word pushes the other and the resistance offered by the one being pushed.

Semantic specialisation is explored in a by-competitor basis in the following section.

4.5. Competition by competitor

4.5.1. Introduction

The forms classified in this book as in competition show some overlap in meaning in that they are both used to express the same semantic category, according to the OED. Nevertheless, a more fine-grained analysis of the context where they are used reveals semantic differences. This analysis could not be performed by process, but it needed to be performed for each cluster individually. The results reveal that some competitors have become semantically specialised (e.g. *clip/clipper*, §4.5.4), whereas others still show a considerable overlap in meaning (e.g. *wrap/wrapper*, §4.5.4) (see discussion in §4.5.6 below).

4.5.2. *-ation* vs. zero-affixation: ACTION

Results regarding distribution have so far been presented by grouping competitors by affix. However, it could be the case that individual doublets behave differently to what is observed for the word-formation patterns as a whole (see Lara-Clares 2017 and Lara-Clares & Thompson 2019). For this reason, one doublet among the ones with the highest frequencies was selected at random for further analysis: *importation/import*^{N} for the sense ACTION.

In the doublet *importation/import*^{N}, the figures obtained from the computation of the C* values seem to prime *import*^{N} (0.45 vs. 0.05) (Table 4.3). However, it could be the case that *importation* is limited to a domain where *-ation* is preferred over zero-affixation. In order to verify whether that is the case, the frequencies of both forms are examined below.

The sense ACTION is conveyed in *importation* in c. 72% of concordances, and nearly 6% were classified as *unclear*. The remaining 22% express a sense other than ACTION. No tagging errors were recorded. In the case of *import*^{N}, nearly 42% of concordances convey the competing sense, whereas c. 40% express a sense other than ACTION. The remaining concordances were classified as *unclear* (c. 16%) and as tagging errors (c. 2% of verbs tagged as nouns).

The analysis by register reveals that *import*^{N} is more likely to prevail consistently. The register distribution, in turn, of *importation* shows that most occurrences are in 'W_non-academic' (c. 28%), 'W_academic' (c. 24%) 'W_miscellaneous'

(c. 23%) (Figure 4.14). In the three registers, the frequency of *importation* is higher than it would be expected considering their size, whereas it is lower in 'W_fiction' and 'Spoken'. In 'Spoken', *importation* is in fact not attested for the sense ACTION. *Import*^{N} is attested in all registers for the competing sense, and most occurrences are in 'W_non-academic' (c. 27%) and 'W_miscellaneous' (c. 23.5%). Regarding register sizes, the zero-affixed form is attested less frequently than expected in 'Spoken', 'W_fiction', and 'W_academic'.

Figure 4.14: Register distribution of importation *(blue) and* import^{N} *(patterned blue) for the sense* ACTION. *The size of each register in the BNC is presented in dotted yellow for easier comparison.*

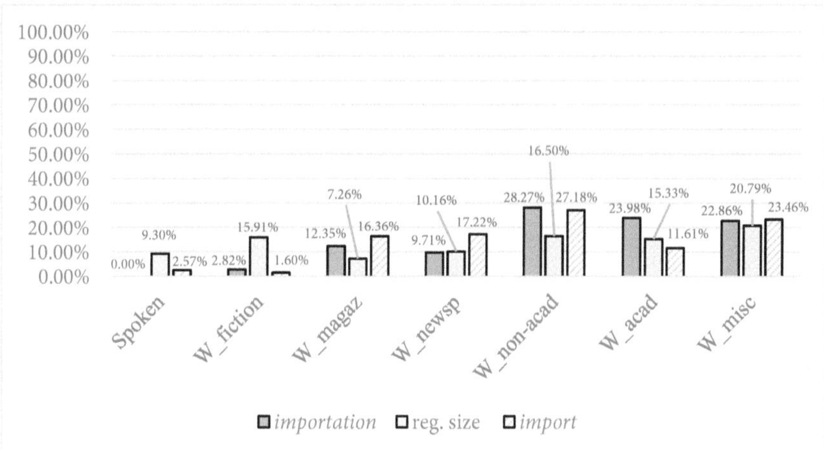

Pearson's chi-square test reveals that *importation* and *import*^{N} differ significantly as regards register ($\chi 2$ (6) = 26.84, p < .001). The overall effect, however, is very weak (Cramer's $V = 0.09$). The standardised residuals (Table 4.11) show that the difference is only significant for the registers 'W_newspaper' and 'W_academic'. In the former, the frequency of *import*^{N} is lower than expected and, in the latter, it is higher than expected.

Table 4.11: Standardised residuals of the chi-square test for importation *and* import^{N} *for the sense* ACTION *across registers in the BNC*

	Spoken	**W_fict**	**W_magaz**	**W_newsp**	**W_non-acad**	**W_acad**	**W_misc**
importation	−1.69	1.11	−1.1	−2.22	−0.15	4.42	−0.72
import	1.69	−1.11	1.1	2.22	0.15	−4.42	0.72

In order to further explore these two competitors, their descriptions in four PDE reference dictionaries were examined. Table 4.12 shows:

i) whether the sense ACTION is listed for each form,
ii) if it is listed, whether it is classified as of any particular use (register, dialect, etc.), and
iii) whether the two forms are classified as synonymous as regards the competing sense in the dictionaries, either explicitly or by means of their glosses.

Table 4.12: The sense ACTION *in the gloss of* importation *and* import^{N} *in dictionaries*

	importation		*import^{N}*		**Synonymy**
	ACTION	**Use**	**ACTION**	**Use**	
Merriam-Webster	+	general	+	general	+
Longman	+	formal; technical; business	+	business	+
Collins	+	American English (general); commerce	+	American English (general)	+
Cambridge	+	general; computer	+	general; business	+

The results show that the two competitors are attested in the four dictionaries, and that all of them describe them as synonymous for the competing sense. Besides, three of them provide a general definition describing an action, not related to any specific use, and three of them classify at least one ACTION sense as being of the business or commerce domain. The Cambridge dictionary also assigns one competitor to the specialised domain of computing: *importation*. An exploration of the cooccurrences of the two competitors might shed additional light on possible differences of use.

The top-ten collocates of *importation* in the BNC mostly refer to the characteristics of the product or the action carried out: *foreign*, *temporary*, *illegal* and *toxic*. Others are related to what is being imported: *coal*, *goods*, *waste*, *equipment*. Two collocates refer to the characteristics of the product or action, that is, *foreign*, *temporary*, *illegal*, *banned* and *toxic*. The other two collocates are *ban* and *banned*. The collocates of *import*^{N} contrast with those of *importation*. The only two collocates in common in the top-ten list of the two competitors are *ban* and *foreign* (although *goods*, for example, is found further down the list). The top collocate of *import*^{N} is *exports*^{V}, followed by *oil*. Three collocates describe the importation, that is, *foreign* and *cheap*, and one refers to a place, that is, *EC* (European Commission). The rest are quantities (*million*, *per cent*) and *export* appears also as a noun.

In COCA, the collocates of *importation* are also related to what is being imported (*slaves*, *goods*) and to characteristics of the product or the action (*foreign*, *illegal*). There are also collocates relating to processes related to the products (*production*, *manufacture*, *sale*) and the words *ban* and *banned* are again in the top-ten. As regards *import*^{N}, *exports* and *oil* are again at the top of the list. There are also collocates related to places (*U.S.*, *China*, *Chinese*). As in the BNC, *export* and *exports* are in the top-ten of the list.

The collocates extracted from the web interface of the two corpora, however, are not limited to the sense ACTION, but they are obtained from all the attestations of the competitors in both corpora. A graph of the cooccurrences of both competitors was thus created using the concordances from the BNC classified as showing the sense ACTION (Figure 4.15).[54] Table 4.13 shows some of the cooccurrences of each competitor and the ones both have in common.

Figure 4.15: Graph of cooccurrences of importation *and* import^{N} *for the sense* ACTION. *Cooccurrences of* import^{N} *are in light blue and those of* importation *in dark blue.*

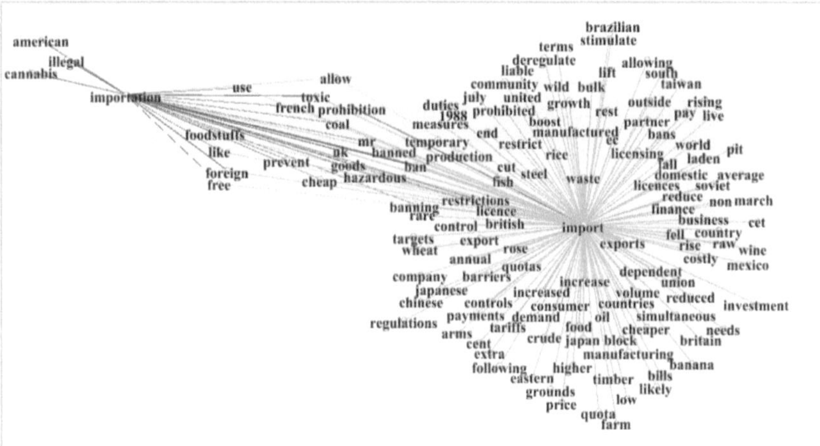

54 The graph of cooccurrences is available in Appendix 1.B for *importation* and in Appendix 1.C for *import*^{N} for easier visualisation.

Table 4.13: Cooccurrences of importation *and* import^{N} *for the sense* ACTION *(BNC)*

	importation	**both**	*import*^{N}
Origin or destination	American	foreign, French, UK	Brazilian, domestic, Mexico, Soviet, Japan, Taiwan, United States
Limitations		ban, banned, banning, prevent, restrictions	prohibited, restrict
Product	cannabis	coal, foodstuffs, goods	arms, banana, crude, fish, oil, steel, waste, wheat
Description	illegal	free, hazardous, toxic	cheap, manufactured, rising
Other			duties, quotas

The cooccurrences of both competitors are very similar. They both refer to the origin or destination of the import(ation), to limitations to the action (e.g. *ban*, *restrictions*) and to the products that are imported (e.g. *coal*, *goods*) and their characteristics (*toxic*, *illegal*, *manufactured*). It seems, however, that there might be a difference between the two forms: *importation* is used frequently to refer to the importation of cannabis or illegal products, whereas *import*^{N} is used for a wider variety of products, such as food (*banana*, *fish*) or materials (*steel*, *oil*). Still, some products are common to both competitors, such as *foodstuffs* and *coal*. Another difference in use is that only *import*^{N} is used in some collocations, such as *import duties* and *import quotas*.

In sum, regarding the doublet *importation/import*^{N}, the use of both competitors is very similar overall, as shown by their definition in dictionaries and their cooccurrences. Regarding register, the doublet shows that there is a register difference, such that *importation* prevails in academic register and *import*^{N} in printed media (newspaper).

4.5.3. *-er* vs. zero-affixation: AGENTIVE

The results of the analysis by affix suggest that *-er* may prevail when in competition with zero-affixation for the expression of AGENTIVE, but there may be some register specialisation. This section tests whether an analysis by competitor yields the same results.

Two doublets were selected for further analysis: *cheater*/*cheat*^{N} and *sweeper*/*sweep*^{N}. The results obtained from their analysis will be compared throughout this section.

The C* value obtained for both doublets (Table 4.4) points to a clear prevalence of *cheat*^{N} when in competition with *cheater* and of *sweeper* when in competition with *sweep*^{N}, both for the expression of AGENTIVE. The degree to which these competitors show the competing sense is similar in the case of the *-er* forms (76.92% of the *cheater* concordances, and 76.37% of the *sweeper* ones), but unequal in the zero-affixed forms (56.35% of the *cheat*^{N} concordances, and 2.83% of the *sweep*^{N} ones). The unclear tag was given to c. 23% of both the *cheater* and *cheat*^{N} concordances, and to nearly 5% of the *sweeper* ones and less than 0.5% of the *sweep*^{N} ones. There were no tagging errors in the *-er* suffixed forms. Tagging errors amount to c. 4% in *cheat*^{N} and c. 2% in *sweep*^{N}. The rest of concordances were classified as conveying a meaning different from AGENTIVE, as follows: c. 16% of *cheat*^{N}, c. 95% of *sweep*^{N} and c. 19% of *sweeper*. In *cheater*, no concordance showed a different meaning. These results illustrate that the competing sense is expressed to a different degree according to competitor, so there may also be differences in use in a by-competitor basis. This is tested farther below in this section.

A comparison of the frequency of the sense AGENTIVE in each competitor for each register in the BNC shows that, in the doublet *cheater*/*cheat*^{N}, the zero-affixed form prevails in all registers except 'Spoken', where both competitors are attested equally. The opposite is found in *sweeper*/*sweep*^{N}, where *-er* prevails throughout, even if the proportion of use of both competitors are similar in 'W_non-academic' and 'W_academic'.

The register distribution of *cheater*/*cheat*^{N} shows that the frequency of *cheater* comes mainly from 'Spoken' and 'W_academic', and it has lower frequencies than expected in 'W_fiction' and 'W_miscellaneous'. It is not attested in any other register. The zero-affixed form, in contrast, is heavily skewed towards 'W_newspaper', where over 50% of its concordances are found. It shows a similar distribution to that of the corpus part in 'W_fiction' and 'W_magazine', and lower frequencies that expected in the rest of the registers (Figure 4.16).

Figure 4.16: Register distribution of cheater *(blue) and* cheat^N^ *(patterned blue) for the sense* AGENTIVE. *The size of each register in the BNC is presented in dotted yellow for easier comparison.*

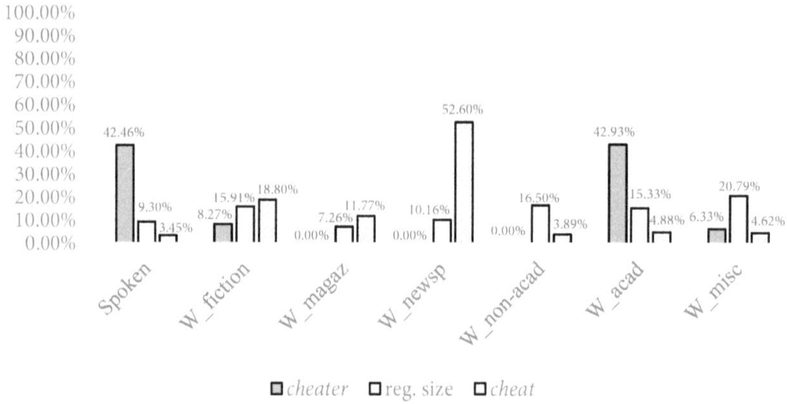

The distribution of *sweeper*/*sweep*^N^ is opposite to that of the other doublet: the *-er* form is heavily skewed towards 'W_newspaper' (nearly 45% of the *sweeper* concordances). The frequency of *sweeper* is slightly higher than that of the corpus part in 'Spoken', 'W_fiction' and 'W_magazine', and lower in the rest of the registers. The competitor *sweep*^N^, in contrast, shows a balanced distribution throughout and is only slightly skewed towards 'W_magazine' (c. 20% of concordances) (Figure 4.17).

Figure 4.17: Register distribution of sweeper *(blue) and* sweep^N^ *(patterned blue) for the sense* AGENTIVE. *The size of each register in the BNC is presented in dotted yellow for easier comparison.*

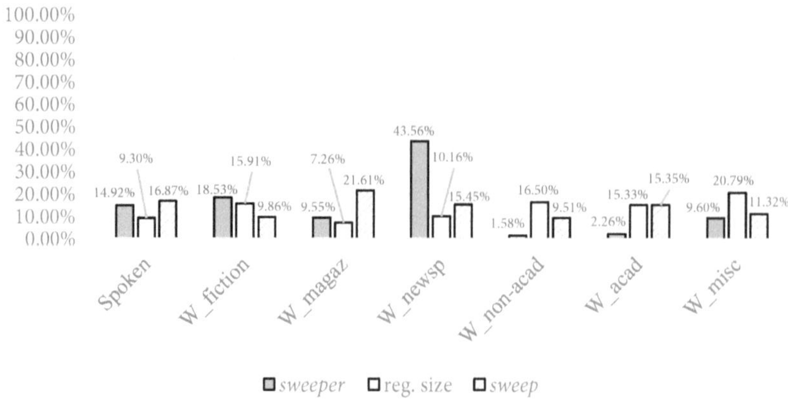

Pearson's chi-square test was performed to test whether the difference recorded is statistically significant. Regarding the doublet *cheater*/*cheat*^{N}, the test reveals that the difference is significant ($\chi2$ (6) = 38.14, p < .01), so the null hypothesis is rejected. The effect is very strong (Cramer's V = 0.56). The standardised residuals are then calculated in order to identify the registers where the difference is significant: the results reveal that they are 'Spoken', 'W_newspaper' and 'W_academic'. In 'Spoken' and 'W_academic', *cheater* is used significantly more frequently than it would be expected, whereas *cheat*^{N} is in 'W_newspaper' (Table 4.14).

Table 4.14: Standardised residuals of the chi-square test for cheater *and* cheat^N *for the sense* AGENTIVE *across registers in the BNC*

	Spoken	**W_fict**	**W_magaz**	**W_newsp**	**W_non-acad**	**W_acad**	**W_misc**
cheater	3.81	−1.08	−0.88	−2.78	−0.75	4.43	0.21
cheat^N	−3.81	1.08	0.88	2.78	0.75	−4.43	−0.21

The results obtained for the doublet *sweeper*/*sweep*^{N} also reveal a significant difference as regards register ($\chi2$ (6) = 17.17, p < .01), and the computation of Cramer's V shows that the overall effect is very strong (Cramer's V = 0.33). The standardised residuals indicate that the difference is only significant in 'W_non-academic' and 'W_academic', where *sweep*^{N} is attested significantly more frequently than expected (Table 4.15).

Table 4.15: Standardised residuals of the chi-square test for sweeper *and* sweep^N *for the sense* AGENTIVE *across registers in the BNC*

	Spoken	**W_fict**	**W_magaz**	**W_newsp**	**W_non-acad**	**W_acad**	**W_misc**
sweeper	−0.12	1.07	−1.04	1.93	−2.22	−2.9	−0.22
sweep^N	0.12	−1.07	1.04	−1.93	2.22	2.9	0.22

The description of the doublet *cheater*/*cheat*^{N} in PDE dictionaries point to a possible prevalence of the zero-affixed form for the expression of AGENTIVE, because *cheater* is not recorded in the Longman dictionary, whereas *cheat*^{N} is. Aside from that, two dictionaries (Collins and Cambridge) indicate that there may be a difference in use between the two competitors such that *cheater* reportedly prevails in American English and *cheat*^{N} prevails in British English. The Merriam-Webster dictionary does not record any difference in use and lists them as synonymous (Table 4.16).

Table 4.16: The sense AGENTIVE *in the gloss of* cheater *and* cheat^N *in dictionaries*

	cheater		*cheat*^{N}		**Synonymy**
	AGENT.	**Use**	AGENT.	**Use**	
Merriam-Webster	+	general	+	general	+
Longman	NA	NA	+	general	NA
Collins	+	mainly US	+	general	+
Cambridge	+	mainly US	+	mainly UK	+

Regarding the doublet *sweeper*/*sweep*^{N}, all dictionaries record the *-er* form for the expression of AGENTIVE. In contrast, the zero-affixed form seems to be restricted to the reference to chimney sweeps. In addition, the Cambridge dictionary classifies the use of *sweep*^{N} to refer to the sense related to chimney sweeps as "old-fashioned" (Table 4.17).

Table 4.17: The sense AGENTIVE *in the gloss of* sweeper *and* sweep^N *in dictionaries*

	sweeper		*sweep*^{N}		**Synonymy**
	AGENT.	**Use**	AGENT.	**Use**	
Merriam-Webster	+	general	+	chimney sweep	~
Longman	+	general	+	chimney sweep	~
Collins	+	general	+	chimney sweep	~
Cambridge	+	general	+	old-fashioned: chimney sweep	~

The differences in use identified so far are further explored by means of the cooccurrences of the competitors in the BCN and in COCA and also in the BNC concordances that were classified as AGENTIVE.

All the top collocates of *cheater* in the BNC[55] show frequency 1. The first is a drug used for sport doping (i.e. for cheating), for which athletes are *penalised. Echoing* collocates with *Cheater* (a surname). In some collocates, cheaters and their *offspring* are *portrayed* as *thieves*. In COCA, they are also portrayed as *liar(s)*. The other collocates characterise cheaters (*serial* cheater) or what may happen to

55 The top-three collocates of *cheater* in the BNC are characters: two symbols ("!" and ":") and one range of numbers (130-1). They are excluded from the list in order to only consider lexical items.

them: they are caught (*catch*) or they never *prosper*. Two forms listed in principle as collocates do not actually collocate, because they appear in a different sentence from that of the keyword (*observer, hey*). There are some collocates in common with the competitor, *cheat*^{N}: *liar(s)/lie, theft*. Most collocates of *cheat*^{N} refer to the type of cheat, be it a person (*drug, tax, welfare*) or an object used for cheating (*sheet, codes*), and some are again related to *steal*ing or *burglary*.

The collocates of *sweeper* are varied: most are related to such position in football (*team, role* as a sweeper, sweeper *system, playing* as a sweeper and *Franco Baresi*). *Webroot* and *Counterspy* are antivirus programs and a *mine* sweeper is a type of ship. The rest of the collocates refer to the instrument used for *clean*ing (*carpet* sweeper), the machine used for cleaning roads (*road* sweeper) or the person who cleans the streets (*street* sweeper). Related to cleaning there are also two collocates of *sweep*^{N} in both corpora: *clean* and *chimney*. The rest of the *sweep*^{N} collocates are related sports (*three/four-game* sweep), movements (*wide, across, arm, foot*) or are/extensions (*broad, gravel*).

The graph of cooccurrences of both doublets for the sense AGENTIVE could illustrate how similar or different each form is with respect to its competitor. Regarding *cheater/cheat*^{N},[56] two collocates are in common: *love* and *cheating*. The former is mainly used to refer to teams that *love* people who cheat, and the latter to the action performed by cheat(er)s. Related to cheaters in sports is *penalize*. The cooccurrences of *cheat*^{N} are also related to sports (*athletics, soccer, cricket, drugs*), to the type of person who performs the action (*player, husband, father, thief*) or their descriptions (*masterminded, dirty, heartless, liar*) (Figure 4.18) (see Appendices 2.B and 2.C for a graph of each competitor).

The graph of cooccurrences of *sweeper/sweep*^{N} illustrates a difference in use between the two forms: there is no cooccurrence in common. Most of the cooccurrences of *sweeper* are related to the Sweeper, a creature with the shape of a man. In the case of *sweep*^{N}, the most frequent cooccurrence is *chimney*, in line with the definitions in dictionaries presented above. In fact, all the concordances classified as AGENTIVE refer to chimney sweeps. Other cooccurrences refer to what chimney sweeps are confused for in the dark (*elephant, seal*), and some do not actually collocate (*advertisement, occupier*). (Figure 4.19)

56 The difference in the number of cooccurrences for each form is due to the difference in frequency in the attestation of the competing sense, which is low in the case of *cheater*.

Figure 4.18: Graph of the cooccurrences of cheater *and* cheat[N] *for the sense* AGENTIVE.

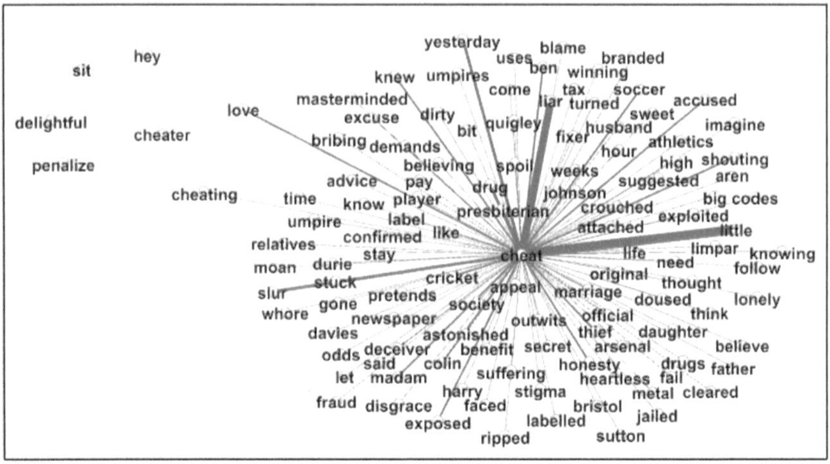

Figure 4.19: Graph of the cooccurrences of sweeper *and* sweep[N] *for the sense* AGENTIVE.

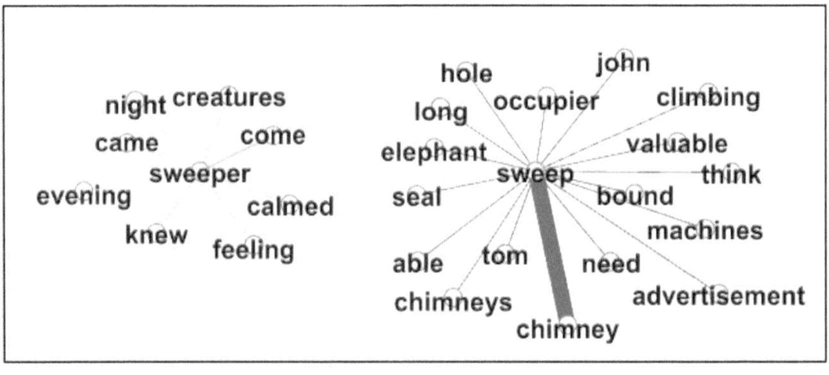

In a by-competitor basis, therefore, opposite results are found, and the competition between *sweeper* and *sweep*[N] seems to be resolved.

4.5.4. *-er* vs. zero-affixation: INSTRUMENT

The results presented so far by affix show that the use of *-er* and zero-affixation for the sense INSTRUMENT may be according to register. However, it should be tested whether the same results are found in a by-competitor basis.

The pairs selected for further analysis are *clipper/clip*[N] and *wrapper/wrap*[N]. The results obtained for each doublet are compared throughout this section.

The C* value obtained for both doublets (Table 4.5) points to a clear prevalence of *clip*^{N} over *clipper*, and a slight prevalence of *wrapper* over *wrap*^{N}. The degree to which these competitors show the competing sense is unequal: nearly 53% of the concordances of *clip*^{N} show the sense INSTRUMENT, whereas only c. 28% of the *clipper* concordances do. In the case of *wrapper/wrap*^{N}, the *-er* form shows the competing sense in nearly 89% of concordances, whereas the zero-affixed form does in c. 37% of concordances. The 'unclear' tag was given to c. 6% of the concordances of both zero-affixed forms, c. 5% to the *wrapper* ones and c. 2.6% to the concordances of *clipper*. No tagging errors were found in the forms with the covert affix, and only 0.02% in the *clip*^{N} keywords. In contrast, nearly 3% of the *wrap*^{N} keywords were wrongly tagged. This shows that the frequency with which the competing sense is expressed by means of these competitors is unequal. Frequencies are then explored to try to ascertain whether there are differences as regards their use for the expression of the sense INSTRUMENT.

In the doublet *clipper/clip*^{N}, the zero-affixed form prevails throughout. It is attested at least four times as frequently as the *-er* form in all registers, and it is the only form attested in 'W_academic'. The opposite profile is found for *wrapper/wrap*^{N}, where it is the *-er* form that prevails in all registers except two: both competitors are attested to the same proportion in 'W_fiction' and the zero-affixed form prevails in 'W_magazine'.

The register distribution of *clipper/clip*^{N} shows that *clipper* is used more frequently than expected in three registers ('Spoken', 'W_fiction' and 'W_magazine'), whereas its frequency is lower than expected in the rest of the registers. Its competitor, *clip*^{N}, shows the same profile of distribution, although it is slightly more balanced, and it is attested in all registers (Figure 4.20).

Figure 4.20: Register distribution of clipper *(blue) and* clip^{N} *(patterned blue) for the sense* INSTRUMENT. *The size of each register in the BNC is presented in dotted yellow for easier comparison.*

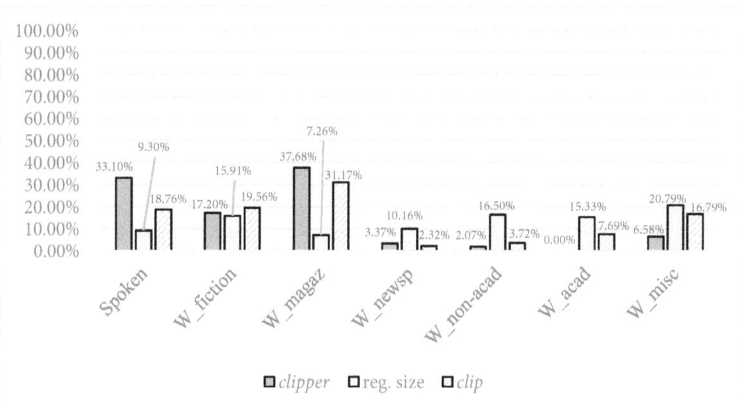

The distribution of *wrapper/wrap*^{N} is quite dissimilar if both competitors are compared: *wrapper* has a somewhat well-balanced distribution throughout, and it is attested more frequently than it would be expected with respect to the register size in 'Spoken', 'W_fiction', 'W_magazine' and 'W_academic'. *Wrap*^{N}, in contrast, is heavily skewed towards 'W_magazine', where nearly half its attestations occur. It is also attested more frequently than expected in 'Spoken', 'W_fiction', and it shows low frequencies in the rest of the registers (Figure 4.21).

Figure 4.21: Register distribution of wrapper *(blue) and* wrap^{N} *(patterned blue) for the sense* INSTRUMENT. *The size of each register in the BNC is presented in dotted yellow for easier comparison.*

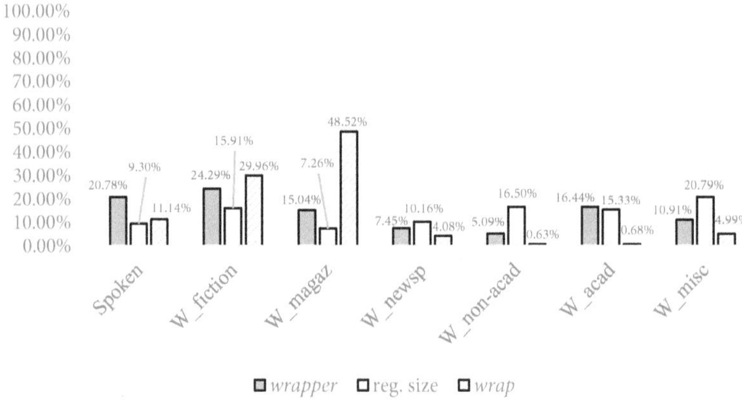

In order to test whether the register difference observed so far is statistically significant, Pearson's chi-square test was performed. For the doublet *clipper/clip*^{N}, it reveals that the difference is *not* significant ($\chi 2$ (6) = 10.74, p < .1), so the difference between the actual frequencies and the expected frequencies may be due to chance. The effect size, however, is medium (Cramer's $V = 0.19$). The standardised residuals indicate that the difference between the two competitors as regards registers is significant only in 'Spoken' (Table 4.18).

Table 4.18: Standardised residuals of the chi-square test for clipper *and* clip^{N} *for the sense* INSTRUMENT *across registers in the BNC*

	Spoken	**W_fict**	**W_magaz**	**W_newsp**	**W_non-acad**	**W_acad**	**W_misc**
clipper	2.22	0.14	1.07	0.51	−0.41	−1.78	−1.77
clip^{N}	−2.22	−0.14	−1.07	−0.51	0.41	1.78	1.77

The results obtained for the doublet *wrapper/wrap*^{N} differ from those of *clipper/clip*^{N}. Here, the computation of the chi-square test shows that there is a significant difference as regards register ($\chi 2$ (6) = 50.45, p < .001), and the computation of Cramer's *V* shows that the overall effect is very strong (Cramer's $V = 0.44$). The standardised residuals indicate that the difference in use is not significant in three registers ('Spoken', 'W_newspaper' and 'W_miscellaneous'). In contrast, *wrapper* is more frequent than would be expected in 'W_non-academic' and 'W_academic', and less frequent than expected in 'W_fiction', 'W_magazine'. The opposite is true for *wrap*^{N} (Table 4.19).

Table 4.19: Standardised residuals of the chi-square test for wrapper *and* wrap^{N} *for the sense* INSTRUMENT *across registers in the BNC*

	Spoken	**W_fict**	**W_magaz**	**W_newsp**	**W_non-acad**	**W_acad**	**W_misc**
wrapper	1.23	-2.39	-4.97	0.71	2.15	4.46	1.76
wrap^{N}	-1.23	2.39	4.97	-0.71	-2.15	-4.46	-1.76

The description of the competitors in PDE dictionaries shows that both *clipper* and *clip*^{N} are used to refer to an instrument (Table 4.20). They reflect a difference in meaning because the type of instrument and their use is different: a *clipper* is used for cutting, whereas a *clip*^{N} is used for fastening things together or for holding them in a specific position.

Table 4.20: The sense INSTRUMENT *in the gloss of* clipper *and* clip^{N} *in dictionaries*

	clipper		*clip*^{N}		**Synonymy**
	INSTRUMENT	**Use**	**INSTRUMENT**	**Use**	
Merriam-Webster	+	general	+	general	~
Longman	+	general	+	general	~
Collins	+	general	+	general	~
Cambridge	+	general	+	general	~

The sense INSTRUMENT is also recorded for both competitors in the doublet *wrapper/wrap*^{N} (Table 4.21). They are described as synonymous to refer to a material used to cover or protect things, but *wrap*^{N} is also recorded as being used to refer to a piece of clothing.

Table 4.21: The sense INSTRUMENT *in the gloss of* wrapper *and* wrap^N *in dictionaries*

	wrapper		*wrap*^{N}		**Synonymy**
	INSTRUMENT	**Use**	INSTRUMENT	**Use**	
Merriam-Webster	+	general	+	general	+
Longman	+	general	+	general	+
Collins	+	general	+	general	+
Cambridge	+	general	+	general	+

Possible differences in use are further explored by means of cooccurrences, both in corpora (BNC and COCA) and in the BNC concordances classified manually as showing the sense INSTRUMENT.

The top collocate of *clipper* in BNC and in COCA is *nail*, which is what is clipped. In both corpora, *ship(s)* is on the top-ten list of *clipper*, which is a type of ship. In the BNC, the collocate *tea* also refers to a type of clipper ship. *Intergraph* is second on the BNC list, which is a manufacturer of Clipper processors. Other collocates for proper names or brands are *hotel*, *chip*, *C400* and *NT*. In COCA, the second most frequent collocate is *yankee*, because the *Yankee Clipper* is the alias of a popular baseball player. Also related to the domain of sports are *Angeles*, *Los* (Los Angeles Clippers), *Lakers* and *season*. Regarding *clip*^{N}, there is no collocate in common with its competitor. The collocates in the BNC mainly relate to the material of the instrument (*paper*, *plastic*, *metal*), the type of clip (*spring*, *bulldog*), the object that is clipped (*ear*) and the place where it is used (*round* (the ear)). In COCA,[57] most collocates are related to videography (e.g. *video*, *audio*, *film*), and description of clips (*begin*, *end*, *commercial* (clip/break)) or their characters (*unidentified*, *king*). The only collocate referring to an instrument is *paper*. Therefore, most collocates do *not* refer to instruments in the competitors.

The collocates of *wrapper* in both corpora are related mostly to what is being wrapped (*chocolate*, *sweet*, *ice* (cream/lolly), *candy* (*bar*), *gum*, *food*, *condom*, *cans*), or the material or colour of the instrument (*plastic*, *paper*, *cellophane*, *brown*). One collocate of *wrapper* can also be found in *wrap*^{N} (*plastic*). The collocates of *wrap*^{N} are varied: at the top it is *under* (for the expression "to keep under wraps"). *Fundic* pertains to the domains of biology or medicine (and *defective* collocates with *fundic wrap*). Two collocates refer to the material of the wrap (*plastic*, *saran*),

57 The first and third collocate on the list are an opening and a closing parenthesis, respectively. They were replaced by the next two collocates in the table in order to consider only the top-ten lexical items.

and four relate to the action of wrapping (*off, keep, kept, cover,* (*to*) *wrap*). The rest are related to what is wrapped (*bubble, gift*). Some items on the list of collocates of both corpora do not actually collocate with the keyword: they appear in separate clauses (*cans, refrigerate*).

A view of cooccurrences restricted to the sense INSTRUMENT of the doublet *clipper/clip*^{N} (Figure 4.22)[58] reveals that *clipper* is used both for the tool used by a barber to cut hair (*barber* clipper) and for outdoor tools (*cordless, outdoor*), probably referring to garden shears or trimmers. The cooccurrences of *clip*^{N} refer to varied types of clips (*alligator, climbing, endoscopic, swivel, surgical*) and their characteristics (*joint, detachable, fitted*). Many cooccurrences are verbs related to the use of the instrument (*hold, lost, puts, fell, let, threw, press, took, opened, connected*) and others are adverbs used to describe their use (*firmly, carefully*). The only cooccurrence in common is *plastic*, referring to the material of the object (see Appendices 3.B and 3.C for a graph for each competitor).

Figure 4.22: Graph of the cooccurrences of clipper *and* clip^{N} *for the sense* INSTRUMENT.

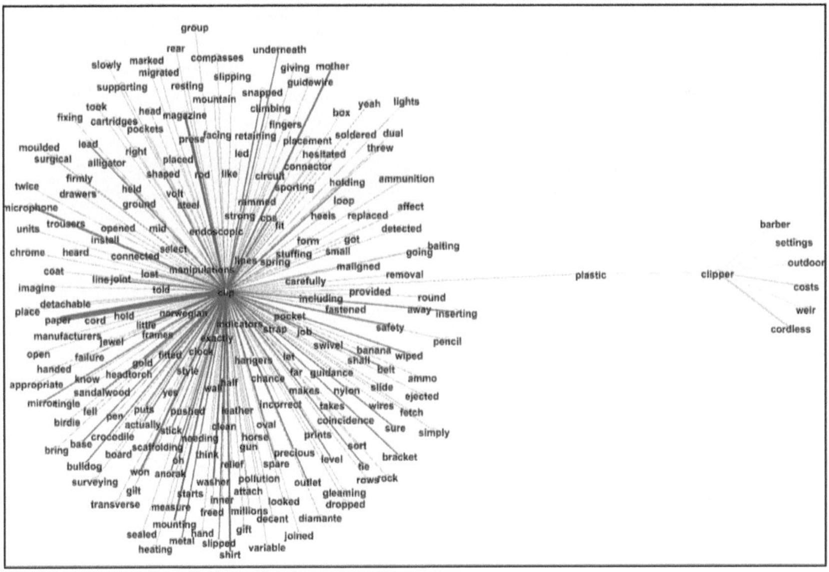

58 The difference in the number of cooccurrences for each form is due to the difference in frequency: *clipper* is atttested for the competing sense nearly 9 times as frequently as *clipper*^{N}.

The cooccurrences of *wrapper*/*wrap*^{N} (Figure 4.23) show that both competitors are used to refer to materials used to cover things, such as *shrink* (cling film), *cellophane* or *plastic*. Another word that cooccurs with both competitors is *cotton*, to refer to the material of a piece of clothing used to cover oneself, and there are also words referring to actions (*peeled*, *pulled*). The cooccurrences of *wrapper* refer to what is being wrapped (*chocolate*, *lolly*, *bread*, *hair*) and also to actions (*destroy*, *scratch*, *collect*, *held*, *lick*). In *wrap*^{N}, some words refer to what is wrapped (*food*) and to actions (*grab*, *tie*, *cover*), but a larger number of words refer to pieces of clothing (*shawl*, *blanket*, *garment*). Some materials are also related to clothing (*silk*, *fibre*) (see Appendices 3.D and 3.E for a graph for each competitor).

Figure 4.23: Graph of the cooccurrences of wrapper *and* wrap^N *for the sense* INSTRUMENT.

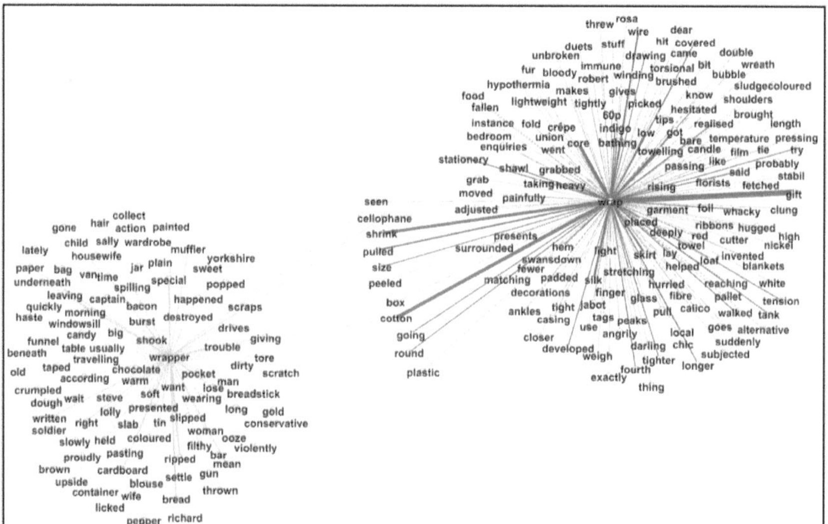

In sum, the analysis of the two doublets point to specialisation in meaning of the competitors. The competition may thus be partly resolved, but in a by-competitor basis.

4.5.5. *-ness* vs. zero-affixation: STATE

The results presented so far, by affix, show that there may be specialisation as regards register for each affix. However, the results may vary in a by-competitor basis. For this reason, two doublets have been selected for further analysis:

alertness/alert^{N} and *darkness/dark*^{N}, both competing for the sense STATE. These doublets will be compared in order to explore whether the same results are obtained for each of them.

The C* values obtained for both doublets (Table 4.7) indicate that the *-ness* form is expected to prevail, but frequencies are explored to see whether there is any difference as regards their use. First, the proportion to which the sense STATE is conveyed for each competitor is described, and then the use by register is compared.

The sense STATE is conveyed in *alertness* in nearly 85% of the concordances, whereas it is conveyed in *alert*^{N} in c. 18% of the concordances. In the latter competitor, c. 17% of concordances were wrongly tagged as a noun, and c. 4.7% were classified as 'unclear'. In *alertness* there were no tagging errors, and c. 7% of the concordances were classified as 'unclear'. In the cluster *darkness/dark*^{N}, the competing sense is conveyed in c. 21% of the *darkness* concordances, and c. 8.7% of the *dark*^{N} concordances. A little over 60% of the *dark*^{N} concordances were wrongly tagged, and c. 1.4% were unclear, whereas none of the concordances of the *-ness* counterpart was wrongly tagged, and nearly 1% were unclear. These results show that, in three of the four competitors, less than one fourth of the concordances conveyed the competing sense.

Regarding their use, *alert*^{N} prevails in 'Spoken' and 'W_newspaper', and the *-ness* competitor does so in the rest of the registers. In the *darkness/dark*^{N} doublet, *dark*^{N} prevails in 'Spoken', and *darkness* in the rest of the registers.

The register distribution of the competitors shows that the distribution is, in general, uneven in both doublets. In *alertness/alert*^{N} (Figure 4.24), the *-ness* competitor shows a similar distribution in all registers except 'Spoken', where it has a lower frequency than would be expected. In 'W_magazine' and 'W_newspaper', the frequency of *alertness* is higher than expected with respect to the size of these corpus parts. Regarding *alert*^{N}, nearly 57% of concordances are in 'W_newspaper', and its frequency is similar to the size of the corpus part in 'Spoken' and 'W_non-academic'. In one register it is not attested ('W_magazine') and in the rest, its frequency is lower than expected. Regarding the doublet *darkness/dark*^{N}, both competitors group c. 50% of their concordances in 'W_fiction'. The *-ness* form is attested less frequently than would be expected in all other registers, and the zero-affixed form is attested for the competing sense in 25% of 'Spoken' concordances. For the rest of the registers, it is also attested less frequently than expected (Figure 4.25).

Figure 4.24: Register distribution of alertness *(blue) and* alert^{N} *(patterned blue) for the sense* STATE*. The size of each register in the BNC is presented in dotted yellow for easier comparison.*

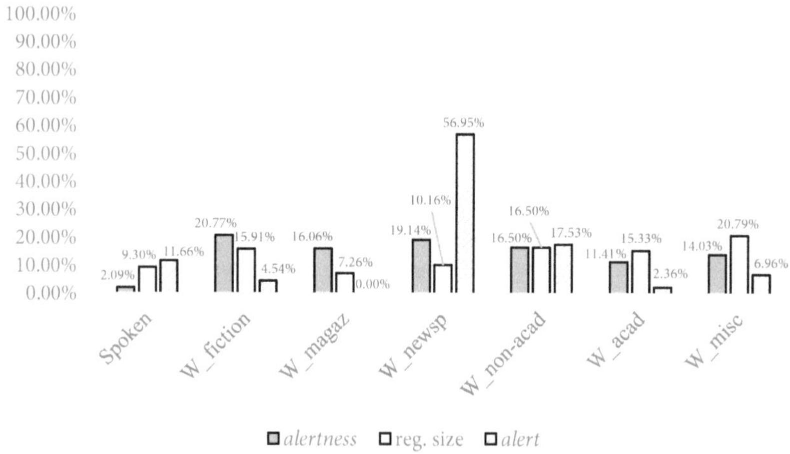

Figure 4.25: Register distribution of darkness *(blue) and* dark^{N} *(patterned blue) for the sense* STATE*. The size of each register in the BNC is presented in dotted yellow for easier comparison.*

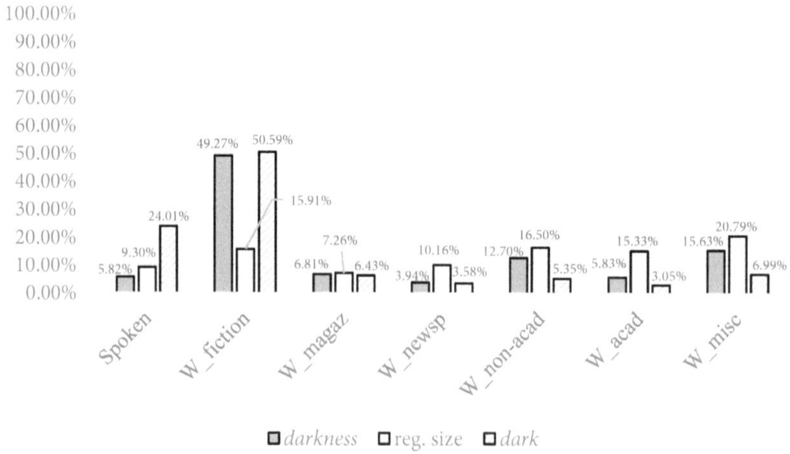

Pearson's chi-square test reveals that *alertness* and *alert*^{N} differ significantly as regards register ($\chi2$ (6) = 24.11, p < .001). The overall effect is very strong (Cramer's *V* = 0.48). The standardised residuals (Table 4.22) show that the difference is significant only for two registers: 'W_fiction' and 'W_newspaper'. In the former, the frequency of *alertness* is higher than expected and, in the latter, it is lower than expected.

Table 4.22: Standardised residuals of the chi-square test for alertness *and* alert^N *for the sense* STATE *across registers in the BNC*

	Spoken	**W_fict**	**W_magaz**	**W_newsp**	**W_non-acad**	**W_acad**	**W_misc**
alertness	−1.87	2.22	1.73	−3.70	−0.48	1.57	1.34
alert^N	1.87	−2.22	−1.73	3.70	0.48	−1.57	−1.34

As regards *darkness/dark*^{N}, the chi-square test reveals that they also differ significantly as regards register ($\chi2$ (6) = 66.57, p < .001), and the computation of Cramer's *V* shows that the overall effect is very strong (Cramer's *V* = 0.27). The standardised residuals (Table 4.23) indicate that the difference is significant for the registers 'Spoken', 'W_fiction', 'W_non-academic' and 'W_miscellaneous'. In the first two, the frequency of *darkness* is lower than expected and, in the last two, it is higher than expected.

Table 4.23: Standardised residuals of the chi-square test for darkness *and* dark^N *for the sense* STATE *across registers in the BNC*

	Spoken	**W_fict**	**W_magaz**	**W_newsp**	**W_non-acad**	**W_acad**	**W_misc**
darkness	−6.74	−2.02	−0.13	−0.03	3.11	1.51	3.78
dark^N	6.74	2.02	0.13	0.03	−3.11	−1.51	−3.78

The description of the doublet *alertness/alert*^{N} in four PDE reference dictionaries shows that both forms are recorded unevenly: *alertness* is recorded only in the Cambridge dictionary, where the sense STATE is glossed. In the other three dictionaries it is listed as a derivative form of *alert*, without any further description. The competing form *alert*^{N} is described in the four dictionaries, but the sense STATE is recorded only in two of them. None of the dictionaries lists these forms as synonymous (Table 4.24).

Table 4.24: The sense STATE *in the gloss of* alertness *and* alert^N *in dictionaries*

	alertness		*alert^N*		**Synonymy**
	STATE	**Use**	STATE	**Use**	
Merriam-Webster	–	–	+	general	–
Longman	–	–	–	–	–
Collins	–	–	+	American English (general)	–
Cambridge	+	general	–	–	–

The sense STATE is, in contrast, recorded for the doublet *darkness/dark^N* in all dictionaries.[59] The definitions pertain to the general domain and, although the dictionaries do not classify these competitors as synonymous, their definitions match (Table 4.25).

Table 4.25: The sense STATE *in the gloss of* darkness *and* dark^N *in dictionaries*

	darkness		*dark^N*		**Synonymy**
	STATE	**Use**	STATE	**Use**	
Merriam-Webster	+	general	~	general	+
Longman	~	general	~	general	+
Collins	+	general	+	general	+
Cambridge	+	general	~	general	+

The cooccurrences of both doublets are assessed to explore possible differences in use, both by looking at the top-ten collocates in BNC and COCA and by examining the cooccurrence graphs generated from the BNC concordances conveying the sense STATE.

The collocates of *alertness* both in BNC and in COCA are mostly related to the senses and to mental states (*ears, concentration, cheerfulness, relaxed, mental, state*). Others are related to gradability, for example, *increase, improve, level* or *high*, and only one collocate is in common with those of *alert^N*: *state*. In *alert^N*, the collocates are related to colour (*red, amber*), cause (*bomb, flood, intruder*) or

59 Note, however, that some of them do not clearly gloss that sense as STATE. For example, the Cambridge dictionary glosses *dark* as "the absence of light". This is interpreted as being a state here, but it is classified as "~" for its ambiguity.

type of alert (*security, police, warning, google, email*). Two verbs are related to the emergence of the alert (*raised, issued*).

The list of collocates of *darkness* shows that the keyword itself is in the top-ten position. The opposite to a state of *darkness*, that is, *light*, is the second most frequent cooccurrence in both corpora. Other forms are related to the process of becoming dark (*fell, into, cover*) and the degree to which this happens (*total*). Two collocates of *darkness*, that is, *heart* and *prince*, are due to the title of a book (Joseph Conrad's *Heart of Darkness*) and a film (John Carpenter's *Prince of Darkness*). Again, only one collocate appears both in *darkness* and its competitor: *light*. The collocates of *dark*^{N} are related to parts of the body (*eyes, hair*), and to states (*afraid, cold, alone*). The rest are related to the process (*getting, gets, growing*) and its result (*dark*).

The manual classification of concordances leads to a view of the cooccurrences of the competitors which is restricted to the sense STATE. In *alertness*/*alert*^{N} (Figure 4.26), both competitors cooccur with *state, wary, people, said* and *face*. The edge connecting *state* is wider than the rest, which means that it is the most frequent cooccurrence in both competitors. However, the rest of cooccurrences are quite dissimilar from one competitor to the other. The widest edges of connecting cooccurrences of *alertness* are for *mental, constant, quick, sudden* and *physical*. The keyword also cooccurs with several states (e.g. *nervousness, disinterestness, receptiveness, cheerfulness, vigilance, wakeful, restful, relaxed*) and actions/processes (e.g. *reduce, maintain, shivers, goes*). The zero-affixed counterpart, in contrast, does not cooccur with states (apart from *hypothermia* and *state*) and there are nearly no actions/processes. Instead, most cooccurrences are related to the type of alert (*flood, security, military, control, red, yellow*), which are also the ones with the widest edges (see Appendices 4.B and 4.C for a graph for each competitor).

Figure 4.26: Graph of the cooccurrences of alertness *and* alert^{N} *for the sense* STATE.

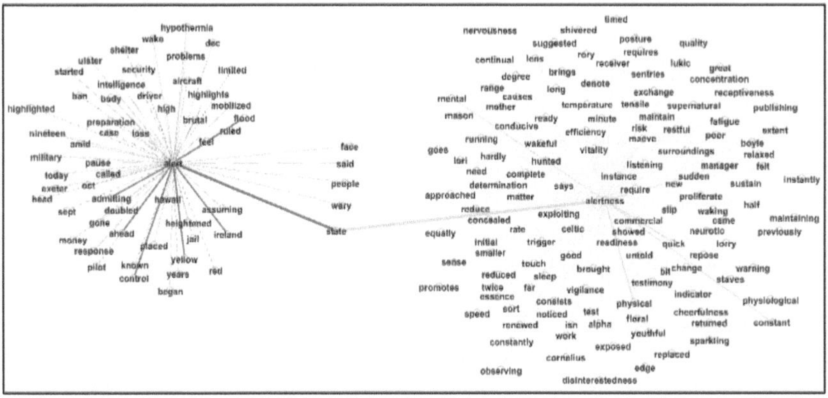

Unlike the doublet *alertness/alert*^{N}, in *darkness/dark*^{N}, there are many elements that cooccur in both competitors (Figure 4.27). Most of them could be used for space and time location (e.g. *winter, night, time, early, suddenly, outside, hall*), and others are used for descriptions (e.g. *light, black, eyes, hated, adjusted, deep*). Specific cooccurrences of darkness are also related to space (*house, tunnel, train, passage, room, earth*) or to time location (*hour, day, daylight, midnight*), as well as to states or feelings (*isolation, frightened, forgotten, despair, terror, locked*). In contrast, in *dark*, most cooccurrences are related to the process of getting dark (*beginning, getting, grow, starts, gone*), and some are used to describe the time (*endless, clock, days*) (see Appendices 4.D and 4.E for a graph for each competitor).

Figure 4.27: Graph of the cooccurrences of darkness *and* dark^{N} *for the sense* STATE.

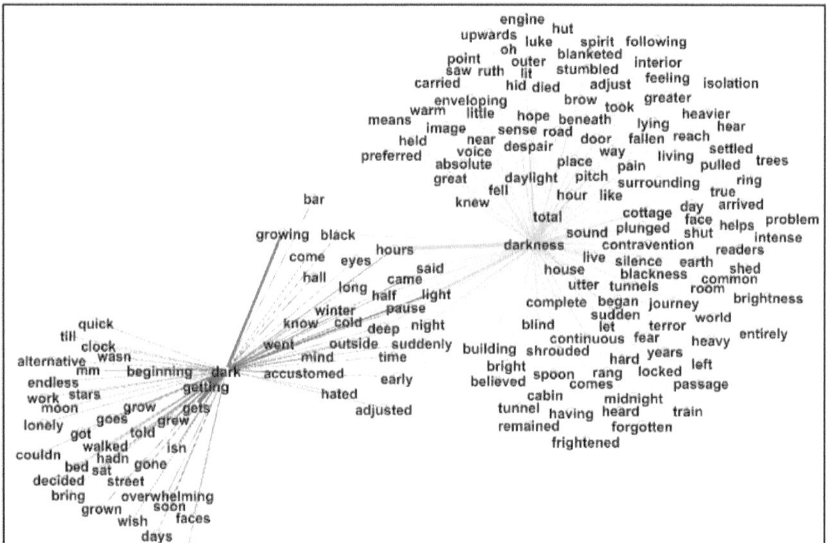

To sum up, then, for the clusters *alertness/alert*^{N} and *darkness/dark*^{N}, the results vary for each doublet: in the former, there is register specialisation and the analysis of cooccurrences supports the idea that there is a difference in use; in the latter, there also is specialisation as regards register, but the cooccurrences and the information extracted from dictionaries suggest that they are used similarly.

4.5.6. Discussion

The third research question deals with tendencies in the resolution of competition and whether they show in every cluster of any given competition pattern. To explore this, Table 4.26 summarises the results obtained from calculation of the C* value (see Table 4.3, Table 4.4, Table 4.5 and Table 4.7), which is used to identify which forms (or which process) have prevailed or may prevail in each cluster. A note of caution is in order for the interpretation of these results: in simple terms, the assumption behind this measurement is that the higher the productivity of a process, the more readily available it will be for the formation of new words. Then, it would be expected that, if a form has a higher C* value (and, thus, productivity) than its competitor, there is a higher chance that it will create new words and, thus, prevail over its competitor.[60] Although this is an assumption that is implicit in any study on the productivity of affixes, certain parameters, such as lexicalisation or pragmatic factors, which may influence the results greatly, cannot be controlled (see, e.g., Bauer 2001: 20–22; Plag 2005: 125–126). For this reason, any statement based on these figures needs to be taken cautiously and only as a potential outcome. This measure is therefore used here only as a starting point to try to identify general resolution tendencies, but it is expected that these may not be followed in some cases, such as when an affix (or a form) becomes specialised.

Table 4.26: Results obtained from computation of the C value by competing pattern

	Senses not attested in cluster	**Clusters in PDE competition**		**Clusters of resolved competition**	
		Overt affixation may prevail	**Zero-affixation may prevail**	**Overt affixation prevails**	**Zero-affixation prevails**
-ation vs. zero-affixation ACTION	1 (13%)	2 (25%)	3 (38%)	1 (13%)	1 (13%)
-er vs. zero-affixation AGENTIVE	1 (5%)	5 (26%)	3 (16%)	10 (53%)	0 (0%)
-er vs. zero-affixation INSTRUMENT	5 (21%)	5 (21%)	6 (25%)	3 (13%)	5 (21%)
-ness vs. zero-affixation STATE	0 (0%)	4 (44%)	1 (11%)	4 (44%)	0 (0%)

60 "According to Corbin (1987:177) a morphological process is *rentable* [...] to the extent that it *may be used* or has been used to produce large numbers of new words" (Bauer 2001: 49; emphasis added).

This said, Table 4.26 shows that not every cluster within each pattern behaves the same way, even if some resolution tendencies can be identified in two patterns: in both *-er*/zero-affixation AGENTIVE and *-ness*/zero-affixation STATE, the overt affix prevails over the zero affix (in 83% of clusters where both competitors are attested in the former, and 89% in the latter).[61] In the two other patterns, zero-affixation prevails, but the proportion of clusters where it does is lower (in 57% of clusters where both competitors are attested for the expression of ACTION, and 58% for the expression of INSTRUMENT).

Taking the expression of AGENTIVE as an example, the overt affix would be expected to prevail when in competition with zero-affixation. This tendency shows, for example, in the doublet *sweep*/*sweeper*, where *-er* is expected to prevail. In contrast, the doublet *cheat*/*cheater* shows opposite results: the zero-affixed form is expected to prevail.

The literature has described three factors which provide hints on which form may prevail over its competitors (see, e.g., Aronoff 1976; Pounder 2000: 322, 669; Bauer 2009; Rifón Sánchez 2011; Fernández-Alcaina & Čermák 2018; Fradin 2019):

i) the earliest attestation date (the earliest form is expected to prevail),
ii) the frequency of the form (the form with the highest frequency is expected to prevail), and
iii) the polysemy of the form (the one that is used to express a wider number of senses is expected to prevail).

If these factors are tested in the two doublets described above, it can be seen that they do not always behave as expected. In the case of *cheat*/*cheater*, the earliest attestation dates of the competing sense in the OED are quite similar for both forms (1664 and 1606, respectively), so this is inconclusive. In the case of *sweep*/*sweeper*, the form with the competing sense which is attested earliest (*sweeper*, in 1657) is expected to prevail (as opposed to *sweep*, where the instrumental sense is attested earliest in 1812), which would follow the expectancy. There are, however, clusters where it is the form attested later that is expected to prevail, for example, *swank*^{N}, attested earliest in 1913 for the expression of INSTRUMENT, is expected to prevail over *swanker*, attested earliest in 1846.

---

61 Note that the percentages provided in the text, as opposed to the table, consider only clusters where both competitors are attested within each competing pattern. The table, in contrast, computes percentages including also clusters where the competing sense is not attested.

Regarding the frequency of the forms, opposite results are found: in *cheat/cheater* the form with the highest frequency is expected to prevail (*cheat*^{N}); whereas in *sweep/sweeper*, it is the form with the lowest frequency that is expected to prevail (*sweeper*). This is because the competing sense is attested in different proportions in each cluster: c. 56% and 77% of the *cheat/cheater* concordances, respectively, attest the sense AGENTIVE, whereas only c. 3% of the *sweep*^{N} concordances do (as opposed to 76% in *sweeper*). The proportion of concordances of *sweep*^{N} showing the competing sense is thus very low, which would explain why *sweeper* is expected to prevail, even if the form shows a lower frequency than its competitor in the corpus.

As for the polysemy of the forms, the results are again opposite. In *cheat/cheater*, the form with the highest number of senses is expected to prevail: *cheat*^{N} has nine senses in the OED and it is expected to prevail, whereas its competitor has four. In contrast, in *sweep/sweeper*, the form with the lowest number of senses is the one expected to prevail: *sweep*^{N} has 34 senses and *sweeper* has 7, but the latter would prevail. This could again be explained by the low proportion of *sweep*^{N} concordances showing the sense AGENTIVE.

Therefore, even if general tendencies can be identified for the resolution of competition, clusters behave differently. Be it as it may, some forms may become specialised and prevail in a domain over its competitor, even if the competitor has been attested earlier, is more frequent (in other domains), or shows a wider variety of meanings. This *niche* of specialisation, as described by Aronoff (2016, 2019), among others, would thus allow forms to remain in use even if only within a restricted domain (see Bauer 2001: 135). The domain is typically of register or semantics, which will be further explored with the two doublets selected.

Regarding register, both *-er* and zero-affixation are skewed towards newspaper samples for the expression of AGENTIVE, and the overt affix occurs significantly more frequently than expected in 'Spoken' and 'W_academic', whereas the zero affix does in 'W_fiction'. The analysis of individual clusters, however, reveals that this general tendency does not always show:

i) *Cheater* is attested significantly more frequently than expected in 'Spoken' and 'W_academic', but *cheat*^{N} is in 'W_newspaper'.
ii) *Sweep*^{N} is attested significantly more frequently than expected in 'W_academic' and 'W_non-academic'. *Sweeper* is not used significantly more frequently than expected in any register.

In both clusters, the association between word-formation process and register is significant, and the effect size is remarkably strong. Therefore, the competition between the two doublets may be partly resolved by register specialisation. However, *sweeper* has no niche regarding register, which may mean that it is used in a wide variety of contexts but thus may be the default form to refer to agents who sweep.

As for the semantics of the clusters, the information extracted from PDE dictionaries reveals specialisation for the cluster *sweep/sweeper*: the *-er* form is used to refer to any agent that sweeps, whereas the zero-affixed form is restricted to chimney sweeps. The analysis of the cooccurrences of these forms support the possibility of a semantic specialisation, as there is no cooccurrence in common. Regarding the doublet *cheat/cheater*, no clear semantic specialisation was identified at first: PDE dictionaries gloss both forms with an agentive meaning. Their cooccurrences reveal that both forms can be used to refer to people who cheat in sport and in love affairs, so there is some overlap in meaning. Otherwise, the low frequency of *cheater* does not allow a detailed analysis of the form. Interestingly, dictionaries point to a possible dialectal difference between the two competitors: *cheater* would be used more frequently in American English and *cheat*^{N} in British English. Besides, the OED reports in the gloss of *cheater* a semantic nuance for *cheat*^{N}: "[a] systematic or habitual cheater is now called a cheat n.1". Therefore, even if both forms refer to agents that perform the action of cheating, the zero-affixed form is used for agents that perform the action repeatedly and the *-er* form for those who do so in particular situations. Besides, the *-er* form seems to be more frequent in American English, and the zero-affixed form in British English, which may explain why *cheat*^{N} was expected to prevail in this book, which is based on data from the BNC. It may be concluded, then, that, even if these forms do remain in competition, they seem to be in the process of diverging both in regional terms and in their connotations.

The results presented so far demonstrate that the proportion of pairs which actually compete is not so big as could be expected. In most cases, forms have become specialised or they are in the process of specialisation. This is in line with previous research on competition (Plag 1999; Koehl 2015; Fradin 2019), which demonstrates that a close analysis of competitors may reveal differences in their use, even if some retain some degree of overlap. This leads to the view of competition as a gradient, where forms or processes compete to varying degrees until competition is resolved (Huyghe & Wauquier 2021; Huyghe et al. 2023; Huyghe & Varvara 2023a). Further research is needed to assess the extent to which each factor (phonological, morphological, semantic, stylistic, etc.) influences the way competition is resolved.

4.6. The clash between two models

The fourth research question deals with the potential bias towards transparency or towards economy in word formation. Specifically, the aim is to ascertain whether a transparent or an economic process is primed when a situation of competition arises and if the bias, if any, is context dependent. To explore this, this book analyses the competition between three overt suffixes (transparent) and zero-affixation (economic) for the expression of four different semantic categories.

The expectation is twofold:

i) According to the principle of Naturalness, overt suffixation should prevail over zero-affixation: "affixing WFRs [Word-Formation Rules] are preferred over conversion rules, and morphotactically more transparent ones over less transparent ones" (Dressler 1987: 122).
ii) Zero-affixation should prevail in spoken language and in informal contexts, whereas overt affixation would prevail written language and formal contexts: "[t]his is because in formal or emphatic speech easy perception takes priority and in casual speech it is easy pronounceability that takes priority" (Dressler 1985a: 86).

To address the second expectation (ii), an analysis of the use of the competing patterns in terms of mode and of register was performed in this book.

In terms of mode, the results show that the association between word-formation process and mode is significant for the four competing patterns, but that the effect size is either weak or very weak (Table 4.27). Therefore, the choice of the word-formation process will be conditioned by the mode, but exceptions are expected. Interestingly, and contrary to what was expected, overt suffixation is attested significantly more frequently than it would be expected in the spoken mode in three of the patterns (for the expression of ACTION, AGENTIVE and INSTRUMENT), while it is zero-affixation that is attested significantly more frequently than expected for the expression of STATE. Uncovering why this is so is outside the scope of this book, but some factors that could play a role and deserve exploration in further research are:

i) the word class of the base, as the patterns derived from the same word class (verb) behave similarly, and different from the one deriving from a different word class (adjective),
ii) phonological factors, as the three suffixes that prevail in the spoken mode start in a vowel, and the other one in a consonant, or
iii) the effect played by the method used, for example, the fact that results are based on BNC data, where the spoken mode is comparatively less represented than the written mode.

Table 4.27: Results from the statistical analysis of the competing patternsas regards mode

	Chi-square	**Effect size**	**Residuals (overt affix)**	
			> expected	**< expected**
-ation vs. zero-affixation ACTION	Significant	Very weak	Spoken	Written
-er vs. zero-affixation AGENTIVE	Significant	Very weak	Spoken	Written
-er vs. zero-affixation INSTRUMENT	Significant	Very weak	Spoken	Written
-ness vs. zero-affixation STATE	Significant	Weak	Written	Spoken

In terms of register, the results presented so far demonstrate that the choice of one process or another is according to register. These results are partly counter to our expectations: zero-affixation was expected to be significantly more frequent in spoken language and in informal contexts, as speed would be primed, whereas overt affixation was expected to be significantly more frequent in written language and formal contexts, where easy processing would be primed. Table 4.10 shows that, in three of the four patterns analysed, the overt suffix is used significantly more frequently than expected in 'Spoken', and in two patterns in 'W_fiction' and 'W_academic'. The zero affix, in contrast, shows higher frequencies than expected in 'W_newspaper' in two patterns, and the rest of the registers differ in each pattern. Such variability does not lead to a firm conclusion in terms of word-formation process and the degree of formality of the texts, although a tendency is clear: within written registers, overt suffixation is used more frequently than expected in formal and fiction texts, whereas zero-affixation is used more frequently in more informal writing (newspaper and non-academic). This is in line with what was expected, but a more fine-grained analysis of the degree of formality or technicality of the texts is needed to confirm these results.

4.7. Methodological aspects

The results presented so far in this chapter are undoubtedly influenced by the methodological decisions taken in this book. For this reason, some key aspects of the methodology are first discussed, so the results obtained are considered with these in mind. This section discusses:

i) limitations arising from the versions available of the OED (§4.7.1),
ii) the discrepancies between corpus and dictionary data (§4.7.2), and
iii) limitations due to the use of the BNC as a corpus (§4.7.3) and to the scope of the analysis to doublets (§4.7.4).

4.7.1. Versions of the OED

The OED is unarguably a rich source of information, but the information presented in it is partly influenced by the methodological decisions taken by the lexicographers, and by the data available at the time a dictionary entry is created, revised or edited (see Nevalainen 1999: 337ff.; see also Bauer 2009: 178).

Some of the forms analysed in this book belong to the second version of the dictionary (OED2), so some entries may not have been updated since the 19th century (e.g. *exhort*^{N}/*exhortation*, not updated since 1894 at the time of submitting this book), whereas others belong to the OED3, which means they have been updated after 1990 and published online since 2000 on a quarterly basis (see Simpson 2004; Allan 2012: 18–21). This becomes especially relevant when using attestation dates, as an entry created or last updated before 1950 will not attest a competing sense after that date and, as a result, it would be taken here as an example of a form that has fallen out of use, even if that is not necessarily the case.[62] This is why restricting the searches to the OED3 version could be desirable (as has been done, e.g., in Smith 2020 and Fernández-Alcaina 2021a, 2021b), even at the cost of leaving out some potentially relevant data. This book does not restrict the search to any particular OED version, but it complements the information extracted from the dictionary with data from a PDE corpus, the BNC. Therefore, in order to avoid the limitations emerging from the sole use of a dictionary or of a corpus, dictionary data is used to identify potential competitors and to extract relevant information about them (etymology, range of meanings, lifespan, etc.), and corpus data is used to identify which clusters remain in use in PDE and to explore how they are used in each context.

4.7.2. Discrepancies between dictionary and corpus data

This book uses dictionary and corpus data to identify patterns of competition and to explore their use in PDE. For most clusters, dictionary and corpus data agree, but there are exceptions. This section briefly discusses two such cases.

One example where both sources of information, dictionary and corpus, agree is the cluster *savage*^{N}*/savageness/savagery/savagism*: the four forms are

62 Attestation dates are used for an analysis of the diachronic profile of competition. Whether the competing senses of the forms are in use in PDE is decided based on corpus data, that is, depending on whether the form is attested in the BNC and, if so, whether the *sense* is attested in the corpus. This is why a competitor may be classified as obsolete in the diachronic analysis, and as in use in PDE.

attested in the OED for the expression of STATE. The zero form, however, counts as an instance of incidental competition, as it is attested only once in the dictionary for the competing sense (in 1487; see discussion below in this section on single attestations in the OED). The other three competitors are attested for the competing sense after 1950, so they seem to remain in competition for the expression of STATE. A search in corpora reveals that the four forms are attested in PDE corpora (but note *savagism* is not attested in the BNC) (Table 4.28).

Table 4.28: Absolute frequencies of the competing cluster savage^{N}/savageness/savagery/savagism *in PDE corpora without sense separation*

	savage^{N}	*savageness*	*savagery*	*savagism*
BNC	306	1	150	0
COCA	3,062	21	856	11
iWeb	23,229	229	6131	13

The semantic classification of concordances reveals that there are no examples of *savage*^{N} for the competing sense in the BNC, whereas *savageness* did show a stative meaning in the corpus (see §4.5.5). An analysis of the concordances of *savagery* in the BNC shows that this competitor is also attested for the competing sense: 82 of the 150 concordances express STATIVE. Therefore, even if the competition between zero-affixation and *-ness* for the expression of STATE on the base *savage*^{Adj} may be resolved, the *-ness* form remains in competition with *savagery*. The use of other corpora could also give insight on the competition with *savagism*: both the COCA (16) and the iWeb (17) attest instances of this form for the expression of STATE:

(16) *Dvorak pursued the hyperrealities of tribal cultures, the structured ceremonies at the tenable borders of civilization in a small town, imagined tribal music as an instance of nationalism, and worried about his daughter too close to* ***savagism***. (COCA)

(17) *Without investigation some might reject the idea that man could have lived on the earth one hundred thousand years in a state of* ***Savagism***. (iWeb)

Thus, these results agree with the information in the OED: *savageness*, *savagery* and *savagism* are instances of ongoing competition for the expression of STATE, whereas *savage*^{N} has fallen out of use for the expression of that sense (which is tagged as *obsolete* in the dictionary).

The other case worth presenting here obtains whenever the OED tags the competing sense of a form as *in use*, but it is not attested in the BNC. One example would be *reloader*, which is not attested in the corpus, even if there is one quotation in the OED dated 1989 for the sense INSTRUMENT. The fact that it is only one quotation raises again the question of whether single attestations should count as proof of availability, or whether they may actually be the result of the inclusivity of the dictionary (see Fernández-Alcaina 2021b: 75–77; see also Hoffmann 2004; Bauer 2009: 181–182).

There are also cases where the OED tags the competing sense of a form as *obsolete* or *dated* but it is attested in the BNC. For example, the meaning INSTRUMENT is attested in the BNC in both *bolt*^{N} and *bolter* (see §4.5.4), but the latest OED attestations for this sense for both competitors are dated 1847 and 1880, respectively.

The exact procedure or standpoint for each case is not resolved in this book, partly because it deserves a lot more attention than can be given to it here, and partly because the relevance of such cases in the dataset is low. The procedure used here was to rely on:

i) OED data for the diachronic analysis, where competitors are considered as in use in a particular point in time depending on the dates of the quotations provided for the competing sense, and
ii) BNC data for analysis of PDE, where competitors are considered as in use in PDE if they are attested with the competing sense in the corpus.

The procedure for each case may well have to be decided on an individual basis and is therefore left to be discussed in further research. At this point, this section is intended to show specific difficulties in data processing for this book and concludes that no single source of information should be taken as being a 100% representative by itself.

4.7.3. Corpus frequencies

Previous research on competition used the frequencies of competitors as an indicator of the prevalence of one process over another (e.g. Rainer 1988, cited in Bauer 2009: 182). However, the semantic classification of the concordances carried out in this book (§3.3.2.2.1) shows that not all forms attest the competing sense in the corpus. Table 4.29 shows the proportion of forms that do and do not attest the competing sense for each of the competing patterns.

Table 4.29: Number of clusters where both members, no member or only one member attest(s) the competing sense in the BNC

	None attests competing sense	**Only one attests competing sense**		**Both attest competing sense**
		Only zero-affixation	**Only overt suffixation**	
-*ation* vs. zero-affixation ACTION	1 (13%)	1 (13%)	1 (13%)	5 (63%)
-*er* vs. zero-affixation AGENTIVE	1 (5%)	0 (0%)	10 (53%)	8 (42%)
-*er* vs. zero-affixation INSTRUMENT	5 (21%)	6 (25%)	5 (21%)	8 (33%)
-*ness* vs. zero-affixation STATE	0 (0%)	0 (0%)	4 (44%)	5 (56%)

The results show that approximately only 50% of clusters of each competing pattern attest the competing sense in both cluster forms. The proportion of attestation of the competing sense is unequal for each pattern too: while c. 63% of the -*ation*/zero-affixation ACTION clusters attest the competing sense in both members, only 33% do so in the -*er*/zero-affixation INSTRUMENT clusters. Where only one of the two members of the cluster is attested for the competing sense, it is usually the overt suffixed form (amounting to approximately 50% in two patterns), while the clusters attesting the competing sense in only zero-affixed forms amounts to 13% and 25% of the clusters of those two patterns. A similar proportion is found with respect to clusters where only zero-affixation is attested for the competing sense in the other two patterns (for the expression of ACTION and INSTRUMENT). The competing pattern with the highest proportion of clusters where no form in the cluster attests the competing sense is found for the expression of INSTRUMENT (c. 21%).

These results prove that an analysis of competition without sense classification is bound to give misleading results. If the attestations of these forms in the corpus had been taken as evidence of competition per se, and the analysis of the competition had been done with the absolute frequencies of the forms in the corpus without any semantic classification, results would have varied greatly. Lara-Clares & Thompson's (2019) comparative analysis of competition taking the absolute frequencies of the competitors in the BNC and the frequencies after sense separation shows that the results were not just different, but even opposite in some cases. Therefore, the value of the results presented in this book lies mainly in the semantic analysis of concordances which, to the best of my knowledge, is not available in the specialised literature of competition in English, even if semantics has been central to research on competition (e.g. Riddle 1985; Schulte 2015; Fradin 2019; Nagano 2022; Huyghe et al. 2023).

The manual classification of concordances is an extremely time-consuming task, which explains why some authors are testing computational methods that would allow analysis of large datasets (Lapesa et al. 2018; Bonami & Thuilier 2019; Wauquier et al. 2020a; Huyghe & Wauquier 2021; Mititelu et al. 2023, and references therein), even if some acknowledge that manual annotation would be desirable:

> In fact, a robust, systematic morphosemantic annotation of derived verbs would be a considerable endeavour in itself, that neither previous work nor the present paper has pursued (Bonami & Thuilier 2019: 6)

These methods are promising, but they are still subject to limitations (see, among others, Baayen et al. 2013; Bonami & Guzmán Naranjo 2023: 249–250; Huyghe & Varvara 2023a; Kotowski & Plag 2023: 5–7; Thuilier et al. 2023), which makes it desirable still to combine different methods in order to attain a more complete picture of the competition. This is the reason why LLMs seem to open new possibilities for analyses of competition, as they may allow the automatic annotation of concordances. Still, the creation of adequate prompts is also a very time consuming task, which needs a lof of development yet. In a test done by Lara-Clares & Fernández-Alcaina (2024) for the doublet *wrap*^{N}/*wrapper*, the results show that the agreement in annotation between two humans and between the humans and GPT-4o was generally similar, even if the LLM rated lower in some cases. The results also suggest that the two forms are currently in competition, as they overlap in meaning for some senses, for example, 'material', 'loose_clothing' or 'indoor_garment', while keeping some differentiation (e.g. only *wrap* has been found to refer to a pack of drugs in the BNC). These results further support the need for a sense-level analysis of competition, and prove the need for the development of less time-consuming methods to do that.

4.7.4. Restriction to doublets

Most research on competition has limited the analysis to pairs of competitors, that is, to doublets (e.g. Aronoff 1976; Kaunisto 2007, 2009; Bauer et al. 2010; Saïlly 2011; Fradin 2019; Smith 2020; Lieber & Plag 2022). This is partly because they make most of the cases (Fernández-Alcaina 2021b: 81) but maybe also for methodological convenience, as it is easier to control variables when only two elements are at play, and it uses a smaller quantity of data. Similarly, this book restricts most of the analysis to doublets:

i) for manageability reasons, as an analysis of concordances of all the competitors in each cluster would prove too time consuming,
ii) because they represent nearly 80% of the sample,[63] and
iii) because statistical comparisons are usually carried out with minimal pairs, and the inclusion of triplets or bigger clusters would imply the use of much more complex statistical measures (see Huyghe & Varvara 2023a: 15).

However, a need to consider derivational paradigms and derivational series in studies on competition has been recently addressed in the literature (see, among others, Pounder 2000: 669–672; Fradin 2016; Fernández-Alcaina & Čermák 2018; Bonami & Thuilier 2019; Fernández-Alcaina 2021b: 31–33; Huyghe & Varvara 2023a: 8). Ideally, then, in order to get a complete picture of competition, not only clusters should be analysed in full: the whole derivational paradigm should be considered (see Štekauer 2014 on derivational paradigms and their complexity). What is more, searches should not be restricted to affixal processes, but every word-formation process available should be included (see Štekauer 2017). Admittedly, such an approach would be extremely complex to tackle at a large scale from a methodological point of view. This is why, for now, a more fine-grained analysis of doublets may be considered to yield relevant results and it can be used to test the adequacy of different methods for research on the resolution of the competition.

4.8. Summary

The potential limitations due to the methodological decisions taken in this book described in this chapter limit the degree to which the results obtained can be generalised to other competition patterns or to other varieties of English, but even the results obtained provide insights into the resolution of competition in PDE nominalisations at a sense level. This chapter discussed the four main research questions of this book, showing that diachronic competition is resolved by the obsolescence of both competitors in approximately half of the clusters. In PDE, it seems that the competition between zero-affixation and *-ation* (for the expression of ACTION) and zero-affixation and *-er* (for the expression of AGENTIVE

63 The proportion of doublets is unequal in the sample, depending on the competing pattern: in *-er*/zero-affixation INSTRUMENT and AGENT, c. 95% of the clusters are made up of two forms. In *-ness*/zero-affixation STATE, c. 80%. In contrast, in *-ation*/zero-affixation ACTION, the proportion is much lower: c. 45%.

and INSTRUMENT) are closer to resolution than the competition between zero-affixation and *-ness* for the expression of STATE. All competing patterns show specialisation as regards register, but each cluster needs to be analysed separately for an analysis of resolution in terms of semantic specialisation. In terms of the conflict between economy and transparency when in competition, expectations prove true only to a limited degree.

5. Conclusions

5.1. Introduction

In §1.3, it was stated that the aim of this book is to explore whether and how the competition between overt affixation and zero-affixation in PDE for the formation of nouns is resolved. To this end, this book focused on four competing patterns:

i) *-ation*/zero-affixation for the expression of ACTION,
ii) *-er*/zero-affixation for the expression of AGENTIVE,
iii) *-er*/zero affixation for the expression of INSTRUMENT, and
iv) *-ness*/zero-affixation for the expression of STATE.

It may be worth recalling at this point, as the background of this book, that, despite the attention given to the topic of competition in word formation, there is quite some variability on how its study is approached:

i) Some authors restrict competition to a situation where two or more forms are derived from the same base and express the same meaning in the same domains, whereas others take a more inclusive approach whereby competition depends only on the word class of the outputs (e.g. nominalisations).
ii) Most research has focused on identifying how derivation is constrained or facilitated by, for example, the profile of the base, in order to find niches of specialisation (e.g. *-ical* prevails over *-ic* in bases ending in *-olog-*, Lindsay 2012: 193). Few references have restricted the analysis to the sense level, that is, in which contexts may one process be preferred over another for the expression of a given semantic category.
iii) Previous research has focused mainly on affixal processes, but zero-affixation has largely been left out of research.

The present chapter is structured as follows: §5.2 draws conclusions, and §5.3 is a description of the limitations of the book and of further research.

5.2. Conclusions

The main conclusions of this book with regard to the study of the competition between overt affixation and zero-affixation for the formation of nouns can be presented from a methodological and a descriptive point of view.

5.2.1. Methodological

From a methodological point of view, this book shows that a combination of corpus (e.g. BNC) and dictionary (e.g. OED) data is needed, as they complement each other and allow for a more fine-grained analysis. In this book, the OED has been used to:

i) identify forms in competition for the expression of four semantic categories (ACTION, AGENTIVE, INSTRUMENT, STATE), and
ii) extract relevant information such as etymology, a description of senses over time, and the lifespan of forms and senses.

Corpus data has been used to explore the use of competitors in PDE to:

i) quantify to which extent they are used for the expression of the semantic categories under study,
ii) analyse the context of use of the competitors as regards register, and
iii) compare their meanings by way of the analysis of their glosses in PDE dictionaries, and their cooccurrences in the concordances classified as showing the competing sense.

The manual classification of concordances has proved that the use of frequencies of the forms without semantic classification leads to inaccurate results: only between 2% and 40% of the concordances in the sample attest the competing sense, but this proportion varies according to the competing pattern. Therefore, if absolute frequencies are used without semantic classification, between 60% and 98% of attestations which are not actually in competition will mistakenly be included in the count. The proportion of concordances attesting the competing sense also varies according to the word-formation process: c. 50% of the concordances of the overt affixed forms attest the competing sense, whereas only 15% of the concordances of the zero-affixed forms do. Thus, conclusions drawn on BNC data without semantic classification bias the frequencies of use of both processes for the expression of the competing sense, especially in the case of zero-affixation.

The restriction of the analysis to forms derived from the same base is useful for better control of the variables that may play a role in the resolution of competition, as it eliminates the effects played, for example, by blocking or by phonological restrictions. This is because corpus attestation evidences to some extent that the forms in question are not subject to constraints that *preclude* derivation. It does not allow, however, for an analysis of factors such as potentiation (see Aronoff 2023: 57), because the study is limited to *attested* forms derived from the same base and by different affixes and, thus, does not explore *potential* forms. Therefore, this kind of analysis helps compare processes which are used for derivation from the same bases, but it does not allow comparison of their potential for derivation independently on the profile of the base.

5.2.2. Descriptive

From a descriptive point of view, the results obtained in this book support the claim made in the literature that competition is not so widespread as it might seem (see Plag 1999; Fernández-Alcaina 2021a, 2021b):

i) after analysis of a sample of c. 1,150 entries from the BNC frequency list, 36 clusters of competition in PDE were identified (c. 3% of the entries in the list), and
ii) following the analysis of nearly 10,000 entries in the OED, 144 clusters (c. 1.5% of the OED entries) were identified in diachrony, of which 60 clusters are attested in PDE (c. 0.6% of the OED entries).

This confirms the hypothesis that the system avoids two forms or processes for the same meaning. More importantly, the results presented in this book give competition in the profiles under study a size and, considered alongside Fernández-Alcaina (2021), allow to envisage how and how fast the system filters redundant forms.

As regards the resolution of competition, the possibilities are:

i) The obsolescence of one or more competitors in the cluster. The diachronic results show that this is the case in 75% of clusters in the sample. This is in line with results from an analysis of competition between verbs: "Despite the heterogeneity of competition, resolution is always the most common outcome independently of the number of competitors, the degree of overlap, the patterns in competition and the meaning expressed." (Fernández-Alcaina 2021a: 228).
ii) The specialisation of one or both competitors. This book explores mode, register and semantic specialisation:
   a. Specialisation as regards mode was found, but the effect size was very weak for the four patterns. Interestingly, the overt suffix has significantly higher frequencies than expected in the spoken mode in three patterns (for the expression of ACTION, AGENTIVE and INSTRUMENT), whereas the zero affix does in the other pattern (for the expression of STATE);
   b. specialisation as regards register was found for the four patterns under analysis, and the effect size was very strong in two, medium in one and very weak in another pattern. Overt suffixation is used more frequently

than expected in formal and fiction texts within the written mode, whereas zero-affixation is used more frequently in more informal writing (newspaper and non-academic); and

c. semantic specialisation was explored in specific clusters, and it led to uneven results: some pairs of competitors (e.g. *sweep*^{N}/*sweeper* for the expression of AGENTIVE) seem to be semantically specialised, so each competitor is used to express a different meaning, whereas others (e.g. *wrap*^{N}/*wrapper* for the expression of INSTRUMENT) retain some degree of overlap.

iii) The coexistence of the processes for a period of time. No pattern or cluster was identified where there was no hint of resolution, that is, where no specialisation as regards register, mode, or semantics was found. However, some patterns seem to be closer to resolution than others: zero-affixation/*-ation* for the expression of ACTION and zero-affixation/*-er* for the expression of AGENTIVE and INSTRUMENT show a higher degree of specialisation than zero-affixation/*-ness* for the expression of STATE.

The profile of resolution varies greatly from pattern to pattern, and even more for individual clusters, which evidences how complex competition is. There is a large number of factors that influence competition and its resolution: from general tendencies of natural languages to economy or transparency, to very specific phonological restrictions. To date, it does not seem possible to control for every variable in a systematic way.

This book thus concludes that the system avoids two forms for the same purpose, but the way in which this happens varies greatly. If the potential for word formation is considered in general terms, formal constraints are key, as they establish which forms can be created or not (e.g. *-ize* precludes derivation with *-ment*, *-al* or *-age*; see §2.3.3.2.3). If competition of forms derived from the same base is examined, then differences of use can be identified, mainly depending on the degree of formality of the text, or also on the meaning of the forms (e.g. overt suffixation seems to prevail in formal and fiction texts, whereas zero-affixation does in informal writing). However, the differences that are identified do not lead to clear-cut choices for word formation, but rather to a preference system that evolves over time.

5.3. Limitations and future research

The limitations of this book I am aware of are mainly methodological and, thus, partly also descriptive as regards the results obtained:

i) The 'Spoken' part of the BNC amounts to only c. 10% of the corpus. This becomes especially relevant when an analysis in terms of mode is taken into consideration because, even if frequencies have been normalised according to the size of each corpus part, some forms or patterns may be underrepresented in that mode. This is particularly relevant for a book where mode influences the resolution of competition as heavily as expounded here.

ii) For the analysis of competing patterns, frequencies have been grouped by affix. However, the frequency of each individual form is unequal, so a word with a very high frequency will influence the results obtained for the whole process. This is why an analysis by doublet may give results that are quite different to the results of the competing pattern.

iii) The semantic classification of concordances, even if it has proved necessary for a more fine-grained analysis of competition, is of necessity subject to a certain degree of subjectivity on the part of the annotator. For most of the data, no measure of inter- or intra-rater reliability has been performed due to the limitation of resources available in this book, but the annotation has been supervised by and consulted with an additional informant. Besides, the test performed on a small proportion of the data (Lara-Clares & Fernández-Alcaina 2024) show a fair agreement of annotation between two humans on Krippendorff's alpha). This book thus assumes that the remaining variability in the annotation (both inter- and intra-rater) is preferable over an analysis based on the frequencies of the forms disregarding their polysemy.

iv) The frequencies of the forms after semantic classification are low for the majority of the competitors, and this makes statistical analysis difficult (see, e.g., Bonami & Thuilier 2019: 6). Nonetheless, it was not possible to manually classify larger numbers of data due to the time limitations inherent to this book.

This book does not exhaust all possibilities of analysis of the data obtained and there are also various ways in which the sample could be expanded. In what follows, some research avenues are listed for further research:

i) An examination of the role played by a larger number of constraints and how they are interrelated, as in Varvara (2020), in particular as regards the effects of:
   a. the semantics and argument structure of bases (as in Iordăchioaia et al. 2020; Huyghe et al. 2023) or derivatives (Alexiadou et al. 2013; Iordăchioaia 2019; Schirakowski 2020),
   b. language varieties, in order to explore potential regional preferences, and
   c. other factors, such as borrowing or lexicalisation.

ii) An exploration of the role played by other forms within the derivational paradigm (see Fernández-Alcaina 2021a, 2021b) and by derivational series (see Fradin 2019).
iii) A comparison of the results obtained from the BNC and the results available in more up-to-date corpora, such as *News on the Web* (NOW, Davies 2016–), or better balanced corpora as regards mode.
iv) The sample could be enlarged by:
   a. increased number of senses and affixes analysed, or
   b. additional word-formation processes such as compounding (see Štekauer 2017).
v) A comparison of the results obtained from corpus research with results from speakers' questionnaires (as in Schirakowski 2020). This would allow complementing the analysis of larger quantities of data with information on:
   a. the speakers' intuitions on the differences between word-formation processes, or
   b. the decisions speakers of different backgrounds take when choosing a method for word formation (see Štekauer et al. 2005; Körtvélyessy et al. 2015).

The main specific findings are, therefore, that the four competing patterns show specialisation as regards register and that, when pairs of competitors are examined, semantic differences are frequent (as claimed by Aronoff 2023: 57). However, the limitations of corpus research, especially when manual annotation of data is involved, cannot be overlooked. It should also be recalled that language evolution may cause changes in the preference system and, thus, a natural or productive process may become dispreferred (see, e.g., Luschützky 2015: 124). For these reasons, it is not possible to predict whether one pattern will prevail over another; it is only possible to examine how the competition is resolved up to PDE.

Appendices

Appendix 1: Data of *-ation*/zero-affixation ACTION

A. Template of the competing pattern *-ation*/zero-affixation for the sense ACTION in PDE (all bases are verbal)

Competing forms	Sense OED	Meaning	Senses				Freq.	Timeline	
		Def. (OED)	*In use*	*Obs./ Dat.*	*Dial.*	*Reg./ Dom.*	*BNC*	*Earliest*	*†*
registration	1	the action of registering or recording something	3				2,302	?1566	
register	6	registration; the action of registering	8	3	2	2	2,633	1563	
exhortation	1	the action or process of exhorting, of earnestly admonishing or urging to what is deemed laudable conduct	3				187	1382	
exhort		exhortation		1			3	c1475	1829
alimentation	1	provision of a means of living	1			1	1	1590	
aliment	2	provision for the maintenance of a person	1			1	4	1563	
disputation	1a	action of disputing or debating (questions, etc.)	1	3			23	1489	
dispute	1a	the act of disputing or arguing against	3	1			4,435	[a1400	
curation	1	the action of curing		2			5	c1374	1677
cure	6a	the action or process of healing a wound, a disease, or a sick person	4	5		1	1,095	c1300	
experimentation		the action or process of experimenting or making experiments	1				361	1674	
experiment	4a	the process or practice of conducting such operations; experimentation	3	3			5,585	1678	
importation	1	the action or practice of importing a commodity, merchandise, goods, etc., from another country or territory for use or resale in the domestic market	2			1	172	a1558	
import	3 (II)	the action of bringing something in from elsewhere	5				2,814	1592	
transportation	1a	The action or process of transporting	2	1	1	1	552	1540	
transport	1a	the action of carrying or conveying a thing or person from one place to another	3	2			7,996	1611	

B. Graph of cooccurrences of *importation* for the sense ACTION

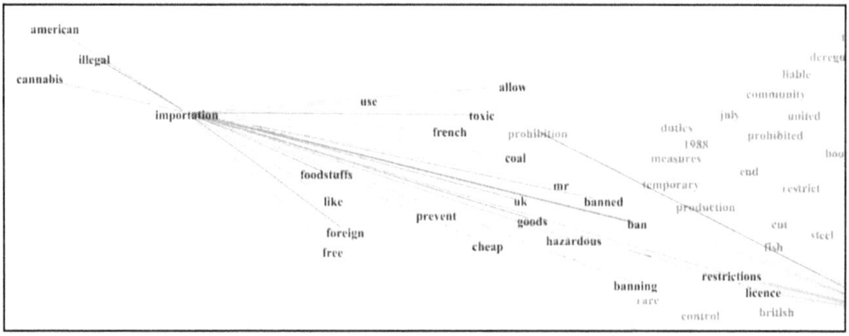

C. Graph of cooccurrences of *import*[N] for the sense ACTION

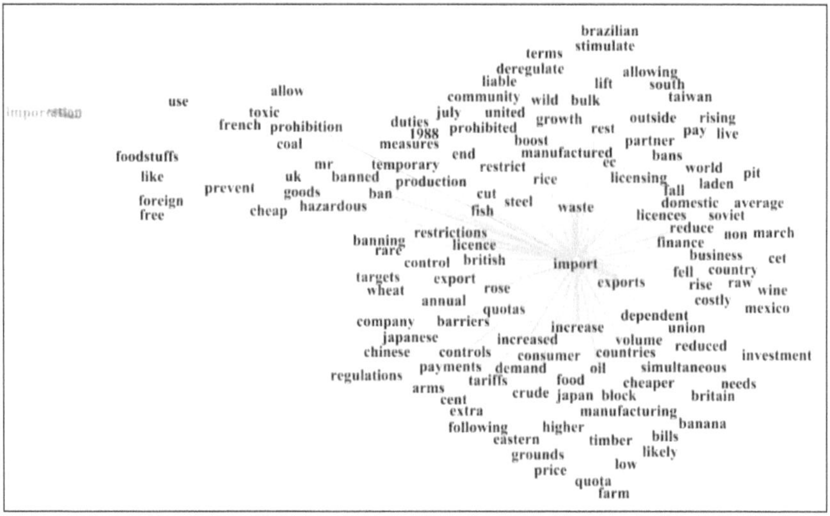

Appendix 2: Data of *-er*/zero-affixation AGENTIVE

A. Template of the competing pattern *-er*/zero-affixation for the sense AGENTIVE in PDE (all bases are verbal)

Competing forms	Sense OED	Meaning	Senses				Freq.	Timeline	
		Def. (OED)	*In use*	*Obs./ Dat.*	*Dial.*	*Reg./ Dom.*	*BNC*	*Earliest*	*†*
adulterer	1, 2	a person who commits adultery/a person who adulterates, corrupts, or debase	2				32	a1382	
adulter		an adulterer, esp. a male one.		1			1	c1384	1994
aider		A person who, or thing which, provides aid or assistance	1				34	1483	
aid	3b	A person who provides assistance or support, esp. to a person in authority	4			2	7,545	1569	
bilker		One who practises cheating; esp. one who evades payment of a cabman's fare.				1	1	1717	
bilk	4	A person who bilks or cheats; a cheat.	1	2		1	4	1790	
cheater	3	One who cheats or deals fraudulently; a deceiver; a swindler. A systematic or habitual cheater is now called a cheat n.1	1	3		1	11	1606	
cheat	5b	One who cheats; a swindler.	3	6			206	1664	
crammer	2a	One who 'crams' pupils for an examination, etc.	1			2	16	1814	
cram	4b	= crammer n. 2	2			3	7	1861	
gouger	1b	One who gouges: (b) one who cheats, a swindler.	1		1		31	1790	
gouge	3b	A cheat, swindle (cf. gouge v. 4). 'Also, an impostor'	1			2	64	1845	
grabber		One who or that which grabs; esp. in (or short for) the combination land-grabber n.	2			1	172	a1558	
grab	3	One who grabs	5				2,814	1592	

(*Continued*)

Appendix 2: **(*Continued*)**

Competing forms	Sense OED	Meaning	Senses				Freq.	Timeline	
		Def. (OED)	***In use***	***Obs./ Dat.***	***Dial.***	***Reg./ Dom.***	**BNC**	***Earliest***	***†***
grubber	3	One who gets together wealth by sordid or contemptible methods. Now usually money-grubber	2	1	1	1	552	1540	
grub	2c	Perhaps: a money-grubber.	3	2			7,996	1611	
kicker	1a	One that kicks; spec. a horse or other animal given to kicking.	3			4	58	1574	
kick	3	One who kicks. Usually with adjective: A (good or bad) kicker, esp. in football.	6	1			1,618	1530	
lifter	1b	One who takes up dishonestly	2				56	a1592	
lift	6	One who lifts or takes away and appropriates (something); a thief.	2	1	1	3	2,699	1591	1630
nagger		A person who nags; something which nags at or bothers one continuously.	1				2	1881	
nag	n2	A person who habitually nags or finds fault.	2				72	1850	
nipper	3	Originally: a stealer of purses, etc. (see nip v.1 7b). Later (more generally): a thief; (also) a swindler.	4	3		1	35	1585	1899
nip	7a	A pickpocket; a cutpurse.	3	2		6	85	1591	1658
scrubber	1	One who, or something which scrubs.	2				47	1839	
scrub	3	One who scrubs; a hard-worked servant, a drudge. Perhaps with some reference to scrub n.1 5a.	4				274	1707	
shadower	3	One who follows another in order to keep watch upon his actions, a spy.	2	1			4	1889	
shadow	8b	A spy or detective who follows a person in order to keep watch upon his movements.	8	2		4	4,236	1859	

Competing forms	Sense OED	Meaning	Senses				Freq.	Timeline	
		Def. (OED)	*In use*	*Obs./ Dat.*	*Dial.*	*Reg./ Dom.*	*BNC*	*Earliest*	*†*
skulker	1	One who skulks, in various senses. †Also as a name for the hare.	2			1	1	1387	
skulk	1	One who skulks or hides himself; a shirker.	2	1			3	c1320	
snipper	2	One who snips or clips; spec. a tailor.	3				1	1611	
snip	7	A tailor. Also employed as an allusive personal name for a tailor.	7	1		2	94	1600	
snooper	1	One who pries or peeps; spec. one who makes an intrusive official investigation.	1	1			21	1889	
snoop	1	= snooper n. 1; spec. one who makes official or other investigation, a detective.	1			1	13	1891	
swanker		One who swanks.				1	1	a1846	
swank	2	-= swanker n.2				2	8	1913	
sweeper	2a	A person employed in sweeping a room, chimney, house, ship, etc.; spec. in India, a person of the lowest caste. Also in combination, as chimney-sweeper n., crossing-sweeper n. at crossing n.	3	2	1	1	180	1657	
sweep	VI, 33a	A chimney-sweeper.	26	3		5	570	1812	

B. Graph of cooccurrences of *cheater* for the sense AGENTIVE

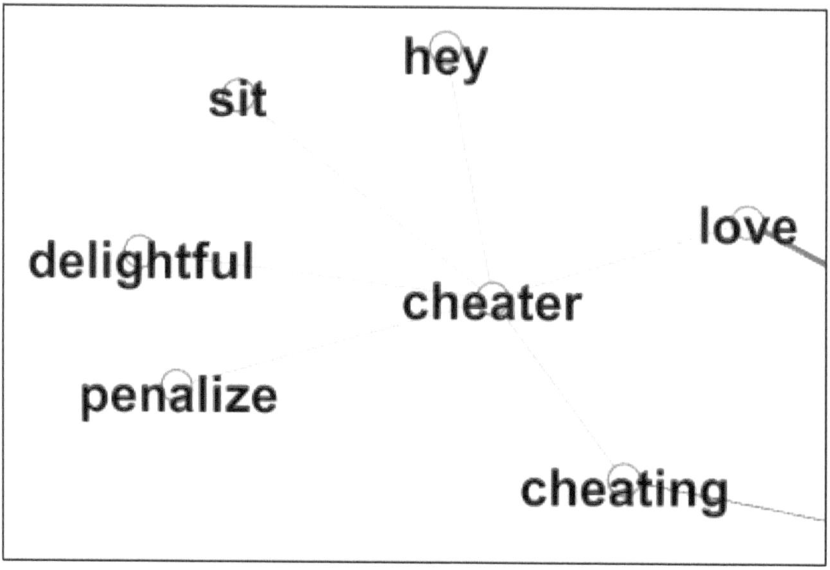

C. Graph of cooccurrences of *cheat*[N] for the sense AGENTIVE

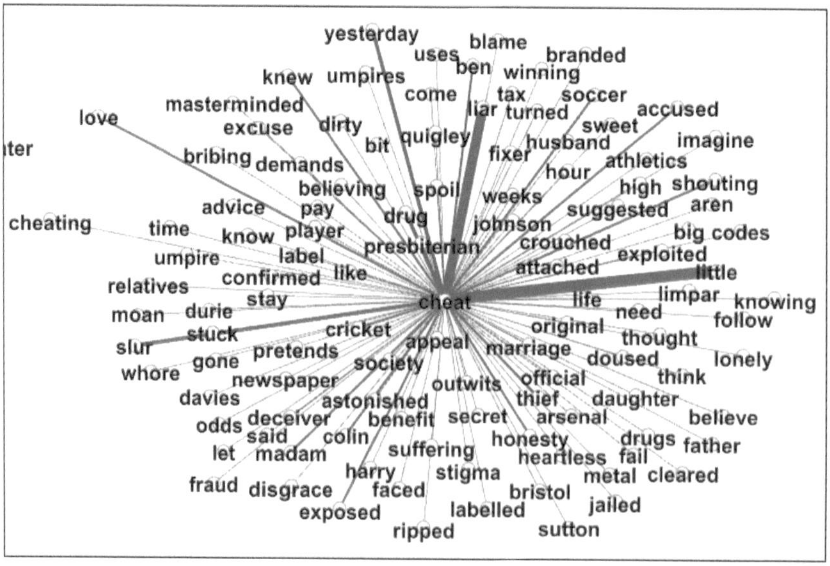

Appendix 3: Data of -ER/zero-affixation INSTRUMENT

A. Template of the competing pattern *-er*/zero-affixation for the sense INSTRUMENT in PDE (all bases are verbal)

Competing forms	Sense OED	Meaning	Senses				Freq.	Timeline	
		Def. (OED)	*In use*	*Obs./ Dat.*	*Dial.*	*Reg./ Dom.*	*BNC*	*Earliest*	*†*
bolter	2	A piece of cloth used for sifting; a sieve, strainer; a bolting-machine.	3				6	1530	
bolt	1	A flour-sieve, a boulter.	2				1,199	c1425	
bracer	1	That which clamps, binds, etc.; a cincture, bandage, brace; †also a pair of braces (*obsolete*).	1	1		1	1	1579	
brace	II	That which clasps, tightens, secures, connects	9	5		5	392	c1440	
clapper	1	the clack n. or clap n.1 of a mill.	4	2		2	30	1340	
clap	9	The clapper of a mill; = clack n. 3, clapper n.1 1.	5	7		2	88	?c1225	
clasper	1a	One who or that which clasps; a means for holding fast: often used more or less technically.	2				8	1551	
clasp	1	A means of fastening, generally of metal, consisting of two interlocking parts.	4	2			99	c1325	
clipper		He who or that which clips or clasps; in plural = clip-hook n.	1				95	1849	
clip	2a	That which clips or clasps; an instrument or device which clasps or grips objects tightly and so holds them fast	1	1			496	1488	
creeper	5	A kind of grapnel used for dragging the bottom of the sea or other body of water.	8	1	1	2	93	?a1400	
creep	5	= creeper n. 5.	7			2	226	1889	
curber	1	One who or that which curbs, or restrains.	1	1			1	1610	

(*Continued*)

Appendix 3: ***(Continued)***

Competing forms	Sense	Meaning	Senses				Freq.	Timeline	
	OED	*Def. (OED)*	*In use*	*Obs./ Dat.*	*Dial.*	*Reg./ Dom.*	*BNC*	*Earliest*	†
curb	I (1, 2)	Something that curbs or restrains.	10	3		1	66	1477	
downer	4	A depressant or tranquillizing drug, especially a barbiturate.	1	1		4	30	1966	
down	1d	A depressant or tranquillizing drug, especially a barbiturate; = downer n. 4. Cf. up n. 7. Frequently in plural.	2	2		3	1,535	1967	
flapper	2	Something flat to strike with; a fly-flap	5				27	1570	
flap	3	Something broad to strike with; esp. a fly-flapper	4	2	1	2	518	c1440	1726
griller	2	A grilling apparatus (in a cooking stove).	2				1	1895	
grill	1b	In modern use: a gas burner (on a gas cooker), or a hot plate or a set of elements (on an electric cooker), which directs radiant heat downwards.	2				451	1907	
hacker	1a	An implement used for hacking, chopping, or cutting; a chopper; spec. an axe or other tool for cutting wood or branches, a cleaver.	2			1	105	c1398	
hack	1	A tool or implement for breaking or chopping up.	6	2			187	1333	
muffler	1a,b	A wrap or scarf (frequently of wool or silk) worn round the neck or throat for warmth. Also gen.: anything used to wrap a part of the body, esp. the head or face.	2	2		1	19	1536	
muffle	1a	Something that muffles or covers the face or neck; a muffler. Also in extended use.	3				5	1539	
pitcher	4, 5	A cutting, rod, or stake planted in the ground in order to take root//An iron bar for making holes in the ground, esp. for setting stakes or hop-poles.	2	2	2	1	106	1707	

Competing forms	Sense OED	Meaning	Senses				Freq.	Timeline	
		Def. (OED)	*In use*	*Obs./ Dat.*	*Dial.*	*Reg./ Dom.*	*BNC*	*Earliest*	*†*
pitch	11	= pitcher n.2 5. /= pitcher n.2 4.	15	3	2	8	2,930	1589	
preserver	2b	In plural. Spectacles for preserving the eyesight.	2				36	1773	1891
preserve	1c	In plural. Goggles used to protect the eyes from dust, bright light, etc.	2	2			234	1883	1893
scraper	4	A scraping instrument held in the hand.	7	1	1	1	66	1552	
scrape	1a	An instrument for scraping, a scraper.	7		1		181	c1440	1688
slicker	1	A tool used for scraping or smoothing leather.//A tool used for smoothing the surfaces of moulds in founding.	2		2		32	1852	
slick	1c	An implement used for slicking; a slicker.	4	1	2	1	231	1883	
slider	5a	A device for holding, and inserting in a microscope, the glass or other plates with the objects to be studied.	4	2		1	33	1703	1855
slide	7a	A slip of glass or other material on which an object is mounted or placed to facilitate its examination by a microscope.	11			1	1,376	1837	
stamper	3	An instrument used in stamping.	3	2			14	1484	
stamp	5/10	An instrument for making impressions, marks, or imprints, on other bodies//A machine for pounding hides to soften them.	9	5		4	1,614	1465	
strainer	1a	A utensil or device for straining, filtering, or sifting; a filter, sieve, screen, or the like.	3				39	1326	
strain	1	A strainer.	7	7		1	2,798	1432	1655
sweeper	1b	A broom for sweeping out an oven	3	2	1	1	180	c1440	1580

(*Continued*)

Appendix 3: (*Continued*)

Competing forms	**Sense OED**	**Meaning**	**Senses**				**Freq.**	**Timeline**	
		Def. (OED)	***In use***	***Obs./ Dat.***	***Dial.***	***Reg./ Dom.***	***BNC***	***Earliest***	*†*
sweep	V, 23	A broom or mop: in oven-swepe.	26	3		5	570	c1475	c1475
twitcher	2d	A device for restraining a horse during shoeing, veterinary procedures, etc.; = twitch n.1 1b.	2	2		1	8	1688	1880
twitch	1b	A loop or noose; spec. a small loop of cord attached to a stick, used to restrain a horse during shoeing, veterinary procedures, etc[…]; (later also) an instrument consisting of two metal branches joined by a hinge, placed on the lip, etc., of a horse for the same purpose.	4	2		2	127	1783	
whisker	1	Something that whisks or is used for whisking: applied to various objects, as a fan; a rod or switch; a bunch of feathers used as a brush	3	2		2	250	c1425	1825
whisk	4	A bundle or tuft of twigs, hair, feathers, etc. fixed on a handle, used for brushing or dusting; also, a water-sprinkler.	4	1		1	54	1745	
wiper	2a	A cloth or other appliance used for wiping; in slang use, a handkerchief	4			2	202	1587	
wipe	4	A handkerchief.	3			2	70	1708	
wrapper	I	Something that wraps or enfolds, and related uses.	2	1	1	4	174	c1460	
wrap	1	A wrapper or covering.	4			1	290	c1460	

B. Graph of cooccurrences of *clipper* for the sense INSTRUMENT

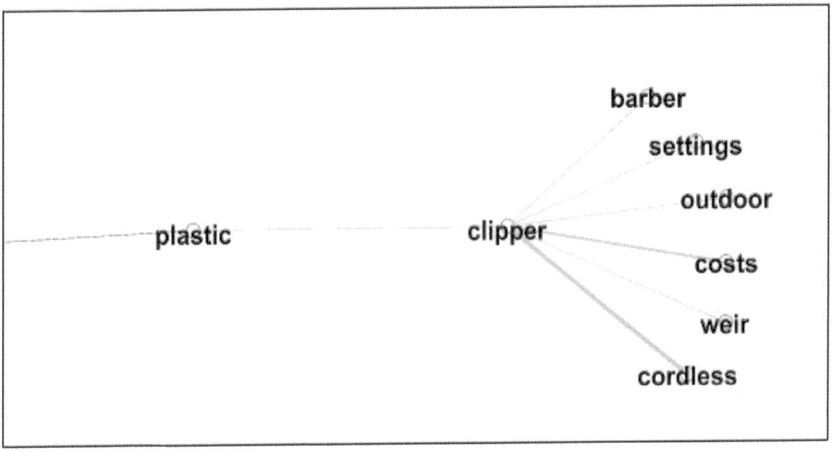

C. Graph of cooccurrences of *clip*N for the sense INSTRUMENT

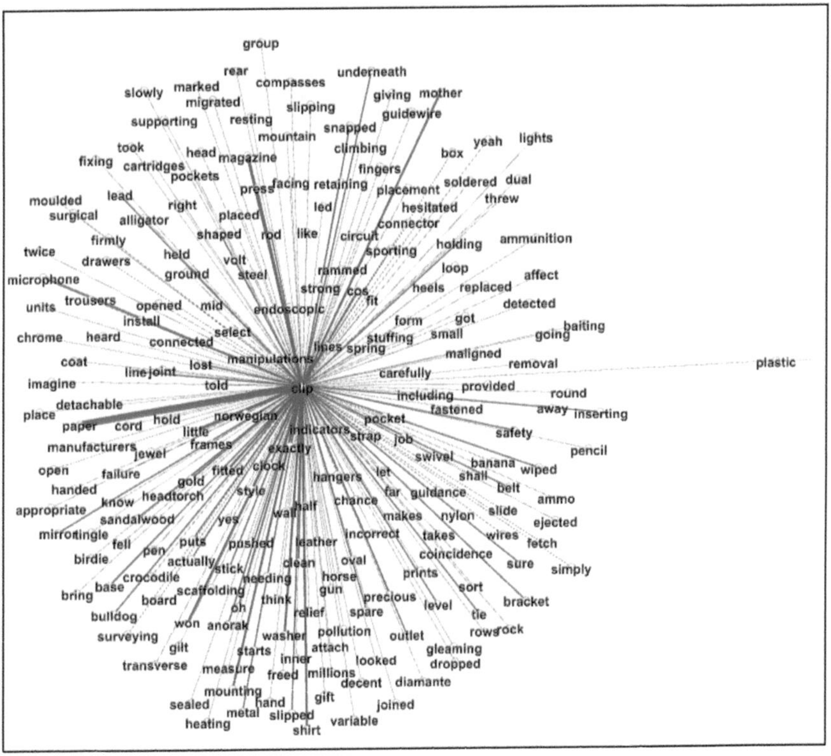

D. Graph of cooccurrences of *wrapper* for the sense INSTRUMENT

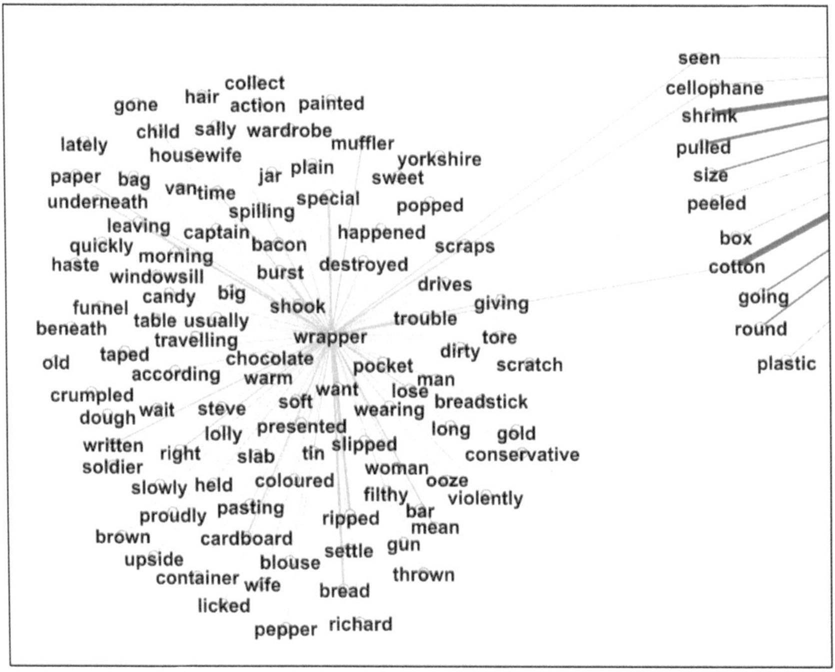

E. Graph of cooccurrences of *wrap*[N] for the sense INSTRUMENT

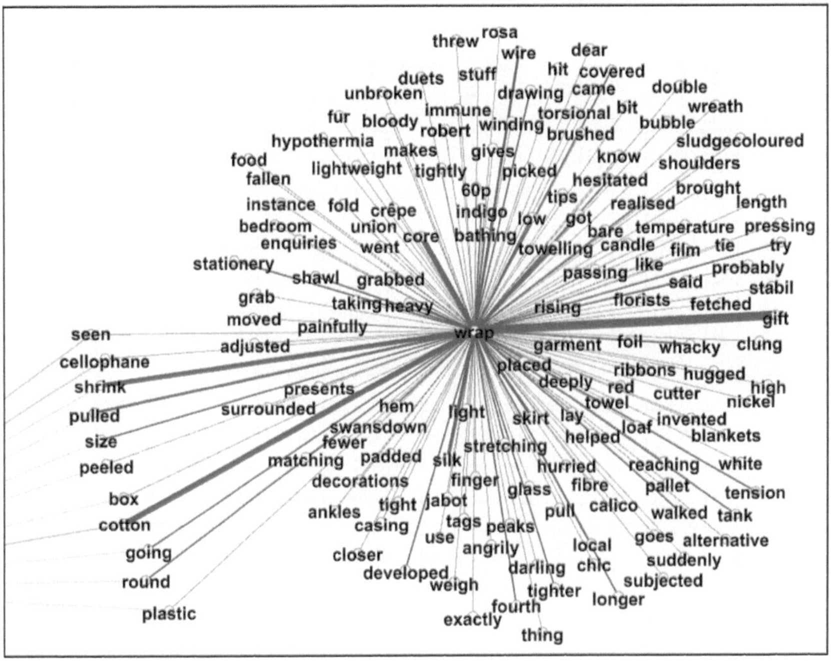

Appendix 4: Data of -NESS/zero-affixation STATE

A. Template of the competing pattern *-ness*/zero-affixation for the sense STATE in PDE (all bases are adjectival)

Competing forms	Sense OED	Meaning	Senses				Freq.	Timeline	
		Def. (OED)	*In use*	*Obs./ Dat.*	*Dial.*	*Reg./ Dom.*	*BNC*	*Earliest*	*†*
alertness		condition of being alert	1				86	1714	
alert	2	state of being alert	3				193	1801	
coolness	1	fact or condition of being or feeling cool; cool quality or sensation	3			1	134	OE	
cool	2b	coolness; cool conditions	2	1	1	2	156	a1500	1905
darkness		quality or state of being dark	7			1	3132	a1050	
dark	1[a]	dark state or condition	5				3139	a1300	
dryness	1[a], 4	quality or condition of being dry	2	1		1	123	1398	
dry	1[a]	dry state or condition	5	1			2	c1200	
faintness		state or condition of being faint	4				19	1398	
faint	1	faintness	1	1			32	c1320	1600
hotness	1	quality or state of being hot	1				16	OE	
hot	1	fact or quality of being hot	1		1	1	40	OE	
lowness	1	low rank or status; humble, poor, or lowly state	7				5	?c1225	
low	2	state or condition of being low; low position	7			2	356	a1225	
savageness		quality or state of being savage ; barbarity, ferocity, cruelty	1				1	a1400	
savage	2	savageness; ferocity	2	2			307	c1487	c1487
warmness		condition of being warm, warmth		5			3	c1000	168
warm	1	a state, or sensation, of being warm	1	1			3	a1250	1839

B. Graph of cooccurrences of *alertness* for the sense STATE

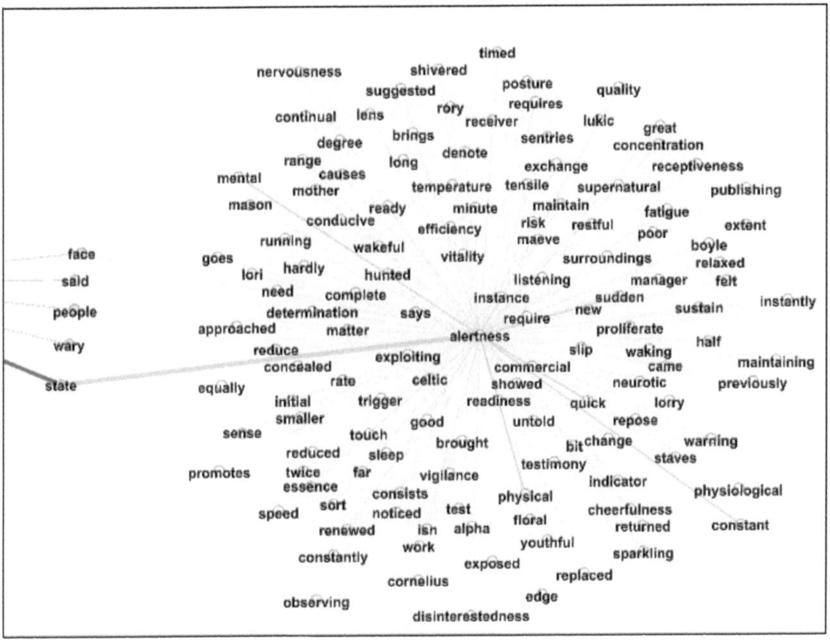

C. Graph of cooccurrences of *alert*[N] for the sense STATE

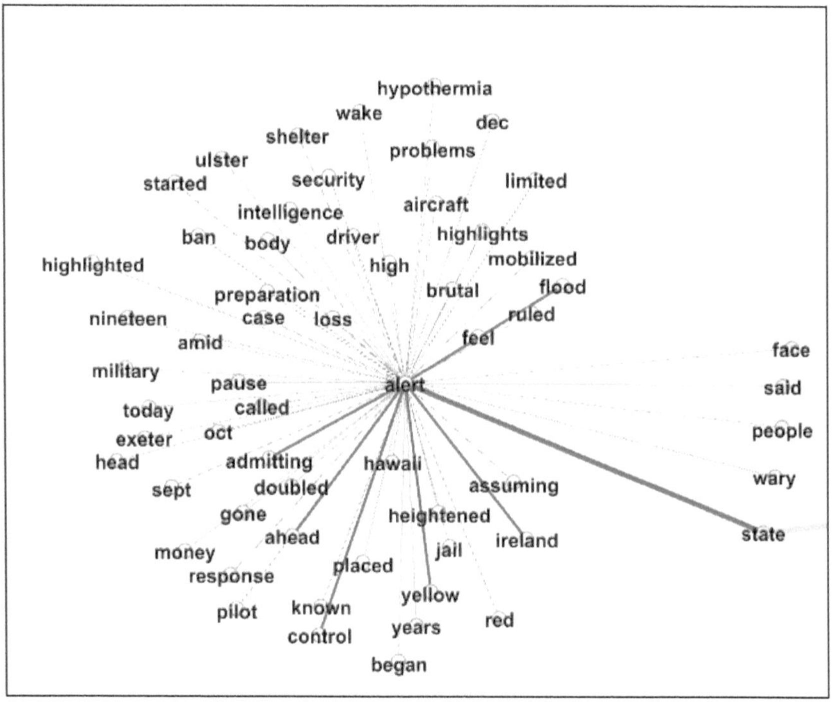

D. Graph of cooccurrences of *darkness*[N] for the sense STATE

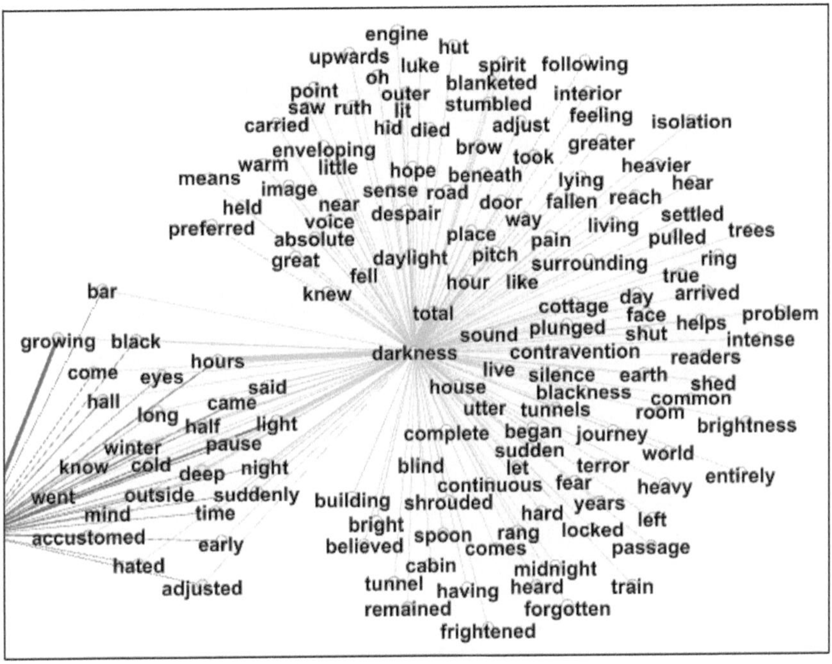

E. Graph of cooccurrences of *dark*[N] for the sense STATE

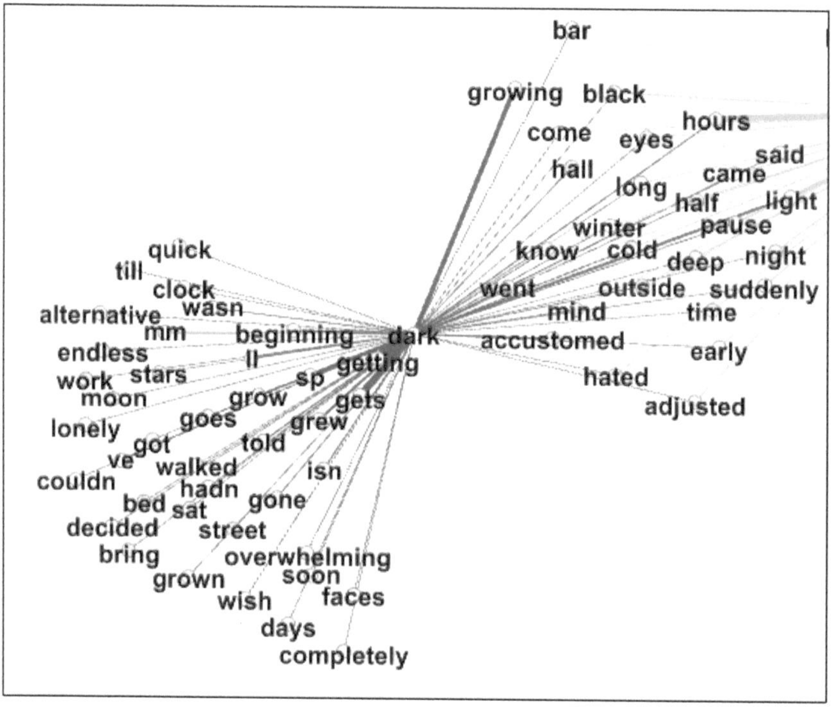

References

Adams, Valerie. 1973. *An introduction to Modern English word-formation*. London: Longman.

Alexiadou, Artemis & Iordăchioaia, Gianina & Cano, Mariángeles & Martin, Fabienne & Schäfer, Florian. 2013. The realization of external arguments in nominalizations. *The Journal of Comparative Germanic Linguistics* 16. 73–95. https://doi.org/10.1007/s10828-014-9062-x

Allan, Kathryn. 2012. Using OED data as evidence for researching semantic change. In Allan, Kathryn & Robinson, Justyna A. (eds.), *Current methods in historical semantics*, 17–40. Berlin: De Gruyter Mouton. https://doi.org/10.1515/9783110252903.17

Amutio-Palacios, Silvia. 2013. Suffix competition in Old English word formation. *Revista Electrónica de Lingüística Aplicada* 12. 45–62.

Andersen, Henning. 2008. Naturalness and markedness. In Willems, Klass & De Cuypere, Ludovic (eds.), *Naturalness and iconicity in language*, 101–119. Amsterdam: John Benjamins. https://doi.org/10.1075/ill.7.07and

Anttila, Raimo. 1972. *An introduction to historical and comparative linguistics*. New York, NY: MacMillan.

Anshen, Frank & Aronoff, Mark. 1988. Producing morphologically complex words. *Linguistics* 26. 641–655.

Antoniová, Vesna & Štekauer, Pavol. 2015. Derivational paradigms within selected conceptual fields – contrastive research. *Facta Universitatis* 13(2). 61–75.

Arndt-Lappe, Sabine. 2014. Analogy in suffix rivalry: The case of English *-ity* and *-ness*. *English Language and Linguistics* 18(3). 497–548. https://doi.org/10.1017/S136067431400015X

Aronoff, Mark. 1976. *Word-formation in Generative Grammar*. Cambridge, MA: MIT Press.

Aronoff, Mark. 2016. Competition and the lexicon. In Elia, Annibale & Iacobini, Claudio & Voghera, Miriam (eds.), *Livelli di analisi e fenomeni di interfaccia. Atti del XLVII congresso internazionale della Società di linguistica Italiana*, 39–52. Roma: Bulzoni Editore.

Aronoff, Mark. 2018. Morphology and words: A memoir. In Namer, Fiammetta & Bonami, Olivier (eds.), *The lexeme in descriptive and theoretical morphology*, 3–20. Berlin: Language Sciences Press.

Aronoff, Mark. 2019. Competitors and alternants in linguistic morphology. In Rainer, Franz & Gardani, Francesco & Dressler, Wolfgang U. & Luschützky,

Hans Christian (eds.), *Competition in inflection and word-formation*, 39–66. Dordrecht: Springer. https://doi.org/10.1007/978-3-030-02550-2_2

Aronoff, Mark. 2023. Three ways of looking at morphological rivalry. *Word Structure* 16(1). 49–62. https://doi.org/10.3366/word.2023.0220

Aronoff, Mark & Anshen, Frank. 1981. Morphological productivity and phonological transparency. *Canadian Journal of Linguistics* 26. 63–72. https://doi.org/10.1017/S0008413100023525

Aronoff, Mark & Cho, Sungeon. 2001. The semantics of *-ship* suffixation. *Linguistic Inquiry* 32(1). 167–173. (https://www.jstor.org/stable/4179141) (Accessed 07-02-2022).

Aronoff, Mark & Lindsay, Mark. 2014. Productivity, blocking, and lexicalization. In Lieber, Rochelle & Štekauer, Pavol (eds.), *The Oxford handbook of derivation*, 67–83. Oxford: Oxford University Press. https://doi.org/10.1093/oxfordhb/9780199641642.013.0005

Baayen, Harald. 1993. On frequency, transparency and productivity. In Booij, Geert & van Marle, Jaap (eds.), *Yearbook of morphology 1992*, 181–208. Dordrecht: Kluwer.

Baayen, Harald. 1994. Productivity in language production. *Language and Cognitive Processes* 9. 447–469. https://doi.org/10.1080/01690969408402127

Baayen, Harald. 2009. Corpus linguistics in morphology: Morphological productivity. In Lüdeling, Anke & Kytö, Merja (eds.), *Corpus linguistics: An international handbook*, 899–919. Berlin: De Gruyter Mouton. https://doi.org/10.1515/9783110213881.2.899

Baayen, Harald & Endresen, Anna & Janda, Laura A. & Makarova, Anastasia & Nesset, Tore. 2013. Making choices in Russian: Pros and cons of statistical methods for rival affixes. *Russian Linguistics* 37(3). 253–291.

Baayen, Harald & Lieber, Rochelle. 1991. Productivity and English derivation: A corpus-based study. *Linguistics* 29. 801–843. https://doi.org/10.1515/ling.1991.29.5.801

Baayen, Harald & Renouf, Antoinette. 1996. Chronicling the Times: Productive lexical innovations in an English newspaper. *Language* 72(1). 69–96. https://doi.org/10.2307/416794

Baeskow, Heike. 2010. His Lordship's *-ship* and the King of Golfdom: Against a purely functional analysis of suffixhood. *Word Structure* 3(1). 1–30. https://doi.org/10.3366/E1750124510000474

Baeskow, Heike. 2012. *-Ness* and *-ity*: Phonological exponents of *n* or meaningful nominalizer of different adjectival domains? *Journal of English Linguistics* 40(1). 6–40. https://doi.org/10.1177/0075424211405156

Bagasheva, Alexandra. 2017. Comparative semantic concepts in affixation. In Santana-Lario, Juan & Valera, Salvador (eds.), *Competing patterns in English affixation*, 33–65. Bern: Peter Lang.

Bagasheva, Alexandra & Nagano, Akiko & Renner, Vincent (eds.). 2024. *Competition in Word-Formation*. Amsterdam: John Benjamins. https://doi.org/10.1075/la.284

Bauer, Laurie. 1983. *English word-formation*. Cambridge: Cambridge University Press. https://doi.org/10.1017/CBO9781139165846

Bauer, Laurie. 1997. Derivational paradigms. In Booij, Geert & van Marle, Jaap (eds.), *Yearbook of morphology 1996*, 243–256. Dordrecht: Kluwer.

Bauer, Laurie. 2001. *Morphological productivity*. Cambridge: Cambridge University Press. https://doi.org/10.1017/CBO9780511486210

Bauer, Laurie. 2009. Competition in English word-formation. In van Kemenade, Ans & Los, Bettelou (eds.), *The handbook of the history of English*, 177–198. Malden, MA: Blackwell.

Bauer, Laurie. 2014. 'What is the plural of mouse?' and other unhelpful questions for morphologists. (Plenary lecture delivered at the *47th Annual Meeting of the Societas Linguistica Europaea* (SLE), Poznań, 11–14 September 2014).

Bauer, Laurie & Lieber, Rochelle & Plag, Ingo. 2013. *The Oxford reference guide to English morphology*. Oxford: Oxford University Press. https://doi.org/10.1093/acprof:oso/9780198747062.001.0001

Bauer, Laurie & Valera, Salvador. 2015. Sense inheritance in English word-formation. In Bauer, Laurie & Körtvelyéssy, Lívia & Štekauer, Pavol (eds.), *Semantics of complex words*, 67–84. Dordrecht: Springer. https://doi.org/10.1007/978-3-319-14102-2_5

Bauer, Laurie & Valera, Salvador & Díaz-Negrillo, Ana. 2010. Affixation vs. conversion: The resolution of conflicting patterns. In Rainer, Franz & Dressler, Wolfgang U. & Kastovsky, Dieter & Luschützky, Hans Christian (eds.), *Variation and change in morphology: Selected papers from the 13th International Morphology Meeting, Vienna, February 2008*, 15–32. Amsterdam: John Benjamins. https://doi.org/10.1075/cilt.310.01bau

Baugh, Albert C. & Cable, Thomas. 2013. *A history of the English language*. London: Routledge.

Benítez-Castro, Miguel-Ángel & Valera, Salvador. 2010. Estudio de corpus sobre la complejidad morfológica en inglés académico escrito. In *Memorias del séptimo Simposium Iberoamericano en Educación, Cibernética e Informática* (SIECI 2010), 175–180. (http://www.iiis.org/CDs2010/CD2010CSC/SIECI_2010/PapersPdf/XA218YL.pdf) (Accessed 07-02-2022).

Benveniste, Émile. 1948. *Noms d'agent et noms d'action en indo-européen*. Paris: Adrien-Maisonneuve.

Bolinger, Dwight. 1977. *Meaning and form*. London: Longman.

Bonami, Olivier & Guzmán Naranjo, Matías. 2023. Distributional evidence for derivational paradigms. In Kotowski, Sven & Plag, Ingo (eds.), *The semantics of derivational morphology: Theory, methods, evidence*, 219–258. Berlin: De Gruyter. https://doi.org/10.1515/9783111074917-008

Bonami, Olivier & Thuilier, Juliette. 2019. A statistical approach to rivalry in lexeme formation: French *-iser* and *-ifier*. *Word Structure* 12(1). 4–41. https://doi.org/10.3366/word.2018.0130

Booij, Geert. 1993. Against Split Morphology. In Booij, Geert & van Marle, Jaap (eds.), *Yearbook of morphology 1993*, 27–49. Dordrecht: Kluwer.

Booij, Geert. 1996. Inherent versus contextual inflection and the Split Morphology hypothesis. In Booij, Geert & van Marle, Jaap (eds.), *Yearbook of morphology 1995*, 1–16. Dordrecht: Kluwer.

Booij Geert. 2007. Polysemy and construction morphology. In Moerdijk, Fons & van Santen, Ariane & Tempelaars, Rob (eds.), *Leven met woorden: Afscheidsbundel voor professor Piet van Sterkenburg*, 355–364. Leiden: Instituut voor Nederlandse Lexicologie.

Booij, Geert. 2010. *Construction Morphology*. Oxford: Oxford University Press. https://doi.org/10.1111/j.1749-818X.2010.00213.x

Booij, Geert. 2020. Principles of word formation. In Putnam, Michael T. & Page, B. Richard (eds.), *The Cambridge handbook of Germanic linguistics*, 238–258. Cambridge: Cambridge University Press. https://doi.org/10.1017/9781108378291.012

Bram, Barli. 2011. *Major total conversion in English: The question of directionality*. Wellington: Victoria University of Wellington (Doctoral dissertation).

Bréal, Michel. 1897. *Essai de sémantique*. Paris: Hachette.

Brezina, Vaclav. 2018. *Statistics in corpus linguistics: A practical guide*. Cambridge: Cambridge University Press.

Bybee, Joan. 1985. *Morphology: A study of the relation between meaning and form*. Amsterdam: John Benjamins. https://doi.org/10.1075/tsl.9

Cambridge Dictionary. 2022. (https://dictionary.cambridge.org) (Accessed 18-07-2022).

Carstairs-McCarthy, Andrew. 1992. *Current morphology*. London: Routledge. https://doi.org/10.1017/S0952675700001640

Carstairs-McCarthy, Andrew. 2010. *The evolution of morphology*. Oxford: Oxford University Press. https://doi.org/10.1093/oxfordhb/9780199541119.013.0047

Cetnarowska, Bożena. 1993. *The syntax, semantics and derivation of bare nominalizations in English*. Katowice: Uniwersytet Śląski (Doctoral dissertation) (https://core.ac.uk/download/pdf/197749102.pdf) (Accessed 10-01-2022).

Collins Online Dictionary. 2022. (https://www.collinsdictionary.com) (Accessed 18-07-2022).

Corbett, Greville G. 2005. The canonical approach to typology. In Frajzyngier, Zygmunt & Hodges, Adam & Rood, David S. (eds.), *Linguistic diversity and language theories*, 25–49. Amsterdam: John Benjamins. https://doi.org/10.1075/slcs.72.03cor

Corbett, Greville G. 2010. Canonical derivational morphology. *Word Structure* 3, 141–155. https://doi.org/10.3366/word.2010.0002

Corbin, Danielle. 1987. *Morphologie dérivationelle et structuration du lexique*. Tübingen: Max Niemeyer.

Crocco Galèas, Grazia. 1990. Conversion as morphological metaphor. In Méndez Dosuna, Julián & Pensado, Carmen (eds.), *Naturalists at Krems. Papers from the Workshop on Natural Phonology and Morphology*, 23–32. Salamanca: Ediciones de la Universidad de Salamanca.

Crocco Galèas, Grazia. 1998. *The parameters of Natural Morphology*. Padova: Unipress.

Crocco Galèas, Grazia. 2001. *What is Natural Morphology? The state of the art*. (https://www.academia.edu/9873677/WHAT_IS_NATURAL_MORPHOLOGY_THE_STATE_OF_THE_ART) (Accessed 06-11-2021).

Darwin, Charles R. 1859. *On the origin of species by means of natural selection, or the preservation of favoured races in the struggle for life*. London: Murray.

Davies, Mark. 2004. *British National Corpus* (from Oxford University Press) (https://www.english-corpora.org/bnc/) (Accessed 06-02-2022).

Davies, Mark. 2008–. *The Corpus of Contemporary American English (COCA)* (https://www.english-corpora.org/coca/) (Accessed 06-02-2022).

Davies, Mark. 2016–. *Corpus of News on the Web* (NOW). (https://www.english-corpora.org/now/) (Accessed 10-02-2023).

Davies, Mark. 2018. *The iWeb Corpus* (https://www.english-corpora.org/iWeb/) (Accessed 06-02-2022).

de Saussure, Ferdinand. 1959 [1916]. *Course in general linguistics*. Translated by Wade Baskin. New York, NY: Philosophical library.

Díaz-Negrillo, Ana. 2017. On the identification of competition in English derivational morphemes. The case of *-dom*, *-hood* and *-ship*. In Santana-Lario, Juan & Valera, Salvador (eds.), *Competing patterns in English affixation*, 119–162. Bern: Peter Lang.

Díaz-Negrillo, Ana. 2020. Neoclassical word formation in English: A paradigm-based account of *-scope* formations. In Fernández-Domínguez, Jesús & Bagasheva, Alexandra & Lara-Clares, Cristina (eds.), *Paradigmatic relations in word-formation*, 213–261. Leiden: Brill. https://doi.org/10.1163/9789004433410_010

Dietz, Friedrich 1838. *Grammatik der romanischen Sprachen II*. Bonn: Weber.

Dokulil, Miloš. 1964. Zum wechselseitigen Verhältnis zwischen Wortbildung und Syntax. In Lipka, Leonhard & Günther, Hartmut (eds.), *Worbildung*, 82–93. Darmstadt: Wissenschaftliche Buchgesellschaft.

Dokulil, Miloš. 1968. Zur Frage der Konversion und verwandter Wortbildungsvorgänge und -beziehungen. *Travaux linguistiques de Prague* 3. 215–239.

Dressler, Wolfgang U. 1985a. *Morphonology: The dynamics of derivation*. Ann Arbor, MI: Karoma Press.

Dressler, Wolfgang U. 1985b. Typological aspects of Natural Morphology. *Acta Linguistica Hungarica* 35(1–2). 51–70.

Dressler, Wolfgang U. 1987. Word formation as part of Natural Morphology. In Dressler, Wolfgang U. & Mayerthaler, Willi & Panagl, Oswald & Wurzel, Wolfgang U. (eds.), *Leitmotifs in Natural Morphology*, 99–126. Amsterdam: John Benjamins. https://doi.org/10.1075/slcs.10.30dre

Dressler, Wolfgang U. 2005. Word-formation in Natural Morphology. In Štekauer, Pavol & Lieber, Rochelle (eds.), *Handbook of word-formation. Studies in natural language and linguistic theory*, 267–284. Dordrecht: Springer. https://doi.org/10.1007/1-4020-3596-9_11

Dressler, Wolfgang U. 2008. Transdisciplinary aspects of morphological productivity. *European Review* 16(4). 457–466. https://doi.org/10.1017/S1062798708000331

Dressler, Wolfgang U. & Mayerthaler, Willi & Panagl, Oswald & Wurzel, Wolfgang U. 1987. *Leitmotifs in Natural Morphology*. Amsterdam: John Benjamins. https://doi.org/10.1075/slcs.10

Efthymiou, Angeliki & Fragaki, Georgia & Markos, Angelos. 2012. Productivity of verb forming suffixes in Modern Greek: A corpus-based study. *Morphology* 22(4). 515-543. https://doi.org/10.1007/s11525-012-9202-4

Fernández-Alcaina, Cristina. 2017. Availability and unavailability in English word-formation. In Santana-Lario, Juan & Valera, Salvador (eds.), *Competing patterns in English affixation*, 163–206. Bern: Peter Lang.

Fernández-Alcaina, Cristina. 2021a. *Competition in the derivational paradigm of English verbs*. Granada: Universidad de Granada. (Doctoral dissertation) (http://hdl.handle.net/10481/71662) (Accessed 21-12-2021).

Fernández-Alcaina, Cristina. 2021b. *The competition of word-formation processes in the derivational paradigm of verbs: Dia-synchronic evidence for the profile and resolution of competition in English*. Berlin: Peter Lang. https://doi.org/10.3726/b19408

Fernández-Alcaina, Cristina & Čermák, Jan. 2018. Derivational paradigms and competition in English: A diachronic study on competing causative verbs and their derivatives. *SKASE Journal of Theoretical Linguistics* 15(3), 69–97. (http://www.skase.sk/Volumes/JTL38/pdf_doc/04.pdf) (Accessed 21-12-2021).

Fernández-Alcaina, Cristina & Molina-Quesada, María Jesús. 2016. Competition in English plural inflection. (Paper presented at the *4th Meeting of Linguistics Beyond and Within – International Linguistics Conference*, Lublin, 20–21 October 2016).

Fernández-Domínguez, Jesús. 2013. Morphological productivity measurement: Exploring qualitative versus quantitative approaches. *English Studies* 94(4). 422–447. https://doi.org/10.1080/0013838X.2013.780823

Fernández-Domínguez, Jesús. 2017. Methodological and procedural issues in the quantification of morphological competition. In Santana-Lario, Juan & Valera, Salvador (eds.), *Competing patterns in English affixation*, 67–118. Bern: Peter Lang.

Fernández-Domínguez, Jesús. 2024. Actional nominalization in Present-Day English in the light of the Referenced Index of Competition. In Bagasheva, Alexandra & Nagano, Akiko & Renner, Vincent (eds.), *Competition in Word-Formation*. 72–103. Amsterdam: John Benjamins. https://doi.org/10.1075/la.284.03fer

Fernández-Domínguez, Jesús & Díaz-Negrillo, Ana & Štekauer, Pavol. 2007. How is low morphological productivity measured? *Atlantis* 29. 29–54. (https://www.jstor.org/stable/41055264) (Accessed 15-12-2021).

Fradin, Bernard. 2016. What can we learn from doublets? (Paper presented at the *17th International Morphology Meeting*, Vienna, 18–21 February 2016).

Fradin, Bernard. 2019. Competition in derivation: What can we learn from French doublets in *-age* and *-ment*? In Rainer, Franz & Gardani, Francesco & Dressler, Wolfgang U. & Luschützky, Hans Christian (eds.), *Competition in inflection and word-formation*, 67–93. Cham: Springer. https://doi.org/10.1007/978-3-030-02550-2_3

Gaeta, Livio. 2006. How to live naturally and not be bothered by economy. *Folia Linguistica* 40(1–2). 7–28. https://doi.org/10.1515/flin.40.1-2.7

Gaeta, Livio & Ricca, Davide. 2003a. Frequency and productivity in Italian derivation: A comparison between corpus-based and lexicographical data. *Italian Journal of Linguistics/Rivista di Linguistica* 15(1). 63–98.

Gaeta, Livio & Ricca, Davide. 2003b. Italian prefixes and productivity: A quantitative approach. *Acta Linguistica Hungarica* 50(1–2). 93–112. (https://www.jstor.org/stable/26189815) (Accessed 20-12-2021).

Gaeta, Livio & Ricca, Davide. 2015. Productivity. In Müller, Peter O. & Ohnheiser, Ingeborg & Olsen, Susan & Rainer, Franz (eds.), *Word-formation: An international handbook of the languages of Europe*, vol. 2, 842–858. Berlin: De Gruyter Mouton. https://doi.org/10.1515/9783110246278-003

Gardani, Francesco & Rainer, Franz & Luschützky, Hans Christian. 2019. Competition in morphology: A historical outline. In Rainer, Franz & Gardani, Francesco & Dressler, Wolfgang U. & Luschützky, Hans Christian (eds.), *Competition in inflection and word-formation*, 3–36. Cham: Springer.

Gause, George F. 1934. *The struggle for existence*. Baltimore, MD: Williams & Wilkins.

Giegerich, Heinz J. 1999. *Lexical strata in English: Morphological causes, phonological effects*. Cambridge: Cambridge University Press.

Fabrizio Gilardi & Alizadeh, Meysam & Kubli, Maël. 2023. ChatGPT outperforms crowd workers for text-annotation tasks. *PNAS* 120(30). 1–3. https://doi.org/10.1073/pnas.2305016120

Givón, Talmy. 1970. Notes on the semantic structure of English adjectives. *Language* 46(4). 816–837. https://doi.org/10.2307/412258

Givón, Talmy. 1979. *On understanding grammar*. New York, NY: Academic Press. https://doi.org/10.1016/C2013-0-10728-3

Gottfurcht, Carolyn A. 2008. *Denominal verb formation in English*. Evanston, IL: Northwestern University. (Doctoral dissertation).

Grandi, Nicola. 2009. Restrictions of Italian verb evaluative suffixes: The role of aspect and actionality. *York Papers in Linguistics* 2(10). 46–66.

Gries, Stefan Th. 2001. A corpus-linguistic analysis of English *-ic* vs. *-ical* adjectives. *ICAME Journal* 25. 65–108.

Gries, Stefan Th. 2003. Testing the sub-test: A collocational-overlap analysis of English *-ic* and *-ical* adjectives. *International Journal of Corpus Linguistics* 8(1). 31–61.

Gries, Stefan Th. 2013. Elementary statistical testing with R. In Krug, Manfred & Schlüter, Julia (eds.), *Research methods in language variation and change*, 361–381. Cambridge: Cambridge University Press. https://doi.org/10.1017/CBO9780511792519.024

Guz, Wojciech. 2009. English affixal nominalizations across language registers. *Poznań Studies in Contemporary Linguistics* 45(4), 447–471. https://doi.org/10.2478/v10010-009-0030-6

Guzmán Naranjo, Matías & Bonami, Olivier. 2023. A distributional assessment of rivalry in word formation. *Word Structure* 16(1). 87–114. https://10.3366/word.2023.0222

Haiman, John. 1983. Iconic and economic motivation. *Language* 59(4). 781–819. https://doi.org/10.2307/413373

Hamawand, Zeki. 2007. *Suffixal rivalry in adjective formation: a cognitive-corpus analysis*. London: Equinox.

Hathout, Nabil & Namer, Fiammetta. 2012. Discrepancy between form and meaning in word-formation: The case of over- and under-marking in French. In Rainer, Franz & Gardani, Francesco & Luschützky, Hans Christian & Dressler, Wolfgang U. (eds.), *Morphology and meaning: Selected papers from the 15th International Morphology Meeting, Vienna, February 2012*, 177–199. Amsterdam: John Benjamins. https://doi.org/10.1075/cilt.327.12hat

Hathout, Nabil & Namer Fiammetta. 2022. ParaDis: A Family and Paradigm model. *Morphology* 32. 153–195. https://doi.org/10.1007/s11525-021-09390-w

Hay, Jennifer. 2001. Lexical frequency in morphology: Is everything relative? *Linguistics* 39(6). 1041–1070. https://doi.org/10.1515/ling.2001.041

Hay, Jennifer. 2002. From speech perception to morphology: Affix ordering revisited. *Language* 78. 527–555. (https://www.jstor.org/stable/3086898) (Accessed 24-10-2021).

Hay, Jennifer & Baayen, R. Harald. 2003. Phonotactics, parsing and productivity. *Revista di Linguistica* 15. 99–130.

Hay, Jennifer & Plag, Ingo. 2004. What constrains possible suffix combinations? On the interaction of grammatical and processing restrictions in derivational morphology. *Natural Language and Linguistic Theory* 22. 565–596. https://doi.org/10.1023/B:NALA.0000027679.63308.89

Hengeveld, Kees & Leufkens, Sterre. 2018. Transparent and non-transparent languages. *Folia Linguistica* 52(1). 139–175. https://doi.org/10.1515/flin-2018-0003

Hock, Hans Heinrich & Joseph, Brian D. 2009. *Language history, language change, and language relationship.* Berlin: de Gruyter Mouton. https://doi.org/10.1515/9783110214307

Hoekstra, Eric & Versloot, Arjen. 2016. Frequency, similarity and the blocking principle. (Paper presented at the *17th International Morphology Meeting*, Vienna, 18–21 February 2016).

Hoffmann, Sebastian. 2004. Using the *OED* quotations database as a corpus – a linguistic appraisal. *ICAME Journal* 28. 17–30.

Hunston, Susan. 2002. *Corpora in applied linguistics.* Cambridge: Cambridge University Press. https://doi.org/10.1017/CBO9781139524773

Huyghe, Richard & Lombard, Alizée & Salvadori, Justine & Schwab, Sandra. 2023. Semantic rivalry between French deverbal neologisms in *-age*, *-ion* and

-ment. In Kotowski, Sven & Plag, Ingo (eds.), *The semantics of derivational morphology: Theory, methods, evidence*, 143–176. Berlin: De Gruyter. https://doi.org/10.1515/9783111074917-006

Huyghe, Richard & Varvara, Rosella. 2023a. Affix rivalry: Theoretical and methodological challenges. *Word Structure* 16(1). 1–23. https://doi.org/10.3366/word.2023.0218

Huyghe, Richard & Varvara, Rosella (eds.). 2023b. Quantitative approaches to affix rivalry. Themed issue in *Word Structure* 16(1). https://doi.org/10.3366/word.2023.0217

Huyghe, Richard & Wauquier, Marine. 2021. Distributional semantics insights on agentive suffix rivalry in French. *Word Structure* 14(3). 354–391. https://doi.org/10.3366/word.2021.0194

Imamovic, Mirela & Deilen, Silvana & Glynn, Dylan & Lapshinova-Koltunski, Ekaterina. 2024. Using ChatGPT for Annotation of Attitude within the Appraisal Theory: Lessons Learned. In *Proceedings of The 18th Linguistic Annotation Workshop (LAW-XVIII)*, 112–123. Association for Computational Linguistics.

Iordăchioaia, Gianina. 2019. The root derivation of psych nominals: Implications for competing overt and zero nominalizers. *Bucharest Working Papers in Linguistics* 21(2). 57–79. https://doi.org/10.31178/BWPL.21.2.3

Iordăchioaia, Gianina. 2022. Paradigmatic aspects of deverbal noun conversion in English. In Ruz, Alba E. & Fernández-Alcaina, Cristina & Lara-Clares, Cristina (eds.), *Paradigms in word formation: Theory and applications*, 155–177. Amsterdam: John Benjamins. https://doi.org/10.1075/slcs.225.07ior

Iordăchioaia, Gianina & Schweitzer, Susanne & Svyryda, Yaryna & Buitrago Cabrera, Camila María. 2020. Deverbal zero-nominalization and verb classes: Insights from a database. *Zeitschrift für Wortbildung / Journal of Word Formation* 4(2). 120–142.

Kastovsky, Dieter. 2000. Words and word-formation: Morphology in the OED. In Mugglestone, Lynda (ed.), *Lexicography and the OED: Pioneers in the untrodden forest*, 110–125. Oxford: Oxford University Press.

Kaunisto, Mark. 2007. *Variation and change in the lexicon: A corpus-based analysis of adjectives in English ending in* -ic *and* -ical. Amsterdam: Rodopi.

Kaunisto, Mark. 2009. The rivalry between English adjectives ending in *-ive* and *-ory*. In McConchie, Roderick W. & Honkapohja, Alpo & Tyrkkö, Jukka (eds.), *Selected proceedings of the 2008 symposium on new approaches in English historical lexis*, 74–87. Somerville, MA: Cascadilla Proceedings Project.

Kilani-Schoch, Marianne. 1988. *Introduction à la morphologie naturelle*. Bern: Peter Lang.

Kiparsky, Paul. 1971 [1982]. Historical linguistics. In Kiparsky (ed.), *Explanation in phonology*, 57–80. Dordrecht: Foris Publications.

Kiparsky, Paul. 1973. Phonological representations. In Fujimura, Osamu (ed.), *Three dimensions of linguistic theory*, 1–135. Tokyo: TEC.

Kiparsky, Paul. 1982. Lexical Morphology and Phonology. In Yang, In-Seok (ed.), *Linguistics in the morning calm: Selected papers from SICOL-1981*, 3–91. Seoul: Hanshin.

Kiparsky, Paul. 1983. Word-formation and the lexicon. In Ingemann, Frances J. (ed.), *Proceedings of the 1982 Mid-America linguistics conference*, 3–32. Lawrence, KS: University of Kansas.

Kjellmer, Göran. 1984. Why *great* : *greatly* but not *big* : **bigly*? On the formation of English adverbs in *-ly*. *Studia Linguistica* 38(1). 1–19. https://doi.org/10.1111/j.1467-9582.1984.tb00733.x

Kjellmer, Göran. 2000. Potential words. *Word* 51(2). 205–228. https://doi.org/10.1080/00437956.2000.11432501

Kjellmer, Göran. 2001. Why *weaken* but not **strongen*? On deadjectival verbs. *English Studies* 82. 154–171. https://doi.org/10.1076/enst.82.2.154.9600

Koehl, Aurore. 2015. Deadjectival nominalizations: Suffix rivalry and synonymy. In Audring, Jenny & Koutsoukos, Nikos & Masini, Francesca & Raffaelli, Ida (eds.), *Morphology and semantics, MMM9 On-line Proceedings*, 54–63. Pasithee: Open Access Electronic Publications. https://doi.org/10.26220/mmm.2269

Körtvélyessy, Lívia & Štekauer, Pavol & Zimmermann, Július. 2015. Word-formation strategies: Semantic transparency vs. formal economy. In Bauer, Laurie & Körtvélyessy, Lívia & Štekauer, Pavol (eds.), *Semantics of complex words*, 85–113. Cham: Springer. https://doi.org/10.1007/978-3-319-14102-2_6

Körtvélyessy, Lívia & Štekauer, Pavol & Kačmár, Pavol. 2021. On the role of creativity in the formation of new complex words. *Linguistics* 59(4). 1017–1055. https://doi.org/10.1515/ling-2020-0003

Kotowski, Sven & Plag, Ingo (eds.). 2023. *The semantics of derivational morphology: Theory, methods, evidence*. Berlin: De Gruyter. https://doi.org/10.1515/9783111074917

Kwon, Heok-Seung. 1997. Negative prefixation from 1300 to 1800: A case study in *in-/un-* variation. *ICAME Journal* 21. 21–42.

Lapesa, Gabriella & Kawaletz, Lea & Plag, Ingo & Andreou, Marios & Kisselew, Max & Padó, Sebastian. 2018. Disambiguation of newly derived nominalizations in context: A Distributional Semantics approach. *Word Structure* 11(3). 277–312. https://doi.org/10.3366/word.2018.0131

Lara-Clares, Cristina. 2016. *Profitability as a measure of competition in present-day English affixation*. Granada: Universidad de Granada. (MA dissertation).

Lara-Clares, Cristina. 2017. Competition in present-day English nominalization by zero-affixation vs. *-ation*. In Santana-Lario, Juan & Valera, Salvador (eds.), *Competing patterns in English affixation*, 207–244. Bern: Peter Lang.

Lara-Clares, Cristina & Fernández-Alcaina, Cristina. 2024. Testing GPT-4o for the semantic annotation of (competing) doublets. (Paper presented at the *Biennial of Czech Linguistics 2024*, Prague, 17-20 October 2024). https://ufal.mff.cuni.cz/~sevcikova/2024/docs/Cristinas_slides.pdf

Lara-Clares, Cristina & Lara-Clares, Alicia. 2016. An online tool for big data sampling in research on competition in English word-formation. (Paper presented at the *4th Meeting Linguistics Beyond and Within – International Linguistics Conference*, Lublin, 20–21 October 2016).

Lara-Clares, Cristina & Thompson, Paul. 2019. Nominal competition in present-day English affixation: Zero-affixation vs. *-ness* with the meaning STATIVE. *SKASE Journal of Theoretical Linguistics* 16(2), 25–49. (http://www.skase.sk/Volumes/JTL40/pdf_doc/02.pdf) (Accessed 24-10-2021).

Lara-Clares, Alicia. 2023. *Aífe: NLP cooccurrence graphs software*. (https://github.com/alicialara/AifeNLP) (Accessed 12-05-2023).

Lara-Clares, Alicia. 2016. *Scáthach: An online tool for big data sampling*. (https://scathach.laraclares.com) (Accessed 14-07-2020).

Laws, Jacqueline & Ryder, Chris. 2018. Register variation in spoken British English: The case of verb-forming suffixation. *International Journal of Corpus Linguistics* 23(1). 1–27. https://doi.org/10.1075/ijcl.16036.law

Lehrer, Adrienne. 1996. Why neologisms are important to study. *Lexicology* 2(1). 63–73.

Lehrer, Adrienne. 2003. Polysemy in derivational affixes. In Nerlich, Brigitt & Zazie, Todd & Vimala, Herman (eds.), *Polysemy: Flexible patterns of meaning in mind and language*, 217–232. Berlin: de Gruyter Mouton.

Lieber, Rochelle. 2004. *Morphology and lexical semantics*. Cambridge: Cambridge University Press. https://doi.org/10.1017/CBO9780511486296

Lieber, Rochelle. 2010. Toward an OT morphosemantics: The case of *-hood*, *-dom*, and *-ship*. In Olsen, Susan (ed.), *New impulses in word formation*, 61–80. Hamburg: Helmut Buske.

Lieber, Rochelle. 2016. *English nouns: The ecology of nominalizations*. Cambridge: Cambridge University Press.

Lieber, Rochelle & Plag, Ingo. 2022. The semantics of conversion nouns and *-ing* nominalizations: A quantitative and theoretical perspective. *Journal of Linguistics* 58(2). 307–343. https://doi.org/10.1017/S0022226721000311

Lindsay, Mark. 2012. Rival suffixes: Synonymy, competition, and the emergence of productivity. In Ralli, Angela & Booij, Geert & Scalise, Sergio & Karasimos,

Athanasios (eds.), *Morphology and the architecture of grammar: Proceedings of the 8th Mediterranean Morphology Meeting*, 192–203. Patras: University of Patras.

Lindsay, Mark & Aronoff, Mark. 2013. Natural selection in self-organizing morphological systems. In Montermini, Fabio & Boyé, Gilles & Tseng, Jesse (eds.), *Morphology in Toulouse: Selected proceedings of Décembrettes 7*, 133–153. Munich: Lincom Europe.

Lloyd, Cynthia. 2011. *Semantics and word formation: The semantic development of five French suffixes in Middle English*. Bern: Peter Lang.

Longman Dictionary of Contemporary English Online. 2022. (https://www.ldoceonline.com) (Accessed 18-07-2022).

Luschützky, Hans Christian. 2015. Word-formation in Natural Morphology. In Müller, Peter O. & Ohnheiser, Ingeborg & Olsen, Susan & Rainer, Franz (eds.), *Word-formation: An international handbook of the languages of Europe*, vol. 1, 123–144. Berlin: De Gruyter Mouton. https://doi.org/10.1515/9783110246254-011

MacWhinney, Brian & Malchukov, Andrej & Moravcsik, Edith (eds.). 2014. *Competing motivations in grammar and usage*. Oxford: Oxford University Press. https://doi.org/10.1093/acprof:oso/9780198709848.001.0001

Malicka-Kleparska, Anna. 1992. Against phonological conditioning of WFRs. In Fisiak, Jacek & Puppel, Stanislaw (eds.), *Phonological investigations*, 423–442. Amsterdam: John Benjamins. https://doi.org/10.1075/llsee.38.17mal

Malkiel, Yakov. 1977. Why ap-*ish* but worm-*y*? In Hopper, Paul J. (ed.), *Studies in descriptive and historical linguistics: Festschrift for Winfred P. Lehmann*, 341–364. Amsterdam: John Benjamins. https://doi.org/10.1075/cilt.4.23mal

Manova, Stela. 2015. Closing suffixes. In Müller, Peter O. & Ohnheiser, Ingeborg & Olsen, Susan & Rainer, Franz (eds.), *Word-formation: An international handbook of the languages of Europe*, vol. 2, 956–971. Berlin: De Gruyter Mouton. https://doi.org/10.1515/9783110246278-010

Manova, Stela & Dressler, Wolfgang U. 2005. The morphological technique of conversion in the inflecting-fusional type. In Bauer, Laurie & Valera, Salvador (eds.), *Approaches to conversion/zero-derivation*, 67–101. Münster: Waxmann.

Marchand, Hans. 1963. On content as a criterion of derivational relationship with backderived words. *Indogermanische Forschungen* 68. 170–175. https://doi.org/10.1515/9783110243109.170

Marchand, Hans. 1964. A set of criteria for the establishing of derivational relationship between words unmarked by derivational morphemes. *Indogermanische Forschungen* 69. 10–19. https://doi.org/10.1515/9783110243116.10

Marchand, Hans. 1969. *The categories and types of present-day English word formation. A synchronic-diachronic approach.* 2nd edn. Munich: Carl Beck.

Mattiello, Elisa. 2017. *Analogy in word-formation: A study of English neologisms and occasionalisms.* Berlin: De Gruyter Mouton. https://doi.org/10.1515/9783110551419

Mattiello, Elisa. 2022. *Transitional Morphology : Combining Forms in Modern English.* Cambridge: Cambridge University Press. https://doi.org/10.1017/9781009168274

Matthews, Peter H. 1974. *Morphology: An introduction to the theory of word-structure.* Cambridge: Cambridge University Press.

Mayerthaler, Willi. 1988. *Morphological Naturalness.* Ann Arbor, MI: Karoma Press. (Translation of Mayerthaler 1981).

Merriam-Webster. 2022. (https://www.merriam-webster.com/dictionary/) (Accessed 18-07-2022).

Mititelu, Verginica Barbu & Iordăchioaia, Gianina & Leseva, Svetlozara & Stoyanova, Ivelina. 2023. The meaning of zero nouns and zero verbs. In Kotowski, Sven & Plag, Ingo (eds.), *The semantics of derivational morphology: Theory, methods, evidence*, 63–102. Berlin: De Gruyter. https://doi.org/10.1515/9783111074917-004

Moder, Carol Lynn. 1992. Rules and analogy. In Davis, Garry W. & Iverson, Gregory (eds.), *Explanation in historical linguistics*, 179–191. Philadelphia: John Benjamins. https://doi.org/10.1075/cilt.84.12mod

Montero-Fleta, Begoña. 2011. Suffixes in word-formation processes in scientific English. *LSP Journal* 2(2). 4–14.

Mörth, Karlheinz & Dressler, Wolfgang U. 2014. German plural doublets with and without meaning differentiation. In Rainer, Franz & Gardani, Francesco & Luschützky, Hans Christian & Dressler, Wolfgang U. (eds.), *Morphology and meaning: Selected papers from the 15th International Morphology Meeting, Vienna, February 2012*, 249–258. Amsterdam: John Benjamins. https://doi.org/10.1075/cilt.327.17mor

Nagano, Akiko. 2022. Affixal rivalry and its purely semantic resolution among English derived adjectives. *Journal of Linguistics.* 1–32. https://doi.org/10.1017/S0022226722000147

Nevalainen, Terttu. 1999. Early Modern English lexis and semantics. In Lass, Roger (ed.), *The Cambridge history of the English language*, vol. 3, 332–458. Cambridge: Cambridge University Press. https://doi.org/10.1017/CHOL9780521264761.006

Ogilvie, Sarah. 2015. *Words of the world: A global history of the Oxford English Dictionary.* Cambridge: Cambridge University Press.

OED Online (Oxford English Dictionary online). Oxford University Press. (https://www.oed.com) (Accessed 18-11-2021).

Palmer, Frank & Huddleston, Rodney & Pullum, Geoffrey K. 2002. Inflectional morphology and related matters. In Huddleston, Rodney & Pullum, Geoffrey K. (eds.), *The Cambridge grammar of the English language*, 1565–1620. Cambridge: Cambridge University Press. https://doi.org/10.1017/9781316423530.019

Plag, Ingo. 1996. Morphological haplology in a constraint-based morpho-phonology. In Kehrein, Wolfgang & Wiese, Richard (eds.), *Phonology and morphology of the Germanic languages*, 199–215. Tübingen: Max Niemeyer. https://doi.org/10.1515/9783110919769.199

Plag, Ingo. 1999. *Morphological productivity: Structural constraints on English derivation*. Berlin: Mouton de Gruyter. https://doi.org/10.1515/9783110802863

Plag, Ingo. 2000. On the mechanisms of morphological rivalry: A new look at competing verb-deriving affixes in English. In Reitz, Bernhard & Rieuwerts, Sigrid (eds.), *Anglistentag 1999 Mainz Proceedings*, 63–76. Trier: Wissenschaftlicher Verlag Trier.

Plag, Ingo. 2002. The role of selectional restrictions, phonotactics and parsing in constraining suffix ordering in English. In Booij, Geert & van Marle, Jaap (eds.), *Yearbook of morphology 2001*. Dordrecht: Springer. https://doi.org/10.1007/978-94-017-3726-5_11

Plag, Ingo. 2003. *Word-formation in English*. Cambridge: Cambridge University Press.

Plag, Ingo. 2004. Syntactic category information and the semantics of derivational morphological rules. *Folia Linguistica* 38(3–4). 193–225. https://doi.org/10.1515/flin.2004.38.3-4.193

Plag, Ingo. 2005. Productivity. In Brown, Keith (ed.), *Encyclopedia of language and linguistics*, 2nd edn, vol. 10, 121–128. Oxford: Elsevier.

Plag, Ingo. 2016. English. In Müller, Peter O. & Ohnheiser, Ingeborg & Olsen, Susan & Rainer, Franz (eds.), *Word-formation: An international handbook of the languages of Europe*, vol. 4, 2411–2427. Berlin: Mouton de Gruyter. https://doi.org/10.1515/9783110379082-002

Plag, Ingo & Dalton-Puffer, Christiane & Baayen, Harald R. 1999. Morphological productivity across speech and writing. *English Language & Linguistics* 3(2). 209–288. https://doi.org/10.1017/S1360674399000222

Plag, Ingo & Baayen, Harald. 2009. Suffix ordering and morphological processing. *Language* 85(1). 109–152.

Plank, Frans. 1981. *Morphologische (Ir-)Regularitäten*. Tübingen: Gunther Narr.

Plank, Frans. 1994. Inflection and derivation. In Asher, Ron E. (ed.), *Encyclopedia of language and linguistics* 3, 1671–1678. Oxford: Pergamon.

Plank, Frans. 2010. Variable direction in zero-derivation and the unity of polysemous lexical items. *Word Structure* 3(1). 82–97. https://doi.org/10.3366/E1750124510000498

Pounder, Amanda. 2000. *Processes and paradigms in word-formation morphology.* Berlin: Mouton de Gruyter. https://doi.org/10.1515/9783110814378

Quirk, Randolph & Leech, Geoffrey & Greenbaum, Sydney & Svartvik, Jan. 1985. *A comprehensive grammar of the English language*. London: Longman.

Radimský, Jan & Štichauer, Pavel. 2021. Nomina Actionis in the diachrony of Italian: a paradigm-based model of competition. *Lingue e linguaggio* 20(1). 33–55. https://doi.org/10.1418/101112

Raffelsiefen, Renate. 1998. Phonological constraints on English word formation. In Booij, Geert & van Marle, Jaap (eds.), *Yearbook of morphology*, 225–287. Dordrecht: Kluwer. https://doi.org/10.1007/978-94-017-3720-3_10

Raffelsiefen, Renate. 2004. Absolute ill-formedness and other morphophonological effects. *Phonology* 21. 91–142. https://doi.org/10.1017/S0952675704000144

Raffelsiefen, Renate. 2015. Phonological restrictions on English word-formation. In Müller, Peter O. & Ohnheiser, Ingeborg & Olsen, Susan & Rainer, Franz (eds.), *Word-formation: An international handbook of the languages of Europe*, vol. 2, 894–917. Berlin: De Gruyter Mouton. https://doi.org/10.1007/978-94-017-3720-3_10

Rainer, Franz. 1988. Towards a theory of blocking: The case of Italian and German quality nouns. In Booij, Geert & van Marle, Jaap (eds.), *Yearbook of morphology 1988*, 155–185. Dordrecht: Foris. https://doi.org/10.1515/9783112329528-010

Rainer, Franz. 2005. Constraints on productivity. In Štekauer, Pavol & Lieber, Rochelle (eds.), *Handbook of word-formation*, 335–352. Dordrecht: Springer. https://doi.org/10.1007/1-4020-3596-9_14

Rainer, Franz. 2014. Polysemy in derivation. In Lieber, Rochelle & Štekauer, Pavol (eds.), *The Oxford handbook of derivational morphology*, 338–353. https://doi.org/10.1093/oxfordhb/9780199641642.013.0019

Rainer, Franz. 2015. Quality nouns. In Müller, Peter O. & Ohnheiser, Ingeborg & Olsen, Susan & Rainer, Franz (eds.), *Word-formation: An international handbook of the languages of Europe*, vol. 2, 1268–1284. Berlin: De Gruyter Mouton. https://doi.org/10.1515/9783110246278-028

Rainer, Franz & Dressler, Wolfgang U. & Gardani, Francesco & Luschützky, Hans Christian. 2014. Morphology and meaning: An overview. In Rainer, Franz & Gardani, Francesco & Luschützky, Hans Christian & Dressler, Wolfgang U. (eds.), *Morphology and meaning: Selected papers from the 15th International*

Morphology Meeting, Vienna, February 2012, 3–46. Amsterdam: John Benjamins. https://doi.org/10.1075/cilt.327.02rai

Rainer, Franz & Gardani, Francesco & Dressler, Wolfgang U. & Luschützky, Hans Christian (eds.). 2019. *Competition in inflection and word-formation*. Cham: Springer.

Raosoft Inc. 2004. Sample size calculator. (http://www.raosoft.com/samplesize.html?nosurvey) (Accessed 12-06-2018).

Renner, Vincent. 2020. An ecosystem view of English word-formation. *The Mental Lexicon* 15(1). 4–20. https://doi.org/10.1075/ml.00011.ren

Riddle, Elizabeth M. 1985. A historical perspective on the productivity of the suffixes *-ness* and *-ity*. In Fisiak, Jacek (ed.), *Historical semantics: Historical word-formation*, 435–461. Berlin: De Gruyter Mouton. https://doi.org/10.1515/9783110850178.435

Rifón Sánchez, Antonio. 2011. Nominalizations of transfer verbs: Blocking, constraints and competition between affixes. In Cifuentes Honrubia, José Luis & Rodríguez Rosique, Susana (eds.), *Spanish word formation and lexical creation*, 233–254. Amsterdam: John Benjamins.

Rodríguez-Puente, Paula & Säily, Tanja & Suomela, Jukka. 2020. New methods for analysing diachronic suffix competition across registers: How *-ity* gained ground on *-ness* in Early Modern English. *International Journal of Corpus Linguistics* 27(4). 506–528. https://doi.org/10.1075/ijcl.22014.rod

Romaine, Suzanne. 1985. Variability in word formation patterns and productivity in the history of English. In Fisiak, Jacek (ed.), *Current issues in linguistic theory, vol. 34. Papers from the 6th International Conference on Historical Linguistics*, 451–467. Amsterdam: John Benjamins.

Romaine, Suzanne. 2004. Change in productivity. In Booij, Geert & Lehmann, Christian & Mugdan, Joachim, in collaboration with Stavros Skopeteas (eds.), *Morphology: An international handbook on inflection and word-formation*, 1636–1644. Berlin: Mouton de Gruyter. https://doi.org/10.1515/9783110172782.2.17.1636

Ruz, Alba E. & Cetnarowska, Bożena. 2023. Directionality in affixation: the applicability of Marchand's (1964) semantic criteria. *Linguistica Pragensia*, 33(1). 7–44. https://doi.org/10.14712/18059635.2023.1.1

Saïly, Tanja. 2011. Variation in morphological productivity in the BNC: Sociolinguistic and methodological considerations. *Corpus Linguistics and Linguistic Theory* 7(1). 119–141.

Säily, Tanja. 2018 Change or variation? Productivity of the suffixes *-ness* and *-ity*. In Nevalainen, Terttu & Palander-Collin, Minna & Säily, Tanja (eds.), *Patterns* *of change in 18th-century English: A sociolinguistc approach*, vol. 8, 197–218. Amsterdam: John Benjamins. https://doi.org/10.1075/ahs.8.12sai

Samuels, Michael Louis. 1972. *Linguistic evolution: With special reference to English*. Cambridge: Cambridge University Press. https://doi.org/10.1017/CBO9781139086707

Santana-Lario, Juan & Valera, Salvador (eds.). 2017. *Competing patterns in English affixation*. Bern: Peter Lang. (https://www.peterlang.com/document/1055047) (Accessed 04-09-2021).

Santilli, Enzo. 2014. Italian comparatives: A case of overabundance? (BA dissertation) (https://www.academia.edu/9307153/Italian_Comparatives_a_Case_of_Overabundance) (Accessed 15-01-2022).

Schirakowski, Barbara. 2020. (No) competition between deverbal nouns and nominalized infinitives in Spanish. *Borealis – An International Journal of Hispanic Linguistics* 9(2). 257–283. https://doi.org/10.7557/1.9.2.5215

Schneider, Edgar W. 1987. Beobachtungen zur Paradigmatik der verbbildenden Suffixe *-en*, *-ify* und *-ize* im Englischen. *Sprachwissenschaft* 12(1). 88–109.

Schulte, Marion. 2015. Polysemy and synonymy in derivational affixation: A case study of the English suffixes *-age* and *-ery*. *Morphology* 25(4). 371–390.

Simpson, John. 2004. The OED and collaborative research into the history of English. *Anglia* 122(2). 185–208. https://doi.org/10.1515/ANGL.2004.185

Smith, Chris A. 2020. A case study of *-some* and *-able* derivatives in the OED3: Examining the diachronic output and productivity of two competing adjectival suffixes. *Journal of English Lexicology* 16. 1–40. https://doi.org/10.4000/lexis.4793

Spencer, Andrew. 2019. The nature of productivity (including word formation versus creative coining). In Aronoff, Mark (ed.), *Oxford Research Encyclopedia of Linguistics*, 1–27. Oxford: OUP. https://doi.org/10.1093/acrefore/9780199384655.013.587

Soares Rodrigues, Alexandra. 2015. Semantic rivalry between affixes: The case of Portuguese nominalisers. In Audring, Jenny & Koutsoukos, Nikos & Masini, Francesca & Raffaelli, Ida (eds.), *Morphology and semantics, MMM9 on-line proceedings*, 134–137. Pasithee: Open Access Electronic Publications. https://doi.org/10.26220/mmm.2274

Štekauer, Pavol. 1996. *A theory of conversion in English*. Frankfurt am Main: Peter Lang.

Štekauer, Pavol. 2005. *Meaning predictability in word-formation*. Amsterdam: John Benjamins. https://doi.org/10.1075/sfsl.54

Štekauer, Pavol. 2014. Derivational paradigms. In Lieber, Rochelle & Štekauer, Pavol (eds.), *The Oxford handbook of derivational morphology*,

354–369. Oxford: Oxford University Press. https://doi.org/10.1093/oxfordhb/9780199641642.013.0020

Štekauer, Pavol. 2017. Competition in natural languages. In Santana-Lario, Juan & Valera, Salvador (eds.), *Competing patterns in English affixation*, 15–32. Bern: Peter Lang.

Štekauer, Pavol & Valera, Salvador & Körtvélyessy, Lívia. 2012. *Word-formation in the world's languages: A typological survey*. Cambridge: Cambridge University Press. https://doi.org/10.1017/CBO9780511895005

Štekauer, Pavol & Chapman, Don & Tomaščíková, Slávka & Franko, Štefan. 2005. Word-formation as creativity within productivity constraints: Sociolinguistic evidence. *Onomasiology Online* 6. 1–55.

Stockwell, Robert & Minkova, Donka. 2001. *English words: History and structure*. Cambridge: Cambridge University Press.

Stump, Gregory T. 1998. Inflection. In Spencer, Andrew & Zwicky, Arnold M. (eds.), *The handbook of morphology*, 13–43. Oxford: Blackwell.

Sweet, Henry. 1891–1898. *New English grammar: Logical and historical*, vol. 1. Oxford: Clarendon Press.

Thornton, Anna M. 2011. Overabundance (multiple forms realizing the same cell): A non-canonical phenomenon in Italian verb morphology. In Maiden, Martin & Smith, John Charles & Goldbach, Maria & Hinzelin, Marc-Olivier (eds.), *Morphological autonomy: Perspectives from Romance inflectional morphology*, 358–381. Oxford: Oxford University Press. https://doi.org/10.1093/acprof:oso/9780199589982.003.0017

Thornton, Anna M. 2012. Overabundance in Italian verb morphology and its interactions with other non-canonical phenomena. In Stolz, Thomas & Otsuka, Hitomi & Urdze, Aina (eds.), *Studia typologica: Irregularity in morphology (and beyond)*, 251–269. Berlin: Akademie Verlag. https://doi.org/10.1524/9783050059587.251

Thornton, Anna M. 2019. Overabundance: A canonical typology. In Rainer, Franz & Gardani, Francesco & Dressler, Wolfgang U. & Luschützky, Hans Christian (eds.), *Competition in inflection and word-formation*, 223–258. Cham: Springer. https://doi.org/10.1007/978-3-030-02550-2_9

Thuilier, Juliette & Tribout, Delphine & Wauquier, Marine. 2023. Affix rivalry in French demonym formation: The role of linguistic and non-linguistic parameters. *Word Structure* 16(1). 115–146. https://doi.org/10.3366/word.2023.0223

Trips, Carola. 2009. *Lexical semantics and diachronic morphology: The development of* -hood, -dom *and* -ship *in the history of English*. Tübingen: Max Niemeyer.

van Marle, Jaap. 1985. *On the paradigmatic dimension of morphological creativity*. Dordrecht: Foris.

Varvara, Rossella. 2020. Constraints on nominalizations: Investigating the productivity domain of Italian *-mento* and *-zione*. *Zeitschrift für Wortbildung / Journal of Word Formation* 4(2). 78–99. https://doi.org/10.3726/zwjw.2020.02.05

von der Gabelentz, Georg. 1901. *Die Sprachwissenschaft, ihre Aufgaben, Methoden und bisherigen Ergebnisse*. Tübingen: Gunther Narr.

Wauquier, Marine & Hathout, Nabil & Fabre, Cécile. 2020a. Contributions of distributional semantics to the semantic study of French morphologically derived agent nouns. In Audring, Jenny & Koutsoukos, Nikos & Manouilidou, Christina (eds.), *MMM12 on-line proceedings: Rules, patterns, schemas and analogy*, 111–121. (https://pasithee.library.upatras.gr/mmm/article/view/3254/3514) (Accessed 11-12-2021).

Wauquier, Marine, & Hathout, Nabil & Fabre, Cécile. 2020b. Semantic discrimination of technicality in French nominalizations. *Zeitschrift für Wortbildung / Journal of Word Formation* 4(2). 100–119. https://doi.org/10.3726/zwjw.2020.02.06

Williams, Edwin. 1981. On the notions *lexically related* and *head of a word*. *Linguistic Inquiry* 12(2). 245–274. (https://www.jstor.org/stable/4178218) (Accessed 22-10-2021).

Wurzel, Wolfgang U. 1987. System-dependent morphological naturalness in inflection. In Dressler, Wolfgang U. & Mayerthaler, Willi & Panagl, Oswald & Wurzel, Wolfgang U. (eds.), *Leitmotifs in Natural Morphology*, 99–126. Amsterdam: John Benjamins. https://doi.org/10.1075/slcs.10.22wur

Wurzel, Wolfgang U. 1989. *Inflectional morphology and Naturalness*. Dordrecht: Kluwer. (Translation of Mayerthaler 1984).

Wurzel, Wolfgang U. 1992. The Structuralist heritage in Natural Morphology. In Lieb, Hans-Heinrich (ed.), *Prospects for a new Structuralism*. Amsterdam: John Benjamins. https://doi.org/10.1075/cilt.96.13wur

Wurzel, Wolfgang U. 1996. On similarities and differences between inflectional and derivational morphology. *STUF: Sprachtypologie und Universalienforschung* 49. 267–279.

Yu, Hao & Yang, Zachary & Pelrine, Kellin & Godbout, Jean Francois & Rabbany, Reihaneh. 2023. Open, Closed, or Small Language Models for Text Classification? *arXiv:2308.10092* https://doi.org/10.48550/arXiv.2308.10092

Zipf, George K. 1949. *Human behavior and the Principle of Least Effort: An introduction to human ecology*. Cambridge, MA: Addison-Wesley.

Subject index

ACTION 47, 58–60, 80, 83–84, 86–87, 90–97, 100–103, 109–114, 129–136, 155–156, 164
adjective 45–49, 57, 59
adverb 49, 59, 147
agglutinating 40, 87
affixation 40, 44–45, 58–60
  overt affixation 35, 40–41, 51, 53, 87–88
  zero-affixation (or conversion) 35, 40–41, 51, 53, 71, 76, 88
AGENTIVE 80, 82–84, 87, 104–105, 108–109, 114–118, 128–131, 136–142, 155–158
analogy 43, 50–51, 56–57
association 93–94, 112–114, 117, 121–122, 125–131, 157–159
-ation 47–48, 57–59, 74, 82, 87, 90–94, 100–103, 108–114, 116, 129–132, 155, 160, 164

BNC (*British National Corpus*) 53–54, 68–70, 73–74, 76–80, 95, 128, 161–165, 170–173
blocking (or preemption) 38, 55–57, 170
borrowing 37–38, 40, 64, 80

cluster 42–43, 51–52, 60, 63–64, 68, 72–74, 80–81, 88–89, 166
COCA (*Corpus of Contemporary American English*) 68, 76, 95
coexistence 38, 43–44, 106–107, 127, 172
coindexation 48–49
collocation 81, 95
combining form 72, 77
competition (or rivalry)
  incidental 102, 104–106, 162
  ongoing 43–44, 62–63, 102–103, 104–108, 127–129, 155, 163
  partial 109, 131
  past 43–44, 102–108
  resolved 43–44, 51, 89, 96, 102–108, 110, 118, 120, 123–124, 131, 142, 148, 155, 157–158, 162, 166
compounding 40, 53, 70–71, 77
constraint (or restriction) 42, 44–57, 59, 73, 86–88, 169
context (or domain) 30-31, 36–37, 40–44, 48–49, 53–54, 61–63, 67–69, 73, 89–90, 94–97, 123–124, 128–129, 131–132, 134, 146, 152, 157–161
cooccurrence 94–97, 134–136, 141–142, 146–148, 152–154, 158
creativity 50, 55, 57

deadjectival 47, 51, 56, 61–63, 79, 86–88, 108–109, 159
denominal 47, 49, 63
deverbal 47, 79, 87, 108–109
diachrony 33, 62, 64, 69–70, 81, 107–108, 161–163, 166–167, 171
dialect 36, 39, 64, 73, 128, 134, 158
distribution
  complementary 34, 37, 43–44, 46, 62, 64
  register 31, 44, 52–54, 68, 89–94, 111–113, 116–118, 121–123, 125–127, 130, 132–133, 137–138, 143–144, 149–151

economy 34–35, 38–41, 55, 159–160, 167, 172
  Principle of Least Effort 41, 64

-er 34, 39, 49, 71, 80–82, 87, 100, 104–106, 108–109, 114–123, 129–131, 136–148, 155–164, 166–167, 172
etymology 47–48, 69, 74, 77, 161, 170

frequency 37, 40, 44, 49–55, 63, 65, 68, 70–71, 77–79, 81, 88–97, 100, 111–114, 116–118, 120–123, 125–127, 129–131, 133, 137–146, 149–153, 156–160, 163–165, 170–174

iconicity 41, 64
INSTRUMENT 74–75, 78–80, 82–85, 87–88, 100, 105, 108, 118–123, 128–131, 142–148, 155–156, 159–160, 163–164, 172
isolating 40
iWeb Corpus 76, 162

Latinate 45–46, 48, 62, 65
lexicalisation 52, 63, 76, 155, 173

mode 37, 89–94, 111–112, 116–117, 121–122, 124–127, 131, 159–160, 171–174

Naturalness 41, 64, 86–88, 159
-ness 38, 45, 49, 53–54, 56–58, 60–63, 65, 78–80, 82, 85–88, 106–108, 123–130, 149–150, 155–156, 160, 162, 164, 167, 169, 172
niche 43, 61–63, 116, 157–158, 169

obsolescence 64, 166, 171
overabundance 35–37

paradigm 35–36, 43, 57, 60, 64, 166
polysemy 63, 81–82, 156–157, 173
potentiation 48, 61, 170
prefixation 39, 47, 49, 54, 59–60, 100
productivity 27–28, 33, 37, 41, 44, 48–59, 61–62, 65, 79, 86, 88–89, 100, 155, 174
  availability 50–51, 57, 108–109, 155, 163
  profitability 50–52, 57

semantic
  annotation 53, 81–82, 164
    automatic 85–86, 165
    manual 83–85, 165, 173–174
  specialisation 36, 39, 56, 63–64, 131–132, 148, 158, 167, 172, 174
STATE (or stative) 78–80, 82–83, 85–89, 100, 106–109, 123–131, 148–156, 159–160, 162, 164, 166–167, 171–172
synonymy 34, 37–39, 42–43, 54–56, 59, 62, 64, 73, 134, 139–140, 145–146, 151–152
  avoidance 34, 38, 44, 171–172

transparency 35, 40–41, 61, 99, 159, 167, 172
  morphosemantic 41, 55, 87–88
  morphotactic 40–41, 87–88

variant 36, 71, 89
verb 36, 40, 45–47, 51–52, 58, 65, 165, 171

Hallesche Sprach- und Textforschung
Language and Text Studies
Recherches linguistiques et textuelles

Herausgegeben von / Edited by / Dirigée par Alexander Brock & Daniela Pietrini

Bd./Vol. 1	Annette Schiller: Die présentatifs im heutigen Französisch. Eine funktionale Studie ihrer Vielfalt. 1992.
Bd./Vol. 2	Gertrud Bense (Hrsg.): Diachronie – Kontinuität – Impulse. Sprachwissenschaftliches Kolloquium Halle 1992. 1994.
Bd./Vol. 3	Wolfgang Boeck (Hrsg.): Sprache, Literatur und Landeskunde slavischer Völker. Funktionale Aspekte in der Beschreibung und Didaktik. 1994.
Bd./Vol. 4	Gertrud Bense (Hrsg.): Kommunikation und Grammatik. 1996.
Bd./Vol. 5	Gisela Hermann-Brennecke / Dietmar Schneider (Hrsg.): Dona Anglica. 120 Jahre Anglistik in Halle. 1997.
Bd./Vol. 6	Max Hans-Jürgen Mattusch: Vielsprachigkeit: Fluch oder Segen für die Menschheit? Zu Fragen einer europäischen und globalen Fremdsprachenpolitik. 1999.
Bd./Vol. 7	Christiane Schiller: Bilinguismus. Zur Darstellung eines soziolinguistischen Phänomens in der Literatur. Dargestellt an Beispielen der regionalen Literatur Preußisch-Litauens: Hermann Sudermann *Litauische Geschichten*, Ieva Simonaityte *Vilius* Karalius. 2000.
Bd./Vol. 8	Gertrud Bense: „Giedojam taw – Wir singen dir". Zur Textgeschichte der preußisch-litauischen Gesangbücher im 18. Jahrhundert. Mit besonderer Berücksichtigung der Liedersammlung von Fabian Ulrich Glaser (1688–1747) und ihrem Umfeld. 2001.
Bd./Vol. 9	Gertrud Bense / Gerhard Meiser / Edeltraud Werner (Hrsg.): August Friedrich Pott. Beiträge der Halleschen Tagung anlässlich des zweihundertsten Geburtstages von August Friedrich Pott (1802–1887). 2005.
Bd./Vol. 10	Julia Balakina: Anglicisms in Russian and German Blogs. A Comparative Analysis. 2011.
Bd./Vol. 11	Thomas Bremer / Annette Schiller (Hrsg.): Dialekt und Standardsprache in Italien und Europa. Edeltraud Werner zum 60. Geburtstag. 2012.
Bd./Vol. 12	Anne Ammermann / Alexander Brock / Jana Pflaeging / Peter Schildhauer (eds.): Facets of Linguistics. Proceedings of the 14th Norddeutsches Linguistisches Kolloquium 2013 in Halle an der Saale. 2013.
Bd./Vol. 13	Anja Neuber: Perspektiven des Friaulischen. Eine soziolinguistische Untersuchung am Beispiel junger Erwachsener. 2015.
Bd./Vol. 14	Peter Schildhauer: The Personal Weblog. A Linguistic History. 2016.
Bd./Vol. 15	Alexander Brock / Peter Schildhauer (eds.): Communication Forms and Communicative Practices. New Perspectives on Communication Forms, Affordances and What Users Make of Them. 2017.
Bd./Vol. 16	Alexander Brock / Jana Pflaeging / Peter Schildhauer (eds.): Genre Emergence. Developments in Print, TV and Digital Media. 2019.
Bd./Vol. 17	Björn Langkopf: Autonomes E-Learning. Effizienz – Didaktik – Perspektiven. 2019.
Bd./Vol. 18	John Marcus Sommer: English and French Online Comments. A Text Linguistic Comparison of Popular Science Magazines. 2020.
Bd./Vol. 19	José Luis Oncins Martínez (ed.): Current Trends in Corpus Linguistics. 2020.

Bd./Vol. 20 Ramón Martí Solano / Pablo Ruano San Segundo (eds.): Anglicisms and Corpus Linguistics. Corpus-Aided Research into the Influence of English on European Languages. 2021.

Bd./Vol. 21 Cristina Fernández-Alcaina: The Competition of Word-Formation Processes in the Derivational Paradigm of Verbs. Diasynchronic Evidence for the Profile and Resolution of Competition in English. 2021.

Bd./Vol. 22 Alexander Brock / Janet Russell / Peter Schildhauer / Merle Willenberg (eds.): Participation & Identity. Empirical Investigations of States and Dynamics. 2022.

Bd./Vol. 23 Daniela Pietrini (a cura di): Lingua e discriminazione. Studi diacronici, lessicali e discorsivi. 2023.

Bd./Vol. 24 Isabel Durán-Muñoz / Eva Lucía Jiménez- Navarro (eds.): Exploring the Language of Adventure Tourism. A Corpus-Assisted Approach. 2024.

Bd./Vol. 25 Cristina Lara-Clares: The Competition Between Overt Suffixation and Zero-Affixation in Present-Day English Nominalisation. 2025.

www.peterlang.com

www.ingramcontent.com/pod-product-compliance
Ingram Content Group UK Ltd.
Pitfield, Milton Keynes, MK11 3LW, UK
UKHW041447071026
15587UKWH00010B/582

9 783631 930632